# MY LIFE

# BURT
# REYNOLDS

# MY LIFE

HYPERION

NEW YORK

Library of Congress Cataloging-in-Publication Data

Reynolds, Burt.
    My Life / Burt Reynolds.—1st ed.
      p.    cm.
    ISBN 0-7868-6130-4
    1. Reynolds, Burt. 2. Actors—United States—Biography.
I. Title.
PN2287.R447A3 1994
791.43'028'092—dc20
   [B]                                    94-27426
                                            CIP

*Designed by Claudyne Bianco*
FIRST EDITION

10  9  8  7  6  5  4  3  2  1

TO QUINTON REYNOLDS

WHO SOMEDAY WILL KNOW
HOW MUCH HIS FATHER
ALWAYS LOVED HIM,
JUST AS I'VE FINALLY
LEARNED HOW MUCH
MY FATHER ALWAYS
LOVED ME.

I WANT TO BE THOROUGHLY
USED UP WHEN I DIE.
FOR THE HARDER I WORK,
THE MORE I LIVE.

—GEORGE BERNARD SHAW

# ACKNOWLEDGMENTS

Alan Margulies, Todd Gold, Dan Strone, Lenore Haas, Logen Fleming, Sally Wagner, Dr. Uhley, Rob Kairalla. And a great group of friends who have stood by me (and who know I love them) through this roller-coaster ride called my life.

To my last wife . . .

And to the stuntmen whose ability and stupidity have, over the years, given me new understanding of the word *pain*.

# AUTHOR'S NOTE

For MANY YEARS—SO MANY THAT I WAS ACTUALLY young when I first started—I talked about writing my autobiography. Back then, I still had beautiful hair, foot speed, and sanity. On two different occasions, I sat down to write *Tom Sawyer Goes Bad*. But my publishers were more interested in the *Confessions of the New Errol Flynn*.

In both cases, I canceled the deal and returned a $1 million advance. But the ego *interruptus* turned out to be enlightening. I realized it was too early to write my life story. I hadn't run all the races, fought nearly all the fights, or chased all the pretty girls.

I guess I've reached the point where I finally don't feel it's imperative for everyone to like me.

And now?

Although my mind tells me that I'm half my present age of fifty-eight, in reality I've broken over forty-three bones in the past thirty-four years, and at present, three of my fingers are newly broken. I've got arthritis in my left and right elbows. I've entered the Rent-A-Wreck era. My best work is probably still ahead of me, but my dream of dying as a ninety-three-year-old stuntman is slipping away.

In place of youth I have perspective. So much has happened to me lately that I was seized by a pressing need to get a few thoughts off my chest. Since Johnny Carson was the closest I ever came to having a psychiatrist, I decided to write a book. David Niven, raconteur extraordinaire, made me pledge to do it someday.

I only had to endure. Many people wondered if I would survive last year's self-immolation by a stream-of-consciousness babble on "Good Morning America: Special Evening Edition," on which I attempted to defend myself after splitting from my unbelievably gorgeous ex-wife Loni Anderson. Or did I plan a public execution?

I knew better. I mean, a purple suit? Challenging her to take sodium pentothol?

I was like a runaway train. It was *Death Wish IV* done as an improv skit. Charlie Bronson could've sued for copyright infringement.

After the interview, GMA's reporter Chantal Westerman knew how damaging it was going to be. I did, too.

She whispered, "You hate it, don't you?"

"It's going to destroy me," I said.

She started to cry and said, "I can't pull it."

"I didn't ask you to pull it," I replied. "It might ruin me, but I'm the one who stuck the gun up my nose."

Anyone who's lived through a divorce or the breakup of an intense relationship knows that the days and weeks immediately following are unadulterated madness. They border on derangement. Somehow, though, you have to deal with it. I unleashed my temper. Unfortunately, I chose to do it on network television. But then, Barbara Walters once said that I had my most intimate conversations in front of 40 million people.

Now that I've entered the third act, I ain't likely to change. My life as a movie star has been an attempt at having fun for everyone who ever sat in a theater, as I once did, and wondered what it would be like to be

Clark Gable or Fred Astaire. Over the years, I'm sorry to say it, but I've slugged people, made some great friends, fallen in love, and have acted as my own worst enemy. I made plenty of mistakes, but I learned some lessons, too. Cary Grant once advised, "Burty, when that stuff stops being fun, just walk away."

I can't imagine that day ever happening. My life, despite its public ordeals, continues to amaze even me. Six years ago I became a father. Gazing into my son Quinton's three-day-old eyes, I experienced something beautiful, timeless, wondrous, and profound in the depths of my soul. Quinton didn't care if I was once a movie star. To him, I was Dad. I looked at him and saw the reason for my being.

For some people, including me, it's hard to approach a little guy like Quinton because of all that he means. At first, I was scared to death to touch him, but I quickly got to where I swung him around with one hand, like a football. When that happened I also realized I had changed. Somehow this helpless little boy forced me to become an adult. A man.

We're a unique bunch, us Reynolds men. My father, a retired police chief, is ninety-something. (He admits to eighty-eight. If I wait any longer to write this book, he'll be younger than I am.) This autobiography is partly a tribute to him—without his strength, I never would've come this far. Yet it's also for me, a lower-middle-class Southern boy at heart who's been fortunate beyond his wildest dreams. But mostly it's for my son, Quinton. I hope one day he'll open this book, have a few laughs, understand his dad a little better, and know that he was loved as much or more than anyone who ever lived.

# INTRODUCTION

As I STEPPED OUT OF MY OFFICE AND WALKED UP the long, brick driveway, past the tennis court and the sign warning "Rabbits & Squirrels Have the Right of Way," I considered the irreparable damage I was about to inflict on the image my wife Loni Anderson and I enjoyed as one of Hollywood's most devoted and seemingly charmed married couples. To the public and our closest friends, we had it all.

It was the stuff of endless magazine covers. Our Beauty and the Beast love affair included an adorable little boy whom we adopted as a newborn, flourishing careers, a dazzling social life, wealth, and immeasurable comforts. Between magnificent homes in L.A. and Florida, it seemed as if we needed the entire country to contain our happiness.

But that picture of conjugal bliss was dislodged

from its gilded frame the night of June 10, 1993, when I climbed up the stairs of the quiet Mediterranean-style house on eight acres of waterfront property which I'd owned for more than twenty years, entered the bedroom, and informed Loni that I intended to file for divorce. After eleven years together—five as husband and wife—there was no easy, painless way to drop the curtain. All other options were exhausted.

"It's over," I said.

Seated on the bed, Loni impaled me with a look of smoldering outrage. She was as aware as I, if not more, of the numerous afflictions suffered by our marriage. Yet I knew from the steely indignation and contempt in her wide, beautiful eyes that she detested me for taking any action that dared eclipse the light illuminating our fairy-tale existence. She was perfectly content to live within the passionless status quo, spending money as though it was as plentiful as sand in a Saudi desert.

Not I. After catching her in a romantic clench with a young man, I lost my desire for her as a woman. The only thing she aroused was my suspicion, which led me to investigate her actions. Following that, I lost my trust in her as a person. We lived together as husband and wife for another two years, yet we shared none of the intimacy of a married couple. Finally, I could stand it no longer.

"I know a whole bunch of stuff and I'm not going to go into it," I said. "You know I'm right."

Loni was as quiet as our big house. Quinton slept in his room down the hall, blissfully unaware that when he awoke the next morning his secure little world would be on the verge of turning upside down. Although the most recent years of our marriage were plagued by quarrels and enmity, I stared at Loni, marveling at her perfectly crafted features and doll-like beauty, and recalled only the best of our shared moments.

"We've been together a long time," I added. "We need to keep our heads. Most importantly, we need to keep the lawyers out of this. I know what's important to you. I'll take care of you. You'll never have to worry. We can work it out and get on with our lives."

That was the plan. It's been almost a year and a half since that evening, and rather than start our lives afresh, the divorce turned out to be a doorway leading straight to hell. It created more problems than it solved. I thought a generous settlement offer of $10 million would forestall such an eventuality. I also assumed that when my attorney came by the next morning with the divorce papers, as I advised Loni during our bedside discussion, we'd handle the unpleasant situation with a certain amount of restraint and class.

Now I realize that I made an error in judgment, resulting from being neither greedy nor devious. She seemed neither crushed nor helpless—as later depicted in the media—while stating her plan to fly to L.A. the next day. I planned to spend the night at my ranch with my dad.

"Will we ever see each other again?" Loni asked.

"Of course," I said. "We have Quinton to think about."

"Oh, yes," she said. "I forgot."


THERE was no doubt that Quinton was the center of my universe. He was a source of limitless joy. The answer to a lifetime of prayer. His dark brown head of hair stopped short of my waist, but he only had to look cross-eyed to make me laugh, or pout to make me cry. When he kicked a football, I felt like we were at the Super Bowl.

I wanted him to have the world, but with Loni and I splitting, I knew I couldn't give him everything. To prepare for the questions I knew he'd ask, I'd read a stack of books on how to talk to children about divorce. Then we went for a walk on the beach.

I'd been delivering lines for almost forty years, almost my whole life, but no amount of acting skill helped me when I tried explaining divorce to my son, because when you deal with kids you can't pretend. Eventually, Quinton saved me from choking on my own jumbled, nervous words.

"Dad, I know what you're trying to say," he said. "The dance is over."

I stared at him and said, "I was just about to say that.

"That's a wonderful way to put it, Quinton," I said. "Because when people marry, they start out with their arms around each other, like a dance. And a divorce is the end of that dance. The music ends, and they go their separate directions."

"Will you still be my dad?" he asked with a tinge of worry in his voice.

"Forever," I said. "I will always be your dad. Nothing, and no one, will ever change that. No one!"

I probably should've suspected something when Loni asked if she could take Quinton with her to L.A. Since I was in the midst of editing *The Man from Left Field*, a TV movie that I starred in and directed, I consented, knowing that I'd be in L.A. within a week or so. The last thing I imagined was that Loni would ever turn our son into a pawn in our divorce.

I had faith that our divorce could be friendly. We'd have to provide statements to the press, but that could be done in cooperation with each other. Our lawyers could work in concert. I wanted our son to be spared the confusion and distress of having his parents skirmish in public. All three of us would have to relearn how to function in our new roles, but we weren't the first family to go through a divorce.

By the next afternoon, though, it was obvious just how stupid I'd been. Maybe not stupid, just naïve, gullible, generous, hopeful—no, stupid. With an entourage that included Quinton's nanny, a security guard from the Gardens Mall who had become more than just a special friend to Loni, our houseman, and Quinton, Loni hid in the Delta VIP lounge until the final boarding call for her flight. As she waited, the nanny spoke to me on the phone.

"You can't believe what she's doing with this security guard," she said. "It's not right. They are all over each other in front of Quinton."

Moments later, Loni emerged into the terminal and was met by an army of photographers and reporters. Normally, when we flew across country, there were one or two paparazzi at most, hanging out in hopes of catching someone well known. But this was a setup. They'd been tipped off. Hidden behind dark sunglasses, Loni strode bravely to the plane. Lana Turner played that same role, but not as well.

For the next week I tried reaching Quinton on the telephone, but Loni wouldn't let me through. People told me that the rag sheets were saying I was ignoring my son, that I didn't even try to call. This wasn't how I envisioned events unfolding, but then I had a lot to learn. Finally, Quinton's nanny called me and described his confusion and sadness.

"It's not right," she said, and then told me she had arranged to take him for a ride the next day and that they'd call me then.

As soon as I heard the ring, I grabbed the receiver. Hearing him say, "Hi, Dad," made me start to cry. I wanted Quinton to think of me as being strong and to know how much I loved him.

"But things are really screwed up right now," I said.

"Boy, are they ever," he replied in a quiet little whisper.

I'd grown up not too far from where I sat while talking to Quinton. I remembered what it was like to gaze up at the sky and see only blue, to race across a sandy beach without care, and to stare at a pretty girl and wonder if you could ever hold her hand. Neither of our lives would ever be as simple as back then.

Some things never change, though. As far as I was concerned, nothing had ever come easy to me.

Nothing had ever come without a fight.

# MY LIFE

# CHAPTER
## 1

As much as I'd like to think everything I've done is based on a lot of luck and some talent—all the movies, TV shows, plays, adventures, and predicaments—it all might've been different, and perhaps never taken place, if not for the outcome of a single footrace. It happened before school. I was fourteen, a quiet, introspective outcast who eyed the cheerleaders from afar and even in hundred-degree heat dreamed of wearing a letterman's sweater. Dick "Peanut" Howser, maybe the best athlete in Palm Beach Central County at the junior-high level, challenged me to race Vernon Rollison, the school's best sprinter. Everyone knew him as "Flash."

What were the odds? I had, after all, outrun the police many times after tipping over outhouses or dumping dog shit on a neighbor's front porch. But

Rollison had never lost a race to anyone in the entire county.

"Well, I'll give it a try," I said, and we all began the long walk to the football field.

I lined up next to Rollison, glanced at the goalposts on the opposite end of the field, and then down at the ground where my fingers dug into the soft earth. Everybody who'd been at Beth's Soda Shop when the challenge was issued had followed us to the field. Peanut looked like Gandhi leading his people. Why had I told him I could hold my own?

I know why. When Peanut came to me and said, "Hey, mullet, I hear you're pretty fast," I saw it as a chance to move over to the jock's side of the street. Peanut was a legend, a three-sport letterman since seventh grade. (He would go on to manage the Kansas City Royals in the World Series, and win.) But his real talent might've been handing out nicknames, because they stuck for life. Recently I attended the wedding of an old school friend and the priest asked, "Do you, Booger, take Francis Lawler to be your wife?"

I mean *forever*.

I didn't want to be known as "mullet" or greaseball. I lived in Riviera Beach, Florida, a weather-battered, rough, waterfront town, which already put me damn close to the bottom of the caste system at Beth's Soda Shop, the school hangout. Cheerleaders, nerds, greasers, and jocks each had their own corners. I looked like a Vaseline ad, but knew I belonged with Peanut and the other jocks who wore the white sweaters with red letters and Wildroot Cream Oil in their hair.

"On your mark," Howser said.

"Lose this race," I told myself, "and you're mullet forever."

"Get set," he said.

I sucked in a deep breath. The entire world stopped.

*"Go!"*

Rollison got off to a better start. I heard his track cleats dig into the turf. My bare feet didn't make a sound. I kept my eyes straight ahead on the goalpost and concentrated on not letting him widen his lead. Three quarters of the way downfield I began thinking about the consequences if I lost: "mullet," forever on the wrong side of the street.

I reached down inside myself for something more. More speed. More guts. Dammit, more of whatever it takes to be a winner. At the five-yard line I flew past Rollison and didn't look back.

Afterward, Rollison congratulated me. He was a good guy, and losing the race didn't make any difference to him. It was just one race. But Howser was astonished. As the other kids rushed over, they saw him shake my hand and pat my back. It was as close to a papal blessing as one could get.

"Nice race, Buddy," he said.

"Yeah, Buddy, nice race," a few others chimed in.

From then on I was Buddy. Buddy Reynolds. It sounds more like a stock-car driver than an actor, but the name followed me well into my acting career, and to this day most of my old school friends still call me Buddy.

Pride can do amazing things. After that race I made better grades and more friends, but winning one race didn't erase years of insecurity. Even though I was accepted by the kids I admired, I never stopped feeling as if I had to keep proving myself. To this day, when it's time to face another challenge, I tell myself, "You have to win or else you start all over. You have to win the race."


MY earliest memory as a youngster is of the dense woods of the Ozarks. It was 1941, and my dad, Burt Sr., was called into the service. He was such a tough, imposing specimen of a man that I figured President Roosevelt had personally summoned him to take on the Nazis. If my dad couldn't whoop 'em, we were in big trouble.

My mom, Fern; my older sister, Nancy Ann; and I followed him from our little house in Lansing, Michigan, to Fort Leonard Wood in Missouri. We spent two years there before my dad received his orders and shipped overseas. It was the Mark Twain period of my boyhood. I was entirely fearless. I roamed the woods, wandered along riverbeds and unexplored caves that extended miles underground.

The base was full of other kids living with their families in the white buildings that all looked alike. I palled around with Guy Bledsoe, whose family had the corner unit in our building. Once we captured a copperhead snake that crossed our path, and I brought it home in my hat as a gift for my mother. She didn't scream; she simply said, "No, thanks."

Surrounded by all the soldiers, trucks, and artillery, my imagination ran wild. I gawked, waved, and learned to salute. My friends and I pretended to be little soldiers. Yet somehow I remained blissfully unaware of war—the actual war raging across Europe as well as the whole concept of it.

I remember those days at the base as a warm, affectionate time in my family, which isn't how I'd always describe us. My dad spoke softly but carried an intimidating set of hands. Hard as steel and big as a loaf of bread. Coiled into fists, they reminded me of unholstered .45s. He didn't say much. Our whole family was sparing with words. One of the best-kept secrets for years was the intensity of my mom and dad's love affair. They always rationed overt affection in front of us.

One of the few occasions I saw them hug and kiss was when Dad received his orders to go overseas. From then on nothing was certain. Flown to New York, he went to see Paul Robeson in *Othello* that night, shipped out on the *Queen Mary* the next day, and began the tense wait for D-Day. Twenty-five years later I would find out that a fifteen-year-old soldier named Charles Durning went to see the same play on that night, and shipped out the next day headed for Normandy Beach with my dad.

As soon as he left, Mom loaded us into the car and returned to Lansing. We took up residence in a tiny metal trailer set behind a house owned by my parents' friends. At six, I didn't mind living like sardines, but I already possessed my father's pride, and I hated being reminded that the property belonged to somebody else. (The kid who lived in the main house once wanted to charge me a nickel to drink from the hose.) He was almost eight, but I whipped his butt.

Fortunately, we soon moved to a little house in northern Michigan. Surrounded by trees and fields, it was across the road from Grandma and Grandpa Miller, my mother's parents, and the old farmhouse where she had been born. The history there went back generations. In a sense, it was our first real home.

IT was called Star City, but the "city" was actually Grandma and Grandpa's farm, along with a few other spreads, set off an unpaved dirt road called Star City Road. My mother and her seven siblings—six boys

6

and a girl, all of whom were unbelievably good-looking and shared the pillowy "Miller lips"—grew up there. Her grandfather Charles, a large, strapping lumberman who fought in the Civil War, had cleared the land and built both the big farmhouse and the little cottage across the street, where we later moved.

Family lore maintained that the cottage had been either a retreat for his demure English wife or a sanctuary where he went to compose music. Nobody knew for sure. But he left an oddly beautiful room with a high domed ceiling that had glass bottles hanging from it, his own invention for bettering the acoustics. I guess musical talent did not run in the family.

As for her family life, my mother said reserve and toughness was bred into their genes. There were too many children and too many chores for much individual attention when she and her siblings were growing up. Maybe she wished there was more hugging and kissing just as I always did during my childhood, but all of us got through on grit and pluck and didn't complain.

Mom developed into a beautiful woman—tall, dark hair, dark-skinned, great figure, and of course those wonderful Miller lips. She followed her older sister, Leona, into nursing and got a job at the hospital in Lake City. Devoted and skilled, she was liked by all the patients. But the odd hours and all-night shifts made it difficult to spend time with my dad.

Their marriage, which lasted sixty-five years, proved there's really something to the staying power of opposites. Where my mother came from a large and stable childhood, my dad lived the sort of adventure that makes for great boyhood stories.

Like my mom, my dad was born on a farm in Michigan, but while he was still a baby his father took a railroad job in Los Angeles, California. In 1911, my grandfather bought a wagon and team of horses and went into the sand and gravel business. He also bought a house in Edendale—now called Silver Lake—where the earliest studios, like Mack Sennett's Keystone Comedy Company, were located.

My dad used to watch them film the westerns and comedies on the vacant lots as he passed on his way to school. He says he was often late because those hand-cranked cameras took forever to operate and he wanted to watch everything. Many of the actors ducked into Larsen's Bakery, where my grandmother waitressed, and so my dad, who always hung out there, met stars like Charlie Chaplin, Fatty Arbuckle, and Mary Pickford—who all called him by name.

My grandfather, John Burton Reynolds, used to rent his wagon and horses to the movies. Charging five dollars a day for the team, he always insisted on driving them himself. As a result, he appeared on the silver screen about fifty years before I made my debut. His acting career was cut short by the advent of trucks—better and cheaper haulers than horses.

Upon selling his business in 1915, my granddad purchased 320 acres in the heart of Utah's Escalante Valley and started a cattle ranch. Suddenly, their lives were defined by the rules of the wild west. The nearest town was Zane—named after western writer Zane Grey. The town's one-room schoolhouse was located about five miles from the ranch. My dad walked to and from school, except for those days when he waited for the train's last mail drop and then ran home so the coyotes wouldn't catch him.

This lifestyle gave my dad the toughness of old rawhide. At twelve years of age, he had his first horse. At sixteen, he worked one whole summer on the rails alongside his father, who blasted tunnels and laid trestles to supplement income from the ranch. Both jobs were tough, hard work. After my dad finished high school, his father gave up on the ranch and moved the family back East to Lansing—back to where they had started.


WHILE shoveling coal in the firing rooms at a local factory, my dad became friendly with Wade Miller, one of my mother's brothers. One weekend Wade invited my dad to go hunting in the woods near his house. The Millers were all great outdoorsmen. My mother was home from nursing school and noticed her brother's new friend, and vice versa. Neither had ever been involved with anyone else, but they didn't waste any time contemplating other options.

In fact, there weren't any. As soon as my mother, then twenty-four (some say twenty-six), finished nursing school, my dad, just twenty years old, popped the question and married her before anything happened to change her mind. They never looked back—just down.

As they left the parsonage, they spotted a shiny, new dime at the end of the stone walkway. It was right in front of Dad's car. Waiting for them. Dad picked it up and stuck it in his pocket. They kept it throughout their entire married life as a symbol of their luck or fate.

I can see why my mother fell for Dad so quickly. In the hardscrabble times of the Great Depression, he inspired confidence. If he stood in a doorway, the light disappeared. On entering a room, all the oxygen seemed to be sucked out. In other words, this man had a presence my friend John Wayne would have envied. He didn't shrink from problems, just grew even larger and more formidable.

He planned on being a toolmaker, but during his apprenticeship, he lost a finger in a lathe. Many years later, I saw him lose another one. While supervising a construction job, a piece of wire got wrapped around his finger. Something happened, and it literally ripped his finger right off at the knuckle. He wrapped the finger in a handkerchief, said "Oh, the hell with it," and kept on working. "I'll go see a doctor when we finish work," he said. He now has two less fingers but the same work ethic.

That sort of determination, which I'd have to try to live up to later on, got him and my mother through the Depression. His responsibilities increased with the birth of my sister, Nancy Ann, in 1930. But Dad didn't buckle. Despite the long unemployment lines, he never missed a day of work. He dug ditches, unloaded steel, worked in the automobile factories—anything it took to put food on the table. My mother lost a son at birth later on, but I was born healthy at home in 1936.

"We just kept percolatin'," my mother told me. "We were never broke; we always had that dime."

# CHAPTER
## 2

TUESDAY, FEBRUARY 11, 1936. MY PARENTS WERE living in a small house on Donora Street when my mother went into labor with me. Her reasoning for having her baby at home was typical of my family. Like any good director, she wanted absolute control, and believed she had it in her own home.

Aside from my father's parents living on the street behind us, those early, formative years on Donora Street might as well have happened to someone else. Even after we moved to Fort Leonard Wood, my dad remained a mysterious presence to me—more akin to a large shadow than an actual person. He was a devoted family man, but every minute he could be he was in training and, knowing my dad, was probably thinking up ways he might take Hitler out himself. Once he shipped out, Dad occupied my thoughts day and night.

After returning to Lansing, Mom set a handsome photograph of him in his uniform on a small table in the sitting room. I wondered about him every time I walked by it. As the months passed, my mom started a collection of things Dad sent home. There were knives, flags, S. S. hats, and assorted souvenirs from the battlefield, all of which I still have today. He was in the first wave to hit the beach at Normandy on D-Day. Seventy percent of his regiment was killed. He later fought at the Battle of the Bulge and three other major battles after that.

A world away, our life had the innocence, charm, and tranquillity of a Norman Rockwell painting. Even though our new house was without electricity or indoor plumbing, and it was a while before an efficient oil heater replaced the wood-burning furnace in the cellar, Mom fixed the place up so it looked great to me.

If my mother needed something she went across the street to Grandma's, a big two-story house with a large, screened-in porch. In front was a beautiful flower garden and six huge, magnificent maple trees that stood like watchmen, reminders of how long the Millers had owned the land.

I spent a lot of time with Grandpa, who had been paralyzed from the neck down in a car accident. I sat on a stool beside his bed and helped him read, quietly listening for him to say, "Now," and then quickly turning the pages of his book, which rested on a huge glass tray connected to his bed. He devoured books; something I would later do myself, I'm sure having learned from him. He also had a mirror above his bed that let him look out the window. When I played in the yard I often looked up at his window and saw his reflection. He gave me a little smile and I waved back at him.

With Dad gone and Grandpa unable to move, both houses were dominated by women. This matriarchy was consumed by cooking, sewing, and related chores—stuff that was fine for my sister. But I imagined myself more like Roy Rogers, Gene Autry, and the other cowboys I saw in the westerns my mom took us to see once a month at the little movie theater in Houghton Lake. I always loved Wild Bill Elliott, who was Red

Ryder, and a young actor who would one day be a dear friend, Robert Blake as Little Beaver.

As long as I was home by dinnertime, my mother let me roam through the woods at will, exploring trails, spotting deer, jumping over porcupines, and playing war. I probably mowed down more Germans in the Michigan woods than Dad's entire unit did in Europe.

School was in the small nearby town of Merritt, which took in all the kids from a wide swatch of surrounding countryside, including many Native Americans. Most were products of very rural upbringings, real rough woodfolks. I felt as if I didn't belong, as I would for many years. As soon as I settled onto the school bus, I remember being overcome by a sick, sinking feeling of being very alone.

Eventually, I made a couple of friends. But I always sensed that I was just walking among props on a stage.

As comfortable as we were in Star City, I never went to sleep at night or awoke in the morning with a sense of permanency or completeness. This little corner of the world was beautiful and secure. There was nothing to complain about, especially in light of the stories I heard about the children in Europe, but I knew deep in my heart and soul that everything was temporary. As soon as my dad came back, everything would change.

# CHAPTER
# 3

ONCE A MONTH, WE GOT A NEW BATTERY FOR MY best friend, the radio. I used to stare at the little green light—as if I could see the people who were speaking. Sundays were great, with "The G-Men," "Let's Pretend," and in the evening, Jack Benny, Lum and Abner, and "The Shadow." We also listened to Gabriel Heatter—"Oh yes, there's good news tonight"—Edward R. Murrow, and one of our favorites, Quentin Reynolds. I thought these guys were great; true journalists in every sense of the word.

All through the war my father wrote long letters to my mother. From foxholes, he told her about the fighting in France, up through Belgium, then Holland, and finally into Germany. He recounted eating cold turkey on Christmas Day in the trenches at the Bulge, and the frigid winter fog that shrouded the Ardennes Forest. We knew he witnessed lots of killing, but spared us the details and described it only as a nightmare.

After the war ended in Europe in May 1945, much to my mom's dismay, my dad had to stay in Germany as part of the U.S. occupying force. In August, Japan surrendered. Three months later, he sent my Mom one last letter. He was coming home.

Dad arranged to arrive at my uncle Keith's home in Lansing. Mom, Nancy Ann, and I drove from the farm to get him. I dressed for the occasion by putting on my little army uniform, including my Eisenhower jacket, cap, brown pants and shoes, and replicas of all the medals I could get—five major battle stars, plus a Silver and a Bronze Star—that my dad had been awarded. I even slung a plastic M1 over my shoulder.

A taxi pulled up in front of the house. Everybody perked up, but only my mother ran outside. My sister stopped me from following. She set me on the sinkboard in the kitchen. Then everybody stared out the window and watched my mom and dad kiss. Mom had on her best blue dress; Dad wore his uniform. It looked like a scene from *The Best Years of Our Lives*.

As they came inside, Mom stepped back to give Dad, Nancy Ann, and me room to say hello. For two years, I had anticipated this reunion. I had rehearsed it countless times in my mind. But now that it had arrived I didn't know what to do. Nor did my dad, who, at six feet three and a half inches and 225 pounds, was the largest man I'd ever seen. He patted me on the head, and for the time being that was enough. It felt like magic all the way down to my toes.

"Here you go, son," my dad said, reaching into his pocket. "Take these."

I looked in my hand. There were more coins than I had ever seen at one time. I ran right to the store and bought him a couple of presents, a small ashtray, keychains, and a wallet. But I wanted to give him more. I wanted to give him something that would show how much we all loved him and missed him—something we weren't able to say.

A few weeks later my parents rekindled their marriage with a second honeymoon to Florida. My dad, who started the war as a sergeant major, the highest rank to be given an enlisted man, was promised a promotion to major general if he reenlisted after the occupation. However, at forty years of age, he didn't want to be a general. He wanted to be a father. He was ready to get on with family life and a career, which he stumbled onto in Florida.

As they enjoyed the warm-weather respite from another chilly Michigan winter, my parents met a man named George Putnam who owned ninety-nine lots in the tiny fishing town of Riviera Beach, where he planned to build a housing development. Eager to get started, he was so impressed with my dad, he signed him on as the general contractor. The lure of steady work and year-round warmth excited both my parents.

Without wasting time, they returned to Star City, arranged for my sister to finish out her school year in Merritt and join us in the summer, and then threw me into the car. Everybody but me was sad as we said goodbye to all the relatives, but the prospect of sun rather than snow helped even my mom get over the sadness quickly.

Except for the day my dad came back from the war, I'd never experienced anything as exciting as the drive to Florida. The backseat of my dad's new 1946 Ford was mine, and I flip-flopped from side to side, staring in awe out the window as we crossed the Smokey Mountains and then hit Highway 1, which extended from New England to the Keys off the tip of Florida.

I got excited every time I reminded myself that my new home was right on the water. Like my dad, I couldn't wait to get there. Both of us, I think, had something to prove. He wanted to make something of his life, and at ten years of age, I wanted to discover mine.

# CHAPTER
# 4

THE FIRST TIME I ACTUALLY SAW THE OCEAN WAS on Highway A1A in Jupiter. It was so green and beautiful. Little did I know what a big part of my life the little town of Jupiter would become someday. In those days it was a truck stop.

As advertised, Riviera Beach was right on the water too, tucked behind a strand of tiny barrier islands that stretch along the entire coast of Florida. When we arrived, the small town had a few thousand residents and two trailer courts: The Sea Breeze and Star Camp. With few belongings, we bought an old trailer and moved into—you guessed it—Star Camp.

Dad went right to work building homes on the far north end of the city, while I resumed fourth grade at Riviera Beach Junior High, a combination elementary school and junior high. I never developed much confidence at school in Merritt, and being the new kid in what seemed like a much bigger place didn't change that. But the situation didn't last too long.

As soon as my dad finished construction on the first house, he took out a GI loan and bought it for $8,000. Located at 28 North 37th Street, the last street in Riviera Beach going north, it might as well have been the edge of civilization. Beyond it was Lake Park. Once called Kelsey City, when it had been a wealthy eccentric's vision of utopia, it had been wiped out in the great hurricane of 1928; all that remained was the city hall, miles and miles of empty streets, and the small school to which I was transferred.

Like all the other homes my dad would build, ours was a wood-framed, Cape Cod charmer, which I was sure was one of the first in Florida. It had three bedrooms and a single bath everybody shared. My parents bought an entire houseful of rattan furniture from someone who needed to sell everything. By the time we moved in, my sister had joined us. Each of us had an attic bedroom, on opposite sides, of course, with a dormer window and window seat facing Highway 1.

Nancy remembers that it thunderstormed the night she arrived. She woke and saw steam rising from the road. At sixteen, the move wasn't easy for her. Seeing the steam, along with the heat and humidity, she said, "Dear God, I'm in hell." For me, it was and always would be paradise.

Most people believed paradise was actually seven miles south and over the bridge—the exclusive island of Palm Beach, where, behind huge walls and royal palm trees, Spanish and Italian villas rose like castles signaling the status of the extremely wealthy. None of that interested me as much as the swampy wilderness to the west. You could've offered me the largest mansion in Palm Beach and I would've turned it down in favor of the mysterious woods that ran all along the northern shore of Riviera and the everglades to the west.

That whole island-dotted waterway was my special place. When I came to the shoreline, I took off my shoes and headed south on the beach, bouncing on tangled mangrove roots, watching fiddler crabs dart in and out of the soft, white sand, and always keeping an eye out for turtles and snakes.

Sometimes I crossed the wooden bridge at Blue Heron Boulevard and went to Singer Island, where I learned to swim. The ocean became my second home. I bodysurfed the biggest waves without any fear. The rougher the sea, the better I liked it.

On these wanderings, I was fascinated by the fishermen and their families who lived in little Key West–type homes and ramshackle huts along the water on the outskirts of Riviera. Most of Riviera was made up of families known as Conchs, after the trumpet-shaped conch shells they brought with them from the islands when they came to Florida. Some settled in Key West, the rest in Riviera Beach. These locals spoke with a clipped, almost indecipherable accent that was the island's native tongue. They were all very strong-looking, the men from working their cast nets and fishing boats. Most were very good but tough people; some were and still are my best friends.

I liked to pretend that I was the Barefoot Mailman, a local legend celebrated on murals on the side of the old post office in West Palm. Everybody knew of him. In the old days, he delivered the mail from Jupiter to Miami, following the beach on the 160-mile round-trip, living off oysters, turtles, oranges, and coconut milk. I only walked as far as the Port of Palm Beach, but I imagined seeing the Barefoot Mailman many times and I told myself that I'd grow up and deliver the mail just like him.

AFTER two years, my dad and his crew had put up twenty-five homes, and the remaining lots were sold off. With the money he saved, my parents bought a little restaurant on Blue Heron Boulevard, just before the Singer Island Bridge. Actually, calling it a restaurant is generous. It was more a counter and sundry store. Yet it was located near a large dock and several of the town's biggest fish houses that cleaned and gutted shrimp, and iced and packed fish. So the place was full early in the morning and then again at lunchtime.

By then, Dad knew almost everybody in Riviera Beach as well as the neighboring towns. As honest as he was well liked, his reputation earned him enormous respect throughout the county. After my parents took over the restaurant, Chief Britt, who was a regular, kept asking my dad to join Riviera's police force.

Dad declined, but Chief Britt just kept after him until he changed his mind. There was no money in police work. Maybe $100 a week if you made chief. But as my dad tells it, he felt he was needed and couldn't resist the challenge. And once he put the uniform on, he says, the work just got in his blood. It became his life.

A few years later, Chief Britt suffered a massive heart attack and died on the job. My father took over and quickly made his mark. In those days, there was gambling from Miami to Palm Beach, all along the Gold Coast, and the big games were controlled by mafia families in New York and New Jersey. If you were the police chief of a small Florida town, it was assumed you might be on the take.

Shortly after my dad took over, he got wind that some New York people were trying to establish themselves in Palm Beach County. One day a well-dressed man he'd never seen before walked into the police chief's office and set a paper sack filled with $15,000 in fresh, crisp bills on his desk.

"I'm gonna leave this here," the man said. "You just ignore us and look the other way."

Big mistake.

My dad reached over the desk and grabbed the guy around his neck, almost tearing out his windpipe.

"I don't tolerate that bullshit in my town," he said.

Tightening his grip, my dad dragged the guy out onto the front porch of the police station. He pushed him down on his knees, threw the bag of money in front of him, and told him to start eating the bills. About that time I passed the station while walking home from school. In one of my most vivid memories I watched this guy take bills from the bag, stuff them into his mouth, chew, throw up, and start over again. No one offered my father a bribe ever again.

At the outset, the job forced him to repeatedly prove himself. There was a group of very tough young men who beat the shit out of every new police chief. It was their way of saying hello and letting the chief know who really ran Riviera. It had been this way for generations—until my dad took over.

Intent on changing these rules immediately, he walked into the Blue Heron bar and introduced himself. He was greeted by derisive laughter. Buoyed by several drinks apiece, a few idiots stepped forward to challenge the new chief.

They obviously didn't know my dad very well. He had a sap—a flat blackjack—strapped under his right sleeve and glove. Before anybody had time to react, he slapped one of the guys across the side of his head. It put him down, quivering with a broken eardrum. Everybody stared at the never-before-floored semiconscious man wiggling like a run-over snake.

"That was just a slap," my dad said. "You probably don't want to know what a punch is like."

They were all very, very quiet. Then he walked out.

He raised me with equally rigid standards. Once, when I was in the fifth grade, four older guys jumped me while I was riding my bicycle home. They beat the hell out of me because my dad was the police chief. When my father came home, he'd heard what had happened.

"Did you take anybody out?" he asked.

"No," I said. "There were four guys."

"I didn't ask you that," he said. "If four guys are going to beat you up, you've got to take one of them out."

My dad only hit me once. I was a powerfully built sixteen-year-old kid, and he overheard me sass my mother after she asked me to do something. (Sass? I said, "Oh, yeah.") I remember him flying into the room. He resembled Dick Butkus in a football highlight film. Then everything went black. When I came to I was sprawled on the floor of my closet. He'd hit me square on the chin and sent me flying through the closet door, tearing it off the hinges. Through the fog, I heard my mom say, "Dear God, Burt, I think you've killed him."

"Nope," my father said. "He's just asleep."

It's never a picnic being the police chief's son. Yet in my eyes no man was greater than my dad. Nobody stood taller or stronger. He was my real-life John Wayne. He defined the rules of manhood. It was like trying to replace Babe Ruth—an impossible task. I suspect this is why

I've spent my whole life thinking that no amount of success would make me as much of a man as my father. I've never lacked for confidence, but I still wrestle with the constant need to prove myself. I can still hear my dad say, "Son, if you're gonna be in a fight, you hit first, and as hard as you can—and *always be the one standing when it's over.*"

# CHAPTER
# 5

In the fifth grade at Lake Park, I could have doubled as Huck Finn. There were maybe a dozen kids in my grade, and none of the boys wore shoes. So I didn't either. As soon as I left my house, I took my shoes off and hid them behind a palmetto bush, and went barefoot until it was time to go home. My parents were amazed at how my shoes lasted, even praised me for being conscientious.

In the sixth grade, I developed my first crush without any warning of the first heartbreak I would suffer. Her name was Marilyn Clark. She had beautiful black hair and one front tooth that was longer than the other. She lived a block away, on Silver Beach Road. I remember the first time her father saw me. I heard him say, "There's a boy out there in the tree."

"Oh, that's just Burt Jr.," his wife answered. "Marilyn's little friend."

Eventually, Marilyn would join me in the tree, where we would talk for hours about nonsense. I loved making her laugh. Nothing was more beautiful, I thought, than that one big tooth in the center of her smile. At parties, we played Spin the Bottle, and I prayed the bottle would stop in front of her. When it did we kissed, a long sweet kiss with everybody looking.

Then Kenny Paramore came on the scene. Kenny was one of those guys who had hair under his arms in sixth grade, drove by the seventh, and shaved by the eighth. He was also a great athlete. One day some guys from Riviera Junior High's basketball team challenged some of our guys to a practice game, even though we didn't have uniforms; in fact, we didn't have a team. But not only did Kenny score a bunch of points, he also made a very big steal—Marilyn.

And so it was. I moped around for awhile, but by the middle of term sixth grade I had turned my eye toward another prize: the school's American Legion Award, a big, shiny trophy. Nobody knew why it was awarded, but it was the school's only prize. Lake Park only went up to seventh grade, and on graduation one boy and one girl won a trophy. When it was handed out the next year, I wanted my name on it. I hadn't ever won anything, but I figured I had a shot. I was the captain of the school safety patrol, and had my own captain's badge and street corner.

I started seventh grade feeling real cocky. My only competition was a fat kid named Norman whose sole purpose between eight a.m. and three p.m. was to kiss every teacher's ass. Well, I knew I had Norman beat, and imagined hearing my name being called out in front of the entire school.

Then someone from the Palm Beach County school board came out, counted all twelve people in the seventh grade, and determined that there weren't enough students to warrant a seventh-grade teacher. As a result, we would be bused to Central Junior High School in West Palm Beach. I couldn't imagine a worse nightmare. Central was enormous. I'd be lost till I graduated. Maybe longer. I might as well be going to Cornell University. Even worse, I'd lost the American Legion Award, something I knew would have made my father proud.

• • •

CENTRAL shared the same school grounds as Palm Beach High, which took in all the students from the ten neighboring junior highs. Each morning whole convoys of buses dropped off students, creating a scene that reminded me of the wartime invasions in Europe. Central stood at the far west end of the immense campus, the high school took up everywhere else. The next six years of my life stretched out in front of me as if I had been drafted into the Foreign Legion.

I doubted whether I could hack it. For the first few days I couldn't even find a seat on the bus. Each one I tried already belonged to someone else. Instead of "Hey, pal, how're you doing today?" I heard, "That's my seat, greaseball." Or "Outta here, mullet." I could always fight, but I figured I'd better give it a week or two. If nothing else, I arrived at my new school with two new additions to my given name.

I was magnificently unprepared. I got lost in the long corridors. The doors confused me. Every time I heard a metal locker bang I was unnerved. Half the time I didn't know where I was, and if you'd have asked me who I was, I would've had a problem with that, too.

At lunch the first day I followed the tide to Beth's Soda Shop, the hangout across the street, where everybody gathered before, during, and after school. Your social standing was determined by where you sat. Beth's had four corners: nerds in one, cheerleaders in another, the greasers, and then the jocks. As I crossed the street, I saw a bunch of greaseballs from Westgate, a tough section of West Palm, on one corner. Among them were some guys I knew from Riviera Beach. A few "mullets." They had Vaseline in their hair and cigarettes rolled up in their T-shirt sleeves. From then on, I ate with them and stared across the street at the swaggering figures in letterman sweaters.

As if my personal identity crisis wasn't enough, others didn't even notice I was alive. In homeroom, kids passed around a black composition book. Someone's name was inscribed at the top of each page. Names like Reggie Studstill and Donald Rott. I didn't know any of them. Beneath the names people scrawled one- and two-word descriptions, like encapsulated movie reviews: "Super guy." "Nice." "Great bod." "Inhuman." That was the best—inhuman. "Inhuman" was like getting thumbs up—from both the fat guy and the skinny guy. You couldn't do better.

I remember the first time the book was passed to me. I paged through it, reading the names, not recognizing any of them, and looking for mine. My heart pounded anxiously as I looked for what was written about me. But I didn't make inhuman. I didn't make nice guy or great bod, either. As a matter of fact, I didn't even make the book.

I was miserable, and the book just added to my misery. I hated where I sat at Beth's. I hated the bus that brought me to school. I hated school, period. As a result, I started skipping. I mean, if someone said, "You want to . . ." I didn't even wait for them to finish asking what. I just said, "Let's go," and took off.

I was the first among my age to sneak into the drive-in. I dove off the big bridge when it was raised when none of my older friends would. I amazed them by accepting a dare to dive off an airboat onto the back of a deer in the Everglades, which could be dangerous and a stupid stunt. After leaping from the cruising boat, you grabbed hold of the deer's soft neck, prayed the animal didn't cut you to ribbons with the razor-sharp edges of its hooves, and then rode it for a few yards into the swamp and hoped you didn't land on a gator.

By age twelve, I didn't have a best friend, but, boy, I had a reputation.

# CHAPTER
## 6

JIMMY HOOKS AND I FOUND EACH OTHER LURKING IN the shadows of both our school grounds, and hit it off immediately, even though he went to Conniston and I went to Central. Like me, he didn't fit in with any of the popular groups. Some of that was because he'd been born with a partial club foot. There was, however, another reason why Jimmy kept to himself, but I didn't learn about that until he finally invited me over to his house.

He'd done so with trepidation, confirming my suspicion, I thought, that he was embarrassed for me to see where he lived. It wasn't great, but I'd seen lots worse. As soon as I walked inside, though, I learned the real story. Jimmy's mom was loud and real drunk, and so was the guy she was entertaining at the time.

I'd heard my father talk about women drunks, but I'd never really been around one.

All of a sudden Jimmy's mom started yelling at him. There was no reason as far as I could tell. She just started screaming. Jimmy held in his anger. Then his mom's companion pushed Jimmy around. Probably because I was standing there, Jimmy felt he had to defend himself. He gave a shove back, and then turned to leave.

As I reached the door, the guy grabbed Jimmy and began hitting him like a punching bag. Jimmy was my age—twelve. I'd never seen a man fight a boy, and in all honesty, it stunned me. I thought kids were supposed to respect grownups, and that's why I didn't jump into the middle of it.

Although Jimmy held his own for a moment, I saw he wanted to get the hell out. So did I. We somehow exchanged panicked glances, and without saying anything, we bolted out the door. Outside, I saw that Jimmy's shirt was torn—half was tattered, the other half completely gone. Neither of us said a word. We didn't have to. In total silence, we walked straight to my house, where my mom was in the kitchen preparing dinner. Never one to beat around the bush, I said, "Mom, Jimmy's going to be my brother and he's going to live here."

I hadn't planned on saying that part until later, but the words just popped from my mouth. I simply said what I felt was right, exactly as I do today.

"Really?" she said, glancing at Jimmy, who looked as if he'd gone a couple of rounds with someone in a heavier weight classification. "Well, I like Jimmy but we'd better talk to Big Burt about that."

While Jimmy and I washed up, we waited for the police car to drive up. Finally, at about 6:30 P.M., I heard Dad pull up the driveway and enter the house. He didn't have to say, "Hello, I'm home." You just knew. All of a sudden, there was less oxygen. The house seemed crowded. The floors shook. Only the gentle, caring look he gave my mother made him seem cut of the same cloth as the rest of us humans.

Nervous but resolute, I approached my dad.

"Pop," I said, "I would like Jimmy to be my brother."

It didn't matter that I was telling an incomplete story. My dad, as police chief, knew most all the personal problems in the town, including Jimmy's situation at home. He took a long look at my friend.

"Is that what you want, Jimmy?" he asked.

Jimmy said, "Yes, sir, if it's all right."

"Well, I'll swing by and talk to your mom tomorrow and see what she says. In the meantime . . ."

My dad turned around and motioned for us to follow him up the stairs. The three of us went into my attic bedroom. Dad opened my closet and stuck his hand in the middle of my clothes. There weren't a lot of clothes, maybe seven or eight pairs of pants and shirts. Still, he pushed half to one side, half to the other, then turned around and faced us.

"If you stay, Jim, these are all yours," he said, pointing to one side. "And these are all yours, Burt Jr."

We listened intently. No questions asked.

"Jim, we have rules here," my dad continued. "If you break them, you're gone. And that goes double for you, son. You understand?"

Jim and I turned slightly toward each other. Our bright eyes and timid smiles reflected both relief and excitement. Jim's mom had no problem with him living where he wanted. Years later, Jim, then in his early twenties, would marry, look up his real mother again and then, after finding she was still on the sauce and wasn't really interested in him at all, asked my parents if he could change his last name to Reynolds. My dad suggested they legally adopt him, which they did. But that first night we knew only that Jim had to stay with us, and so we answered my dad like dutiful soldiers.

"Yes, sir!"

# CHAPTER
# 7

ALTHOUGH WE SELDOM TALKED, I TRULY LOVED MY sister. In many ways I think she raised me, as she was six when I was born. She was so shy and sensitive, yet she had very strong opinions about what was good for me. She had a very tough time communicating because of her shyness and our upbringing, but she raised two of the best kids in the world, and I would die for her.

By the time I was thirteen she had moved out of the house. I was bored with school, and I had a strong premonition that my life was going nowhere. I though I was a nogoodnik. I thought there was adventure somewhere beyond the confines of Riviera, somewhere out in the vast and mysterious *there*, and I decided to search for it.

Two older guys—clearly, not the best role models—who took me under their wing during my first year at Central coaxed me into skipping town with them. Admittedly, it didn't take much coaxing once I heard them talk about hoboing across the country, hopping freight trains, hitchhiking, camping, and taking life day by day as the outlaws we imagined ourselves to be.

"And Burt Jr.," one of them said, "you're in charge of getting us some money for the trip."

"Okay," I said.

What a putz!

Later that night, Dad and I picked up Mom after she closed the restaurant. I scooted into the backseat, where she set her paper bag full of the day's receipts. As they talked, I stuck my hand in, pulled out a wad of bills, and stuck them in my pocket. After saying goodnight to my parents, I counted out nearly one hundred dollars, which was a lot of money back then. Not once did I think how hard my mom had worked for it.

A while later, I heard my mother crying downstairs, a sound I'd never heard before. She'd just discovered the missing money. I didn't know that she always recounted the daily take once she got home. Sneaking out to the staircase, I listened as she told my father about the missing money and then cried that her helper, "the best girl there ever was," had broken her trust.

"Don't worry, Fern," my dad comforted her. "I'll take care of it in the morning."

He didn't have to. Early the next morning, I rolled the cash up inside a note and stuck it in the steering wheel of my dad's car, a place he was sure to look. "It was me who took the money," the note said. "I'm sorry. Burt Jr."

With no intention of sticking around, I joined my two pals up Highway 1 as planned. I told them about the money. Although pissed, they decided to continue the journey anyway, but they made me promise never to screw up again.

We thumbed a ride or two until we got outside of town. Then, emboldened, we hopped a freight train, intending to get off in Vero Beach, about sixty miles away. But the train didn't stop in Vero. It didn't stop until we rolled into Allendale, South Carolina, where we got off, tired, worried, and hungry.

It was morning. Following a two-lane road on foot, we had just crossed a river bridge when a local sheriff pulled up and stopped us for vagrancy. He asked where we were headed. I blurted out Michigan and the other guys said New York. That got his interest. He asked if we had any money.

"Yes, sir, two dollars," I piped up again.

Apparently that wasn't enough. Without asking our ages, he drove us into Allendale.

We spent the night in jail. I didn't mind jail; my dad had one. But the other guys were unnerved, particularly when we weren't allowed a phone call home or any other inkling that we might ever be set free. The next morning we were handed over to a local farmer and ordered out into the field, where we picked tomatoes with lots of migrant workers.

It wasn't so bad, being out in the sun and working up a sweat. I grew attached to one of the migrant families. Their daughter resembled Gene Tierney, whom I'd seen in *Laura* at the theater in West Palm and fallen in love with. I felt similar stirrings toward this dark-haired, teen-age beauty picking tomatoes beside me. Her beautiful brown legs made it so I didn't even notice the work.

I marveled at her family. They lived in an old truck beside the road near the fields, but what they lacked materially they more than made up for in affection. At lunch, they ate together and talked and laughed unlike any family I'd seen, especially mine. And as the day passed, they joked and hugged and kissed. It was the way I always thought families should be, and I envied them.

When the girl's father invited me to eat lunch with them the next day, I jumped at the chance. I listened to their stories about moving from one state to the next, following the pickers. At the end of the day they invited me to join up with them when I got out of jail. I wasn't quite sure how that would work, but the prospect of spending the rest of my life with this young Gene Tierney gave me warmth in an area I'd never felt before.

After our third day in jail, the sheriff came by the cell and told us my father—not theirs, mine—had wired money for three bus tickets back to Riviera. Although I hadn't called, he had been tracking us since we left, asking the sheriffs in the different towns along the highway to keep a lookout for his wayward boys.

The ride home was long, much longer, it seemed, than the trip there had been. Maybe it was because I had so much on my mind. As the bus neared Riviera, I wondered what would become of my Gene Tierney friend. I also wondered what would become of me. What was going to happen when I got home? I had to overcome a lot of fear when I finally asked the driver to stop.

"I live right near here," I said, and hoped that was still true.

The bus pulled to the side of the highway. It was about six o'clock in the morning when I turned the corner onto 37th Street, close enough to see my house. Having been up all night, not to mention in jail for three and a half days, I was quite a messy sight. I was also scared shitless. Still, my dad had taught me to accept the consequences of my actions like a man.

Sucking up my guts, I knocked on the front door. My mom answered in her nightgown. My dad walked up behind her. He was already dressed in his uniform.

I had figured I'd be punished, and I prepared myself for the worst. But it never came.

"Do I still live here?" I asked.

"Yes, son," my mom said, and then she grabbed me in her arms and squeezed tight.

It was the first time I remembered really being hugged, and in that embrace I felt all mom's love, and never forgot the feeling for the rest of my life. Even though I had to remain after school every day for two months as punishment for cutting classes, I didn't care. That hug made everything worthwhile.

# CHAPTER
## 8

I MIGHT'VE CONTINUED STRUGGLING THROUGH
school, biding my time, if I hadn't beaten Vernon
Rollison in that seemingly unimportant race before
school. Afterward, Dick Howser asked if I planned on
trying out for the football team. This year was going
to be different.

It began on unfamiliar ground. On the first day
of football practice I was given a practice jersey,
pants, hip and shoulder pads, and a helmet. But I'd
never played any organized sports, and I didn't know
how to put on any of the gear or what to do afterward.
So I copied Howser. It's a good thing, too, 'cause if
you ever put your thigh pads on backwards, you'd be
a soprano! When he asked someone to pull his jersey
over his shoulder pads, I also asked for help. Same
thing when Coach Carroll drew Xs and Os on the

blackboard. Howser got it all immediately. I pretended to understand, too.

Once we got on the field, I did better. I understood about hitting and running. I loved the sound of colliding helmets, crashing shoulder pads, and gut-busting tackles, and flung myself into the game. Before the first practice ended, I realized that I was pretty damn good at that football stuff. Good enough that no one wanted to tackle me. And good enough to make the team.

Besides raw ability, I had lots of incentive. The pain of playing in the humidity and heat caused guys a lot bigger and more experienced than me to pass out, but it was nothing compared to working in the fish houses gutting shrimp all day. Every time I got the ball, I ran as if getting tackled was one way to get cut from the team and be back chopping sugar cane or gutting shrimp. Like my dad taught me, I made sure I was the last one standing at the end of every day.

Apparently, the coach was impressed. In the first game, which happened to be against Riviera Junior High, I started at halfback. Howser played quarterback. And another new friend, Kreig "Mo" Mustaine, rounded out the backfield at the other running back spot. Mo, who was part Mohawk Indian—hence the nickname—was one of the coolest guys on the team. He taped his socks up, rolled his sleeves just so, and bleached his black hair blond in the front. He had the look down pat. It went with the name Mo Mustaine. So cool.

By halftime, the three of us powered Central to a twenty to seven lead over Riviera, including intercepting two passes and scoring my first touchdown run. During the second half, Howser ran a keeper play and was caught by Spanky Pinder, Riviera's toughest player. Spanky, a big, double-tough Conch kid, was such a bully on the schoolyard he got five spankings a day. Hence the nickname. He didn't just tackle Howser, he stomped on his leg and then ground his face into the dirt with his spiked foot.

Spanky had frightened all the kids my age when both of us attended Riviera Junior High, but as soon as I saw what he did to my new best friend, I exploded. Until then, I'd never known my temper had such a short fuse. On the next play I turned into a guided missile, running straight at Pinder with my shoulders down and head lowered. On contact, I exploded into him. I heard him make a strange noise. It was the air rushing out of him. Spanky was carried off the field on a stretcher, and the game basically ended on that play.

Unbeknownst to me, my dad was in the stands that afternoon, and ironically, he sat next to Spanky's father, a classy man. As Spanky left the field, my dad apologized to Mr. Pinder.

"It's okay," he said. "Spanky started it. He always starts it."

After the game, my dad saw me outside the locker room. He told me that I'd handled the situation well.

"Pinder deserved it," he said. "He started it. You finished it. Good job."

Oddly enough, that was one of the only times my dad commented on one of my games. At the end of the season, I was one of four of Central's players selected to the county's all-star team. I also earned my coveted letterman's sweater. By year's end, I added baseball, basketball and track letters. Yet I would've traded all the honors and trophies just to hear my dad tell me again how proud he was of me. Unfortunately, he didn't give out a lot of "attaboys." I don't know who that hurt more, me, him, or our opponents. Because I took many a guy out of the game just to get my dad to say something.

I had my admirers, though. At school, I walked down the hall and people parted to let me pass as if I was "somebody." People were friendly, and everybody seemed to say hello to me. My white sweater, with three big red Cs stitched on the side, generated popularity. Even Margie Amole, captain of the cheerleading squad, talked to me. But there was no greater indicator of my status than the little black composition book.

Midway through that first season it surfaced again one morning in homeroom. My name was on the first page. Buddy Reynolds. "What a smile." "Fastest guy in school." "Muscles." And then, beneath several other entries, was that coveted word. "Inhuman." I repeated it to myself. *Buddy Reynolds, inhuman.* From then on, my life was never the same.

# CHAPTER
# 9

AFTER FOOTBALL SEASON, MY EDUCATION CON-
tinued. Margie Amole, the sexiest girl on the cheerleading squad, was among my new educators. The
subject was—you guessed it—sex. Back in the 1950s,
that meant my first long, long kiss. We sat under a
tree in the park. The night air was bathwater warm.
Our lips met, pressed together, and it was heaven.
Locked in a passionate embrace, we mashed faces for
what seemed like eternity. If I had died then, I
would've been happy.

But then something strange happened. Without
warning, I felt her lips part and her tongue pushed its
way into my mouth. It almost choked me to death.

I didn't know what to do, how to respond, where
to put my own tongue. Considering how much more
experienced Margie was, I just couldn't believe she

was such a lousy kisser. Later that night I told my friend Mo.

"She was great, but every now and then she had her mouth wide open!" I complained.

Mo cracked up.

"Damn, Buddy," he said. "Welcome to the wet French world. She French-kissed you!"

"Right," I said, but still wasn't sure I was crazy about the idea.

Okay, so I wasn't very sophisticated, but by the time I moved on to Clara Mae Dean and Barbara Jean Moody I considered myself an international kind of guy. With the start of high school in 1951, I still only knew about real sex—the actual deed—through locker-room hearsay. But the sight of the older girls in their tight sweaters with little white pearls and tight skirts made every day at Palm Beach High a joy to behold.

During the first week, Howser urged me to sign up for algebra, biology, and history as an investment for my future, but I had no interest in academics. Nobody on either side of my family had ever attended college, and I didn't plan on being the first. Instead, Mo and I enrolled in print shop, where we made lots of points with girls by printing up personalized name cards for them, and still had plenty of time for football and women.

The whole year turned out to be a wash. Both of us made the varsity team, but we didn't get to play until late in the game. We had the same luck with girls, who wanted nothing to do with benchwarmers. However, during spring practice I gained twenty pounds and turned into an animal. By the end of spring, the team's legendary head coach, H. M. "Red" Whittington, led me to believe I would be his starting halfback the next year.

"You're a tough lad," he said. "You love to run over people. Put on some more muscle this summer."

"I can't wait," I said to Mo and Howser. "How am I going to put on more weight and keep in shape?"

Easier than I ever imagined. From early morning until the afternoon, I worked on the fishing boats, baiting hooks, hauling in the big ones for the Yankees to have their pictures taken with. Then, once the day finished, I hung out at the Alibi, a bar on Palm Beach's hoity-toity

Worth Avenue. The Alibi's owner, Trevor Howell, was an ex-cop who knew my dad and loved football players. Which meant I was welcome anytime.

I didn't drink much, just watched the people, my favorite pastime. Across the street from the bar was a nice antique shop. One day I noticed a beautiful three-masted schooner in the window. It looked like something that would sit in a rich man's study, and several times after that I stopped to admire it.

One of those times the woman who owned the store stepped out and I sensed her watching me. In her mid-forties, she was strikingly beautiful. If I'd have fantasized about an older woman, she would've looked exactly like her. Blond, leggy, well-rounded calves, classily dressed, shoulder-length hair, and perfume that cut through the salt air like a switchblade.

"Do you like the boat?" she asked.

What boat? My eyes riveted on her reflection in the window.

"Yes," I said. "But it's a ship."

She moved closer, interested.

"How do you know that?" she asked.

"Because I have to work on boats every summer," I said.

"What do you do?"

"Bait hooks for rich Yankees. Then they catch a sail fish and I reel it in, so they can have their picture taken with their great new trophy."

"You're very funny," she laughed. "Why don't you come inside the store. I'll show you around."

Nervously, I followed her inside. We introduced ourselves as she showed me around. Her conversation was light, casual but confident. Mine began to remind me of my friend Steve Holzapple, who was a severe stutterer. After a few minutes, she gave me a small shiny tie tack that said Palm Beach Sailfish Club. I looked at it and smiled.

"Boy, is my old man going to get a hoot out of this," I said.

"Why? Who's your father?" she asked.

"Burt Reynolds Sr."

"The chief of police?" she asked, surprised.

That being the case, she suggested I not tell my dad who gave me the pin, or to say it came from a friend at school. Gazing into her beautiful eyes, I agreed to say whatever she wanted me to say. No problem.

"Where are you going now?" she asked.

"The pier," I answered. "I love to dive this time of day. No big deal."

About an hour later I was still doing jackknives, half-gainers, and swan dives off the old wooden pier when I saw her watching me from afar. I pretended not to notice, but suddenly I was trying to become an Olympic-caliber diver. My chest puffed out, my back arched, and my feet pointed straight. I went in without a splash.

The next morning I was outside the antique shop when my friend opened the door. I followed her in. She studied me like a newly acquired piece of art. I didn't mind.

"You're a good diver," she said. "And you have a beautiful body. Of course you know that, don't you?"

"Thank you—and—no!"

"No? How nice. You're a football player, I hear, too, right?"

"Sometimes."

"And what else? What do you have planned for after college? Are you going to be a doctor, architect, lawyer?"

"Oh, no, none of that. I don't have the smarts for that."

"Nonsense," she said. "I think you're one of the smartest people I've met in a long time. For instance, how'd you know I was watching you?"

"I saw you," I said.

"But you never looked at me."

"If I had, you would've walked away."

"See, that's what I mean. You're real smart." Then she touched my arm in a way that sent shivers through my entire body. "Would you like to have dinner?"

"At a restaurant or something?" I asked.

Never having been in restaurants other than my mom's and Mo's uncle's hot dog stand, I couldn't picture myself going to one with this stunning lady on my arm.

"No," she said. "We can have dinner at my house. I'll fix something you'll like. How's Saturday night sound?"

She wrote down the address, and the next Saturday evening Steve

Holzapple drove me to her home in Palm Beach. As Palm Beach residences went, it wasn't large, but when I walked in I realized what money and taste could do. It was one of the most fabulous places I'd ever been in. There were wonderful, exotic chests and pieces of furniture from India, China, and other faraway places. The walls were Chinese red, as were the plates, and the furniture was teak. Dinner ended innocently enough, with an invitation to return.

Every Saturday night for the next month or so she fixed me dinner and I questioned her about her travels around the world. Obviously, she was observing me closely, watching how I reacted to her, and I must've suspected I passed certain tests because I sensed something was going to happen between us. Or maybe I hoped something would happen if I kept coming back for dinner. Maybe I'd be dessert.

Then it happened. After dinner, she brushed my cheek with her lips, innocently, seemingly by accident. But it wasn't an accident. As I sat on the couch, she touched my face, let her finger trace a line down my chest, and pressed her mouth to mine. Silently, surely, she guided my hands, loosening her dress and slip and then effortlessly undressing me.

It was my first time making love, and I couldn't have wished for anyone better to be with. Gentle, tender, and smart enough to make things last for what seemed like forever, she made me feel godlike. Of course, at that age you're perpetually like a marble statue. From then on, she seduced me in countless ways. Before dinner, after dinner, teaching me to also be rough, but that giving is as pleasurable as receiving. Needless to say, I was up for anything. By the end of the summer I was starting to feel like I had the keys to the kingdom. I was also falling in love. I was familiar with all the spots. Unfortunately, my proficiency was the beginning of the end. As soon as she sensed I wanted to take the initiative, she told me we had to say goodbye.

I didn't know what the hell was wrong. I didn't understand that she was one of those women who liked inexperienced boys. It was my first serious lesson in love, sex, and women. I started off with an A, and felt like I'd worked my way up to an F. She'd left me bewildered, confused, and frustrated. But she'd also made me very, very happy.

# CHAPTER
# 1 0

SEPTEMBER 1952. IT WASN'T JUST THE START OF MY junior year. It was the resumption of football season. After the accolades I got at spring practice, everyone expected a lot from me—especially Coach Whittington, and, of course, my dad.

I wanted to be great. By then, I'd accepted that God had given my legs to somebody else. I had a long upper body and short bowed legs. Somewhere I'm sure there is a guy with a short upper body walking around on my long legs. I'm a little over six feet tall, yet I can go into a men's store, stand next to a man who's five seven, and put on his pants. Actually, telling these stories about yourself can backfire. Because of this, and the damn lookalike, many people think I really am five seven (the lookalike is!). However, I tried to make even this positive. I found that most of the great running backs were bowlegged, so I was sure this made me even harder to bring down.

I stayed after practice and hit and hit and hit, and ran around the track pulling a rope tied to several tires. I ran pass patterns till I could do them in my sleep. I intimidated opponents. Instead of cutting away from tackles when I ran the ball, I ran over them, and those I couldn't run over I punished for being in the way. Left tire tracks across their faces.

In the long run, though, none of that extra effort would have mattered if Bobby Riggs, one of the assistant coaches, hadn't dispensed some life-changing advice. Early in the semester, after I got off to a great start, he told me I had a good chance at playing college ball.

"Buddy, you're going to get scholarships, a lot of them, and you're not going to be able to go," he said.

"Why not?" I asked.

"Son, you can't get into any college when your preparation is print shop," he explained. "You have to take all the prerequisites for college entrance exams."

With Coach Riggs's guidance and a lot of help from my teachers, I doubled up on coursework and took both my sophomore and junior years both in my junior year. There was little to my life other than football and study hall. I managed because I knew football was the source of my self-esteem, my ticket to something better than working on fishing boats, and I was willing to do anything it took to make it.

Once school was out, I played just as hard off the field. I remember that summer between my junior and senior years was when I finally entered the enormous estates in Palm Beach. These were the homes of decades, even centuries, of vast wealth and privilege. The country's wealthiest families. There was more money per square foot on this little island of Palm Beach than anyplace in the world.

Yet in the summer the island was deserted. These titans of money and status took their backgammon sets, Geritol, and martinis to Kennebunkport or Newport or wherever else they summered, and unknowingly left their boarded-up homes to us. During the day, we camped on their fabulous private beaches. Later, under the cover of darkness, we snuck inside and behind the hurricane-shuttered windows, lit candles, played our little radios, and danced up a storm.

In those days, the coolest drink was a Purple Passion—vodka and grape juice that we'd mixed in the bathtub. Somebody said it was an aphrodisiac, so we guzzled them as if they were protein drinks and danced to Johnny Ace, Bo Diddley, and Fats Domino.

We partied at the Dodge, Post, and Kennedy estates. The Kennedy place was depressing as hell, but the Post estate, Mar-a-Lago, was unbelievable. Years later, when I started to make it in show business, I was invited to the Dodge estate, though it was weird going through the door rather than the window. Mrs. Dodge, a beautiful woman, said, "Buddy, let me show you around the house."

I said, "No, ma'am, let me show you. The master bedroom's up there. The study is down this way . . ."

"How do you know all this?" she asked, surprised.

And I said, "Mrs. Dodge, I've had more parties here than you have."

For me, those secret parties were a kind of revenge. My dad occasionally earned extra money supervising car parking for these families when they had their social gatherings. Although he got $100 for the night, I didn't think that was the going rate for his dignity. Once I heard someone say, "Hey, Chief, get me my car." I wanted to fly into the guy and beat the shit out of him. But Dad endured this test of pride to support his family. He was by far a better man than I will ever be.


BEFORE my senior year of high school ended, I nearly did, too. Her name was Constance Phipps (a nice name, but not her real one), and she was from one of those exceptionally wealthy Palm Beach families. But I didn't hold that against her. Constance was, and still is, an extraordinarily gorgeous, funny, and bright woman. We met in my sophomore year, but I wasn't ready for her until my senior year. I stood in a corner, playing the bongos and trying to look virile. A little dated now, but it worked for me then. Constance noticed.

On our first date, after being admitted through iron gates, I knocked on the front door of the palatial home where she lived. Her mother answered.

"Buddy, I'm so happy to see you, darlin," she said in a voice so sweet it could give you cavities. "From now on, I wish you would come to the service door to pick up Constance."

"Well, I'd be glad to," I said, "because that's actually what I'm here for."

Mrs. Phipps laughed, but added, "That's very funny. That's really very funny. But you still have to come to the service door."

Constance and I hit it off from the start. She had a body like few I've seen in this or any other life. Her only flaw, if you can call it that, was two deformed fingers. I don't believe anyone ever knew about it, since Constance always held a hankie in that hand. Until I knew better, I thought it was one of her endearing affectations.

Dear God, did she have charm and personality. Despite her wealth, and despite the number of experts she saw and operations her family could afford, she would never have a normal hand. But instead of being insecure or angry because of it, Constance went the other way. She became a joke-cracking clown, rebellious, athletic, wild, and crazy. I thought I was pretty daring till I met her. Constance was into advanced calculus.

Many years later, after I was already well known as an actor, Constance was interviewed as part of a TV special on me. In it, the reporter interviewed Constance at her mansion in Palm Beach. She talked to him by the swimming pool, wearing the smallest string bikini anybody had ever seen. She was forty-something and looked spectacular. The reporter asked how long she had known me.

"Buddy?" she smiled adorably. "Why, when we were just young'uns, he used to bang my brains out right over there against that palm tree. Just banged my brains out."

Once the reporter and the crew recovered, the interviewer explained the restrictions of TV and posed the question again.

"How long have you known Buddy?"

And she said, "Why, Buddy got my cherry."


IN terms of football, 1953 was a vintage year. Voted First Team All State and All Southern at fullback, I received over fourteen scholarship offers. By the senior prom, I'd narrowed my choices down to Miami and

Florida State. About this time I had broken up with Constance and started playing the field. Both of us went to the prom, but with other people. Ironically, we were named King and Queen of the Class of '54 and had to dance together, alone, spotlighted, under a mirrored ball in the middle of the dance floor.

Despite breaking up, I still had a mad crush. I knew I would never get over her—who could? As she looked into my eyes and melted into me, I thought we were going to rekindle things right in front of the entire class. But she had a surprise for me.

"You know, Buddy, when you go to college next year?" she said.

"Yeah."

"Well, they're going to call you B. Papa Reynolds."

We stood under this giant glass ball that reflected light into a million little dots. Music played. It looked like a scene out of *American Graffiti*. But as soon as Constance whispered that, everything disappeared. I might as well have been in the Sahara Desert. I broke out into a cold sweat. At the time, there was a football star at the University of Florida known as J. "Papa" Hall, because he'd fathered a child. So I knew exactly what she meant by B. Papa Reynolds.

She might as well have called me B. Frigging Stupid. But that came later in life.

We stopped dancing. For a moment, we must've looked like wax figures in the middle of the American Legion Hall.

"What are you saying?" I asked.

And she said, "How'd you like to get married under the goalposts?"

"Well, let's talk about that later," I said.

I went back to my date, Marilyn Tear, a perfect name, and Constance went back to the looney bird she was with, some guy in a soldier's uniform. I told Marilyn I wasn't going to be able to take her home—she wasn't pleased—and then went over and got Constance. I told the soldier, "Don't even think about getting up." Then Constance and I walked out, got into the car I'd borrowed, and drove to her house. Outside her door, I said, "I'll pick you up tomorrow night at six. We're going to drive to Georgia."

The next morning I asked my friend Steve Holzapple if I could borrow his car and drive it to Georgia, where the law permitted marriage as young as age sixteen. He was shocked. I don't know by what—that I was going to get married or that I asked to take his car into another state.

"You can't drive it to Ge-Ge-Ge-Georgia," he said. "I'll d-d-d-drive you."

"I'm going to get married, Steve," I said.

"No sh-sh-sh-sh-shit!"

That night I stole a wad of cash from my mother's receipts and then Steve and I drove to Constance's. Petrified but determined to do the honorable thing, I decided to forsake going around to the service entrance and knocked on the front door. Mrs. Phipps answered. As calm and pleasant as ever, she appeared to have been expecting me.

"Hello, Buddy," she said. "Where do you think you're going?"

"Ma'am?" I asked.

"Do you think you're going to Georgia?" she asked.

I looked over her shoulder and saw Constance crying. That made me even more resolute in my decision.

"Yes, ma'am," I said.

"No, you're not," she said matter-of-factly. "Constance isn't going to marry you, darlin', because you're never really going to amount to a hill of beans. We'll take care of this tomorrow, and she'll be back in school in a week and everything will be fine soon."

"Ma'am?" I asked, my will starting to crack.

"Oh, don't worry, Buddy. You two can still date. That's fine. You just can't get married. Now you take that stuttering boy and go home."

I turned around and walked slowly back to the car in a state of shock. Steve and I drove to the Skydome Theater and sat underneath the walking bridge nearby and drank beer until the sun came up. I've never forgiven myself for not being more forceful. It's a sin I will carry to my grave. I (or we) would have a forty-year-old heir!

Her mother took her to Cuba, where she got an abortion. Three days later she was walking across campus, smiling and laughing and being herself as if nothing had ever happened. She never showed me an ounce of anger, and God knows she could have.

I still think of Steve, under the bridge, shaking his head and saying, "W-w-w-w-women." In one very long word, he almost said it all.

# CHAPTER
## 11

MY FATHER DREAMED THAT I'D SOMEDAY HAVE A shot at going to West Point. Mike Easley, one of my best friends in high school who was one year ahead of me, was already there. Mike and Dad both plotted to get me into the uniform he wore so courageously. Through an influential state senator, I was to be given an appointment. But I told my father I knew I didn't have the discipline for it. I would fail him. I told him, "Dad, please don't even consider it." There's no doubt in my mind that hurt him more than anything I've ever done. Now I had even more baggage to carry around.

If I had gone, I wouldn't have lasted more than fifteen minutes as a West Point cadet. Some upperclassman would've come up, slapped me around, and

I would've put him to sleep and my career at the same time. I would've failed—and failed royally.

Instead, I signed a letter of intent with Miami. Howser, who was heading to Florida State on a baseball scholarship, told me I should reconsider—maybe I was making a mistake.

I said, "Peanut, Miami plays Nebraska, Notre Dame, and big-time schools. Who does Florida State play? Stetson? Furman?"

"Not next year," Howser said. "They're moving up. It's gonna be Alabama, Auburn, Georgia."

Despite having signed to attend Miami, I visited the Florida State campus. Why not? The rush parties the university threw for prospective athletes were great. And with fourteen scholarship offers, I got to be pretty good at being entertained. I expected to see a pretty little campus covered with ivy, but not such a charming little town. Then I met one of the slickest, most charismatic men I have ever met, and did he do a number on me.

Tom Nugent, the new head coach, was on a mission. Florida State was going into big-time football. He was an innovative genius; he gave football the I-formation, the typewriter huddle, the lonesome end. In those days, most schools passed very little. FSU passed more than it ran. He also made FSU the first team to wear white shoes—not so innovative, but, like everything else he came up with, it's still around.

He was just as clever as a recruiter of talent. Behind his desk hung a beautiful, wide-angled photo of the FSU campus. I didn't pay any attention to it when we first started talking about what Miami was giving me. In those days, there was no reason not to answer candidly. Cars, jobs, money. It was all routine stuff. Coach Nugent was unfazed by Miami's generosity.

"Buddy, will they give you that?" he asked, swiveling around in his chair and pointing at the school picture. "With your athletic ability and charm—well, son, you'll own this entire campus. You'll start for me as a freshman. You won't start as a freshman at Miami, but that's beside the point. Do you know how many girls there are here?"

"No, sir, I don't," I answered.

He said, "Well, this was a girl's school up until 1948, not that this would have any effect on your decision. But there are fourteen girls for every guy."

"I like this school," I said as earnestly as possible.

Before I left his office, I signed with Florida State. What I didn't know is that Nugent made that same pitch to every prospective player. On the first day of practice, honest to God, there were four hundred guys on the field, all with full scholarships. Most of them were grown men—paratroopers and rangers who'd served in Korea. They were twenty-eight years old. A few of us were just seventeen years old. Only thirty-six guys made the team—the thirty-six who were still standing at the end of three weeks of two-a-days practices. In other words, what they did wasn't really kosher. They couldn't keep four hundred players. It was like the old gladiator days. But those of us who stuck it out were friends for life.

One of the younger guys turned out to be Vic Prinzi. Vic, who would go on to be drafted at quarterback by the New York Giants and to play some for the Denver Broncos, was a star quarterback prospect. We met during a drill where two guys, in this case linemen and backs, stood about fifteen yards apart and then tried to run each other over. I was holding my own against the bigger linemen, some who outweighed me by seventy pounds. So when I glanced up and saw Prinzi, a skinny, Italian kid, I thought, Look at that. It's Gandhi in a football uniform. I'm going to ruin this guy's day.

Vic, on the other hand, saw me and said to himself, Oh, thank God, I can take a breather. This guy's no lineman; how bad can he hurt me?

It turned out I broke his collarbone and two ribs.

I visited him in the infirmary that night and we fell in like at first sight. We've been best friends ever since that night, despite Prinzi's not being able to play until the sixth game of the year because somebody broke some of his bones. Victor finally got back into uniform against Virginia Military Institute. He threw five touchdowns, was back of the week in the nation as a freshman, and finished the '54 season among the top quarterbacks in the country. He never looked back.

For a freshman, I had a wonderful year, too. I broke into the starting lineup in a few games and averaged 9.2 yards per carry.

But all my real seasoning occurred off the field. The jocks joined one of two fraternities, SAE or Phi Delt. I became a Phi Delt, but I wasn't exactly a paradigm of comportment or respectability. One afternoon while I was playing cards, a junior frat brother said, "Reynolds, go wash my car."

When they pulled that shit, all the new pledges were supposed to jump.

"Which car is it?" I asked.

"It's that Pontiac out in front," he said.

"Alrighty," I replied.

So I went out front, stuck the hose in the front seat, rolled up the windows, and returned to my card game. About twenty minutes later, the Brooks Brothers mannequin came back, saw me at the table, and wailed, "Hey, I thought I told you to wash my car."

"I'm washing it," I said. "I'm washing that baby as we speak."

"You are?" he asked.

"Yeah," I said. "I'm doing the inside first."

He ran out to look. There was water up around the middle of the windows. After that, *nobody* asked me to wash their car again.

About halfway through the season, a girlfriend from West Palm Beach sent me a Dear John letter. We'd begun dating during the summer and promised each other a semi-serious commitment. She was impossibly gorgeous, so I was semi-shattered by her letter. I walked down the dorm hall and, in a moment of blinding anger—a feeling I could patent—I punched a hole in a door. My fist went straight through. As I stood there with my arm stuck, I realized the door belonged to Al Mackowicky. Now, "Big Al" was an all-American tackle from Penn. Oh, shit! I thought, of all the people in the world, why am I standing here with my fist through his door?

On a trip to Louisville, the day before the game, the entire team had gone to see *On the Waterfront*. Not only did Brando blow me away, but like Marlon, Mackowicky raised pigeons on the dorm roof. He was from Pittsburgh and said things like, "You know, I love deez pigeons so much that when day don't come back, I get so pissed I want to kill the utter ones. You know what I mean? I'd like to break dare necks."

As I prayed that Mackowicky wasn't in his room, I felt somebody grab my arm. Then the door opened. There was Big Al.

"What are you doing?" he asked.

"I just got a Dear John letter, Al," I said. "I was feeling real bad and I sorta lost my temper!"

"Oh, say, you know, I'm sorry," he said, and then he shoved my arm out and looked through the hole. "What the hell. Now I gotta nice breeze."

As it turned out, Mackowicky was responsible for the longest run of my college career. In a game against Auburn, which was ranked No. 1 in the nation and loaded with all-Americans, Big Al came back to the huddle after a play and told Prinzi that he thought he could handle Auburn's all-American defensive tackle. So Vic said, "Pop left on two." Big Al opened a hole I could drive through, then I ran straight at the linebacker. Nobody did that. I duked him and then zip, it was off to the races. Fob James, a world-class sprinter who succeeded George Wallace as governor of Alabama, brought me down on the one-inch line.

It was a fifty-nine-yard gain, though with each reunion it gets longer. By now, it's over 120 yards; in fact, I've run all the way to the parking lot.

The funny part is that when Fob James became governor, he made a public service announcement for the NCAA and recounted how he ran down this guy who was fast enough to have qualified for the Olympics. He failed to mention that the guy he tackled was Burt Reynolds. (Nobody wants credit for running down a candy-assed actor.) As a result, I made a psa for the NCAA using the same footage. Not only did I point out what a brilliant run it was, I said, "I don't know who this guy is who made the lucky tackle. He had the angle on me though!"

Of course, at the time of the Auburn game, the word *actor* wasn't in my vocabulary. My entire world was football, football, and more football, and after a postseason visit to the Sun Bowl I looked ahead to an even better sophomore year.

# CHAPTER
## 12

THE 1955 PRESEASON WAS FULL OF HYPE. I WAS EX-
pected to be named to the all-everything categories.
Pro teams like the Baltimore Colts and Detroit Lions
scouted me during our spring practice games. In
one, I seemed to confirm a future of pro ball by hur-
dling two would-be tacklers. I was a workhorse who
could carry the ball twenty-five times without breathing hard. My short, powerful little legs were propel-
ling me along right on schedule.

But in our first game against Georgia Tech they
failed. As I started returning a punt upfield, I cut to
the right and went down in excruciating pain. No
one was even close to me, but I felt as if my knee had
been hit with an ax.

Carried off the field on a stretcher, I entered the
locker room still in excruciating pain. But it wasn't as

bad as the embarrassment I felt about being injured without anyone laying a finger on me. Real tough. Our trainer Don Fauls, who we called "Rooster," started to examine my knee.

"It's torn, Buddy. I can feel the cartilage; it's loose."

"Bullshit, Rooster, I can still play."

I played a little in the second half, just to test the knee. Even though I still ran over a few guys, I banged my knee up even worse. I ground it into hamburger and gristle.

After the game, Rooster chewed me out. If I wanted to walk with a limp for the rest of my life, he said, fine, that was my choice. But he suggested finding a great doctor to operate on it, and that perhaps I would have more football in me. He didn't know. Nowadays, the procedure is done arthroscopically, and sometimes you can come back in as little as two to four weeks, but back then knee surgery was a major operation that put you in a cast from toe to butt for months.

It scared the hell out of me. With my football future uncertain, I warned myself, "You'll never be anybody if you're not a football star. Nothing. You'll go back to being on the wrong corner again."

Sheer will, determination, and guts allowed me to make it back for the final two games of the season. I played on the second team, picking up a few yards. But it didn't take long for everyone on both sides to figure out I was a step slower and could only cut to my left. My bursts of speed and power were gone. By the last game my knee was ruined. Any thoughts of ever playing football as a career were over.

Over Christmas break I realized football was a part of my past, and it depressed the hell out of me. The joy ride I'd been on for a few years was over. I'd been found out, my real identity exposed, and I wasn't prepared to deal with the abrupt change in my future.


THE night before Christmas I borrowed my dad's '53 Buick, one of those huge, heavy-duty cars, and spent the whole evening cruising around West Palm Beach. On the way home, I got stopped for going about 105 in a 45 mph zone. It was pure recklessness on my part, but that and everything that followed, I'm sure, was part of a subconscious master plan to wipe myself out.

The sheriff's son, John Kirk, Jr., stopped me and said, "Your old man is going to kick your ass."

"Yeah, I know," I said. "But then again, you could tear up the ticket."

"I ain't that big a football fan, pal," he said, and handed me the ticket.

Mad at myself and everything to do with life, I drove around Riviera aimlessly. I cut down a dirt road where some knuckleheads happened to be in the process of hijacking cement blocks from Rinkers, a huge cement-block company. A flatbed truck with the cab pointed toward me was in the road. Its bright lights shined directly into my eyes. As far as I could tell, it looked like a car traveling in my direction. I was unable to see that the flatbed itself was across the road.

However, the instant I passed the beam of light I saw what was about to happen. In terms of reflexes, I suppose I was in the greatest shape of my life. If I had hit the brakes, my head would've been severed. I would've died instantly. Instead, I dove under the dashboard and let the car crash into the flatbed. The top of the car came off. I got smushed like a sardine in the mangled sheet metal and cement blocks.

You couldn't recognize the Buick. It might as well have been a Morris Minor. The rescuers needed seven and a half hours to carve me out of the wreckage. There were no Jaws of Life then; just welding tools, crowbars, and muscle. Clark Bibler, a lieutenant on my dad's police force, arrived at the scene. I heard his voice and managed to say, "Bib?"

"Who's that?" he asked, flashing a light under the truck.

"It's Buddy, Bib. Don't call my dad."

"Buddy?" he said.

"Don't call my dad. Don't tell him about the car."

Looking at the car, Bib said, "I think he's going to find out anyway."

I didn't realize the gravity of my condition. No one did. When they finally got me out, I didn't have a visible scratch on me. It looked like a miracle. I literally stood up and announced, "I'm all right."

A moment later, though, I coughed and blood streamed out of my mouth. It turned out I'd broken some ribs, shredded my shoulder, and hurt my knee again. But the most serious injury was to my spleen, which was busted. Only nobody could tell. I'd been in such a tight space for so long that the blood had coagulated. But when I coughed, blood came pouring out of my mouth. There was no doubt I was hurt real bad inside.

Somebody threw me in a waiting ambulance. I recognized the attendant in back, Tommy Price, someone I remembered from high school as being a good guy and very religious. I said, "Tommy, pray for me. I'm dying, and I don't know how to pray."

I knew whatever was wrong was real serious. In the ambulance, I hovered on the blurry edge of consciousness, but I remember Tommy held my hand and prayed all the way to the hospital.

Once there, someone asked if I had a doctor. I didn't. The only doctor I knew was Rooster, the FSU trainer. Someone thought to call my old high school football doctor, Lynn Fort. By coincidence, two weeks earlier Dr. Fort had performed a spleenectomy, a rare procedure in the 1950s, on an all-state Palm Beach High player named Abner Bigbee, who'd caught an elbow in his gut during a gym class and busted his spleen. Dr. Fort had saved his life.

Dr. Fort knew me well. His son, Lynn Jr., was a good friend and had started at center back when I played at Palm Beach High. Dr. Fort lifted my hand and pressed on my fingernails. I never knew why. I suppose to see if there was any blood. Then he checked my blood pressure. At that point, I remember hearing him clearly. He turned to one of the nurses and said, "Prep him. This boy's dying."

Then it was Ben Casey time. As they pushed me down the hall, I saw the lights flying by overhead. Then everything went black.


LATER on, as fate would have it, I dated the head nurse, Reba Sterling, and she told me what I already knew—that during the operation I'd flat-lined. I had died. I guess I already knew that, though, because I remembered seeing the light. Being in the corridor, as they say, and seeing the light. I also remember hearing a nurse yell, "We're losing him. I think he's gone." Doc said, "Goddamnit." And I remember myself shouting at the whirling blast of light at the end of the corridor, "The hell with you, I'm going back."

According to Reba, old Dr. Fort screamed, "I know this kid. He's too damn tough to die." All of a sudden he climbed over me, jammed his thick hand up my chest, grabbed my heart, and gave it a big squeeze. Right then, there was a blip on the heart monitor. Heart massage was not an everyday occurrence in the fifties. Dr. Fort saved my life.

On Christmas day I woke up with a big zipper down my stomach. Fifty-nine stitches to be exact. But I couldn't have wished for a better gift. How many people get a miracle for Christmas?

Six days later—January 1, 1956—I was jogging down the beach, wondering what to do with the rest of my life.

# CHAPTER
# 1 3

IN THE AFTERMATH OF RECOVERY, I KNEW FOOTBALL
was out of my life forever. The question was, what the
hell did I want to do with my life? I talked to my dad
about joining the police force, but he discouraged
me.

"You can do better than me, Bud," he said.
"You love kids. Why not be a parole officer?"

With that in the back of my mind, I enrolled at
Palm Beach Junior College. Most of the easy classes,
to which I naturally gravitated, were already full. So I
signed up for the unlikeliest of choices, art appreciation and English Literature. On the first day, I arrived
late—thank you, Dr. Freud—and only one seat was
available: front row, center, under the watchful eye of
Professor Watson B. Duncan III, the best teacher I
ever had.

I was used to coaches who sometimes cussed worse than sailors. Professor Duncan was an erudite gentleman. I thought I'd feel totally out of place in his class. I mean, I read playbooks, not plays or classic novels. As he listed the great writers we'd be studying—Shakespeare, Chaucer, Keats, Shelley, Byron—I wanted to ask, "What position did those guys play?"

I soon learned. Mr. Duncan would assign each student a different book to read in two days. He picked J. D. Salinger's *Catcher in the Rye*. Until then, I'd never read a book from start to finish in my life. I'd written all my book reports from the flap copy on the inside jacket. But halfway through the first chapter of Salinger's classic, I was hooked. I finished it in one day. For the rest of my life, I've always had a book going.

Professor Duncan also ran the drama department. In fact, Palm Beach Junior College's new theater is called the Watson B. Duncan Theater. But at that time, my only awareness of the drama department came from knowing it was a popular course among pretty girls. I barely heard Professor Duncan announce tryouts for a production of *Outward Bound,* but he snapped me from my cloud of indifference.

"Mr. Reynolds," he said, "readings are this afternoon at three, and you'll be there."

"Sorry, sir, I'm not coming," I said, thinking Professor Duncan was out of his mind.

But he'd already decided I was going to be an actor. He admitted this years later, explaining that when we'd read Shakespeare aloud in class, he'd noticed I had some real fire in my belly. He had no idea how much.

"Yes, you will be there," he said and then walked off.

Like other challenges, I couldn't resist this one. He gave me the play, opened to a page, pointed to the part of Tom Prior, and told me to read. I had no confidence whatsoever. You could barely hear me speak the first two words, but Professor Duncan had already made up his mind. As I was about to go on to the third word in the sentence, he interrupted.

"You've got the part," he said.

"What?"

He smiled. "No, you weren't that good, it's just that we don't have a lot of time to whip you into shape. But when you get there, you're going to surprise even yourself, and I think a whole lot of people who think you're just a dumb jock."

I was stunned. More so when Professor Duncan informed me that Tom Prior, the downtrodden alcoholic who was played by John Garfield in the movie, was the lead. Now I realize how remarkable Professor Duncan was as a teacher *and* a director. He gave everybody blocking but me, knowing I couldn't get all that down, give as honest a performance as possible, and also deliver my lines.

After being on stage, something clicked. As was the pattern in my life, I gravitated toward the challenge of participating in drama class. It was no different than football, which I played to prove myself worthy of recognition. Whether sports or drama, I wanted to be good, to try for the triple, not just swing back and forth.

Yet no one was more shocked than I at the end of the year when my performance in *Outward Bound* won the 1956 Florida State Drama Award. I gladly accepted the first-prize scholarship to the Hyde Park Playhouse in Upstate New York. Even though I didn't anticipate acting being anything more than an extracurricular activity, I wouldn't have to spend the summer chopping sugar cane or working on a fishing boat.

TAKING advantage of a bank account Doc Rinker, the wonderful man who owned Rinker's Cement, set up for me following my car accident, I bought a brand-new Dodge. My brother, Jim, and I drove to Waverly, New York, where we visited Vic Prinzi. After a few days, they dropped me off in Hyde Park and then kept my car for the summer. Oh well, easy come, easy go.

My apprenticeship began with supporting roles in productions of *Affairs of State* and *Anniversary Waltz*, which had professionals in the starring roles. Acting is defined by a rigid class system. Apprentices aren't supposed to mingle with the stars, and so on. But I didn't know this, and wouldn't have cared if I did. So one day I saw a very attractive young woman and introduced myself by asking some stupid question.

"Hi, I'm Buddy Reynolds," I said. "I don't know where to go for this reading."

"Are you from the South?" she asked.

"Yes. Florida."

"No kidding. I was born in Georgia."

I didn't recognize her until she introduced herself: Joanne Woodward. I felt even more foolish when she knew who I was. Graciously, Joanne complimented me on my tiny performance, saying I had an interesting face and she bet I could act. We quickly became friends. At the time, she was dating a young actor named Paul Newman, but, darn, he wasn't around. One night she invited me to a party. Sure, I thought, why not.

Little did I know. The party was at Gore Vidal's house, and the guest list was very small. Just Gore, his friend Howard Austin, Joanne, and me. Back then, I may have looked like Marlon Brando, but there was nothing remotely worldly about me. Gore epitomized the brilliant well-traveled, literate intellectual. Moreover, he could be wickedly clever and nasty. Over drinks, just for fun, he chopped me to pieces. Every one of my comments that I thought was borderline witty, he shoved up my nose and made a fool out of me.

"Why do you think you're ever going to be an actor?" I remember him saying. "There are construction workers prettier than you."

I rose from the table and went into the kitchen to get a glass of water and cool off. I wanted to figure out a polite way to excuse myself and get the hell out of there. Then, all of a sudden, Howard Austin's arms were around me. I knew it was Howard because he had on a fringed cowboy jacket, the kind Roy Rogers wore. Earlier, I'd complimented him on it. Howard said, "I think I love you."

I froze. I didn't know how to respond.

"Are you crazy?" I stammered.

And he said, "You can have the jacket."

He'd crossed my ability to cope. I picked Howard up by the front of his jacket and airmailed him into the living room. He flew in on his back, landing right in front of Joanne and Gore. I walked in and said to

Joanne, "I'm going back to the theater. You want to give me a ride?"

"All right," she said. "We'll go."

"Good thought," Gore said.

I didn't say a word in the car till we got back to the theater. "I could have been a little stupid—and unsophisticated," I said. But Joanne was marvelous.

"He's a wonderful man," she said of Gore. "They were just maybe a little drunk and, I think, testing you."

"Well, I didn't pass."

She said, "Oh, you passed. Just in another category."


I had as much to learn about life as I did acting. When we staged the musical *Plain and Fancy*, I developed a crush on the lead actress's best friend, a pretty blonde. I had no idea they were lovers. After going out to dinner with them one night and having a great time, I came back to my dorm and a guy asked if I knew they were dykes.

"What'd you say they were?" I asked.

I'd never heard the work *dyke* before, but it sounded like some kind of racial slur to me.

"They're dykes," he said.

"Look, I don't like that kind of talk," I said. "I'm from the South and I've had to put up with that all my life."

"Dykes? You've had to put up with dykes all your life because you're from the South?"

I grabbed him by the shirt and lifted him off the ground.

"Don't say that anymore."

"Whatever," he said and stumbled away, confused.

Joanne's other introductions were more successful. Through her, the powerful MCA agent Maynard Morris signed me. She also convinced director Wynn Handman, who worked at the Neighborhood Playhouse in New York, to cast me as Al in the next production coming to the Playhouse—*Tea and Sympathy* starring Linda Darnell—even though he'd already hired Mark Rydell, a soap opera star, to play the part. But Joanne worked her magic. Rydell, who later directed *On Golden*

*Pond* and several other films, got paid his wages, but I got the job. Maybe that explains why I've never worked for him. I'm sure he was delighted, and it certainly didn't hurt his career.

Anyway, I also got the reviews. One New York paper said, ''[Buddy Reynolds] looks like Marlon Brando without the fish monger's gestures or mumbling. He steals the scenes, he gets the laugh. We see a star on the horizon.''

I don't remember if my vision was quite that keen. But it was enough to keep me looking up at the sky.

# CHAPTER
# 14

AFTER TOURING IN *TEA AND SYMPATHY,* WHICH IN-
cluded driving the bus as well as playing Al, I took my
Actor's Equity card to New York City full of enterprise
and spirit. But the concrete jungle makes its own
rules. Either it's on top of you or you're on top of it.
There are no in betweens.

I rented an apartment on West 81st Street, a few
blocks away from the Hayden Planetarium. My one-
room place was so small I could cook breakfast,
lunch, and dinner without getting out of bed. If I'd
been Forrest Tucker, I could've peed without moving, too. I couldn't quite make it, though, and had to
take one step. There was no use pretending it was
anything but a closet.

Every day brought a new experience. Just figuring out how to get the gas, electricity, and a phone

hookup required more education than I'd received in three years of college. But it was part of being on my own.

Boosted by the good reviews I'd gotten over the summer, I was serious about giving New York a shot. I began by taking classes with Wynn Handman. After doing *Tea and Sympathy* together, he recognized that I was shier than I looked and that I had a healthy ego leftover from being a star athlete. Because that worked both for and against me, he put me in a class with people who had attained a lot of success in fields other than acting.

On the first day I walked into my new class and met N.Y. Giants football star Frank Gifford, dancer Carol Lawrence, and a few top comedians, including Red Buttons and Jan Murray. After a week or so, Handman singled me out to do an improvisation. Following him into the hallway, he whispered that I was a soldier who was blinded in Korea and returning home for the first time. I didn't know he told the rest of the class something else.

Well, hell, I told myself, I've always worked from the outside in. Now work from the inside out, like a real New York actor.

I closed my eyes and felt my way blindly up the stairs, expecting that Carol would be my girl and imagining how I'd have to tell her I was blind. The class, however, had been told they were at a surprise party, something quite different from what I was mentally gearing up for. I opened the door and said, "Carol, I have something to tell—"

Suddenly, everybody screamed, *"Surprise!"*

I should've been able to switch gears, react and play with the situation, but I might as well have stuck my finger in a light socket. That's how far the unexpectedness of the situation threw me. I was blind. I didn't want a party; I wanted everyone out. I went berserk. I grabbed my classmates and threw them out the door. Red and Jan bounced down the stairs. As I reached for Frank, he gave me one of those I-don't-think-so looks.

When I finally calmed down, Wynn puffed on his pipe, studied the damage, and commented, "I believe that was the shortest improvisation I've ever seen. But it was also quite exciting."

Embarrassed, I didn't know how I could ever show my face in class again. For several days I moped around and considered returning to a more predictable life in Riviera. But I couldn't go back a quitter, defeated. What would that prove? Then—and this is why actors must never give up—I landed a part in the revival of *Mister Roberts,* starring Charlton Heston at the New York City Center Theater. It was a timely break and a very prestigious place for a young actor to work. It paid $85 a week and taught me that nothing revives ambition and enthusiasm like work and a little cash.

Heston, who was finishing *The Ten Commandments,* showed up a week late for rehearsals. Something about parting the Red Sea, I think. Once he arrived, I discovered what it meant to be a movie star. Chuck—it's still hard to call him that—had a towering presence. When I compared myself to him, I thought, Dear God, I will never be a movie star.

The play was a big success. When it closed, John Forsythe, who had directed, arranged a movie audition for me. He really is that nice. He provided little information about the job other than the address of the apartment where I was supposed to meet the director. I remember the elevator that opened right in an apartment, which impressed the hell out of me. Then came reality. Josh Logan, the highly respected Broadway director, walked over to me, took a long look, and started laughing.

Not a good sign.

"What's so funny?" I asked.

"You can't do this picture," he said. "I mean, I'm sorry. But you and Marlon will look like the Bobbsey Twins."

The movie was *Sayonara,* and Marlon Brando had already signed to star. Red Buttons, my classmate, got the job I auditioned for, and later received the Academy Award. All I got was advice.

"You know," Logan added, "you should go to Hollywood."

Hollywood was too far away and too risky compared to New York. I was still in the process of convincing myself that I could survive, and perhaps thrive, as an actor. I didn't want to stray unnecessarily from the opportunity I saw in theater and live television. Hollywood would have to wait until I had built up more confidence.

In the meantime, I learned to survive. Like every struggling actor's résumé, mine included odd jobs waiting tables, washing dishes, and driving a delivery truck. I hated all of them. The only job that suited me was when I worked as a bouncer at Roseland, the upstairs ballroom dancing hall. The interview was a little weird, though.

"You're a little small to be a bouncer here, aren't you?" the manager asked.

"I'm over six feet and weigh 192," I snapped. "And I'm tougher than any son of a bitch you got working here."

"Really," he smirked.

Then I met the two other bouncers—Jack DeMave, whose boxing career inspired *The Golden Boy* and who stood six-five, and Tony "Two Ton" Galento, a brick of flesh and muscle who'd once fought Joe Louis. I gave Tony a brief look up and down and then turned to the manager and showed him what a true asshole I was.

"Do I have to beat the shit out of this fat piece of shit to get the job?" I said.

The next thing I knew Tony bumped into me and I crashed across the floor into a table and chairs. I got up and charged right at him. Tony caught me like a line drive and put me in a headlock, jeopardizing what few brains I had left. That I'm still here shows how much I impressed him.

"Dis guy's got guts," he said. "Give him da job."

Why not? It made his and Jack's lives amusing. Every time a fight broke out, the guys trading punches looked at the two of them, and then went after me. I fought four, five, six times a night. Most of the time I ended up rolling down those stairs with people. Which is how I learned to do stair falls.

As I brushed myself off, Tony would say, "Buddy, youz shouldn't roll down doze stairs like dat. You got to snuff 'em out before you get to da stairs."

Good idea, Tony. But after a month, Jack found me a less bruising job as a dockworker. One day a neatly dressed guy who looked tremendously out of place came around asking if anyone was willing to fling himself through a glass window on a TV show for a few bucks. Everyone laughed, except me.

"How much?" I asked.

"One hundred fifty dollars," he said.

"I'm your guy."

My live television debut came on "Frontiers of Faith," a religious program that aired early on Sunday mornings. I lined up and ran as if I was following Al Mackowicky through the line, and then crashed through a glass window. TV, I thought, ain't that hard.

# Chapter 15

I**F RIP TORN HADN'T TAKEN ME UNDER HIS WING, I'D** probably still be jumping through windows. At that time I really believed Rip was the greatest young actor in New York, bar none. Every time he went up for a part, he made everybody else look like amateurs, including great actors like Paul Newman, Steve McQueen, Robert Redford, and George Peppard. But Rip was also the most self-destructive actor I ever saw walk onto a stage.

Rip and I met at Childs, a restaurant on West 46th Street that served as a hangout for the Actors Studio crowd. They wore black turtlenecks and gathered as close as possible around Lee Strasberg. I desperately wanted to be part of their group, but I knew I wasn't anywhere near ready. Neither was Rip, but not because he lacked talent. He simply didn't care about belonging to anything. Which gave us something in common.

We became roommates for a while. It was truly an experience. Once, while playing basketball together at the YMCA, he told me that he had an eighteen-year-old wife named Ann Wedgeworth, who was pregnant and living back in their Texas home. Till she moved to New York, we shared the rent and our aspirations.

For a while we worked with vocal coach Al Malver to try to get rid of our Southern accents. One of our exercises was to repeat the phrase "Poe-too-la-bay-da-may-ne." We looked as strange reciting it as the phrase itself sounded. But we worked at it endlessly, repeating it every-place we went. On the subway, old Rip didn't care what the hell anybody thought. He'd shout, "Poe-too-la-bay-da-may-ne!" and I'd move to the other end.

He screamed at me, "Boy, you ain't never going to be an actor if you're embarrassed."

Well, I finally lost my Southern accent. But Rip, the talented son of a bitch, who can lapse into French, Cajun, Spanish, or whatever accent he wants, hung on to his native drawl. After weeks and weeks of saying that damn "Poe-too-la-bay" shit, he quit. I knew he did it on purpose, too. One day, I asked why.

"Because, old Buddy, I can't figure out what the hell's the matter with the way I'm talking right now," he said. "I know doctors and law-yers who talk like this. I'll talk the other way when I have to play a Yan-kee."

One day Rip said he had an audition for the Actor's Studio and asked if I wanted to read with him. I was flattered, and then scared shit-less when the day arrived. All went well, though, until right in the mid-dle of the scene Rip threw off his hat and screamed, "Goddammit! I forgot my best line." Then he ran out. The people, including Strasberg, seated behind a long desk, were stunned.

"Go get him," Lee told me. "We want him."

Ripper was unique. I caught up with him on Broadway. He was still cursing.

"Rip, they want you," I said between breaths.

"They do?"

"Yeah."

He looked at me for a moment, cocked his head in thought, and then said, "Fuck 'em. Just fuck 'em."

That was nothing compared to what he did to Kazan. At that time, every New York actor worshiped director Elia Kazan. I'd seen *On the Waterfront* several times since college, and to me, Kazan was the greatest actor's director ever. You realize how good a director really is when everybody in a picture is great but never as good again without that same director. In my opinion, Eva Marie Saint was brilliant, but she never quite equaled that performance again. The same with Karl Malden, Rod Steiger, and Lee J. Cobb. (Well, Lee was always great.) And Marlon, though brilliant in *Streetcar*, was absolutely flawless, I thought, in every second of *Waterfront*. It was one of the most perfect performances I'd ever seen.

Kazan called Rip in to read for *Cat on a Hot Tin Roof*. Like every New York actor, I dreamed of working for Kazan, but on that day it was thrilling enough to simply to sit in the back row and watch Rip. Prepared, both of us knew he was going to be brilliant, which he was. Much to my surprise, though, he walked on stage holding the script, which he knew by heart. He also wore odd little glasses and spoke barely above a whisper.

"Mr. Torn," Kazan said from the front, "we can't hear you."

Suddenly, Rip broke character. He stood alone on stage, lit by a strong white light.

"What'd you say?" Rip asked.

"Oh, shit," I thought.

"We can't hear you, Mr. Torn," Kazan repeated.

Five seconds passed.

"Goddamn you, don't you sell me short until ya hear me read," he shouted through clenched teeth. He threw the book across the stage and began his performance again. It was electrifying in every way. Kazan stood up and started to say, "I want to put you—"

That was all he said before Rip, a great athlete, jumped over the orchestra pit and into the aisle, and walked out. Kazan followed, asking what was happening, complimenting his work, pleading with him to stop and listen. Without breaking stride or turning around, Rip roared, "Don't give me any of your fucking Hollywood bullshit, man. I'm an actor. An actor, goddammit! Fuck you! Fuck you! Fuck you!"

As he passed me, he interrupted his rather colorful departure long enough to say, "Come on, Buddy."

I'd never seen anything like that. Rip, for God knows what reason, thought Kazan had not given him respect. He couldn't have been more wrong. But that's what I mean about being self-destructive. A few years later, Rip played the lead in a touring company of *Sweet Bird of Youth*, met co-star Geraldine Page, fell in love, and married her.

Between storming out of auditions, Rip worked regularly on TV and used his pull, God love him, to get me jobs. If the show had any fights, stunts, or scenes where someone was set on fire, he got me the part. By 1958, my credits included such mainstream TV shows as "Robert Montgomery Presents," "Omnibus," and "Hallmark Hall of Fame." At most, I recited a word or two of dialogue and then got shot, tossed out a window, or thrown down the stairs.

Finally, I landed a showier part. Per my specialty, I played a guy who catches on fire and jumps through a window. But after I landed in the alley and rolled around in a mud puddle, the lead was supposed to ask the fire chief if anybody survived. The chief would nod toward me and say, "That guy over there." Then the lead was supposed to pick me up and, after I recited an entire page of dialogue, I'd die in his arms. It looked like a Best Supporting Emmy to me!

I worked so hard on it, and Rip coached me, helping me to play "moment to moment."

"Don't indicate, Buddy!" he shouted. "Don't indicate, goddammit!"

I had no idea what the hell that meant. But this was the best role I'd had to date and I knew this was the one I wanted my entire family to see. Prior to this, I'd never asked my parents to watch me on anything. But the night before, I called my mom and told her to get everybody together and watch. I described the part, told her it was a great role, beyond all the others I'd done.

My folks didn't have a TV set, but on the big night they went to my Aunt Edna's, where about twenty friends and family gathered around the set to watch Buddy give a performance most actors only dream about.

In those days, fire gags were among the most dangerous of all stunt work. Insulated fire suits hadn't been invented yet, so the possibility of suffering severe burns and doing permanent damage to your lungs was a very real one. In my case, protection included dipping my hat and jacket in water. Nothing else. Then they poured glue over me, and at the appointed moment I was lit up brighter than a Fourth of July torch and thrown out of a candy-glass window.

The fall was about one story. A piece of cake. The hard part was finding my mud puddle of water, and extinguishing the flames. I also had to think about lines.

"Okay," I told myself. "Now listen for your cue."

The lead was to go to the fire chief, played by Paul Ford. One day Ford would be recognized as a great character actor, but then he was a mid-fortyish actor in his very first live television show, and he was painfully nervous. My scene was to be preceded by his only line: "Yeah, that guy over there."

Then the cameras were to swing onto me. Well, they lit me up. I crashed out the window, found my little puddle. Everything was working like clockwork.

"Chief, did anyone make it?" the lead asked.

"Nope," Ford said.

He blew his frigging line.

"Are you sure? Didn't just one person make it?" the lead asked again.

"Nope," Ford said, looking strangely far away.

The camera switched to a close-up of the lead, who improvised, "Well, if he would've made it, this is probably what he would've said." Then he delivered every one of my frigging lines. I couldn't have been more pissed. I thought of the crowd watching back home. Between the flames and the mud, they couldn't even tell it was me. I don't think I called the house again for a month.

But by then, I was on the move again.

# CHAPTER
# 16

DESPITE THAT DISASTER, I REFUSED TO LET WEEDS sprout around my dreams. I don't believe any young actor worth his talent contemplates becoming a star more than he thinks about the work itself. If you're going to be an actor, you concentrate on acting. That's the crux of all satisfaction. Whatever else happens—recognition, reviews, stardom (whatever that is)—is a combination of talent, timing, and luck.

Today, some kids become stars overnight, often before they even shave. Most aren't ready for all the trappings that come with stardom. Few stick around, and fewer still ever develop the substance that lets them walk onto a stage with the command of a Brando, a Charles Durning, or a Yul Brynner.

Yul Brynner—now there was a star. By chance, I saw him up close (without dreaming we'd become good friends years later) and knew without exchanging a single word that he was quite unlike anybody else. Brynner had an incredibly overpowering presence and charisma, as well as a devilish sense of humor. To me, he was a real movie star.

In early 1958, I heard the drum roll of Hollywood for the first time. George Maharis, another young New York actor, and I flew across country to test for the picture *But Not for Me.* Along with a California actor named Barry Coe, we were all up for the part of the very method New York actor who takes the girl, an actress, away from Clark Gable, the producer. George and I spent the flight talking about how we were real "New York" actors and pitying the poor California actors who would go up against us.

The whole way out George talked about how you couldn't trust anyone in Hollywood. Somebody had brainwashed him good. I couldn't believe that an entire industry could be composed entirely of crooks and thieves. I had to work thirty-seven years before I realized he was right.

From the moment we landed I was in love with Los Angeles. It all looked so big, bright, and new. The sky was clear then. The mountains changed colors throughout the day. The Valley was filled with orange groves. At night, the air was filled with the most wonderful smells of orange blossoms and jasmine. It really did look like paradise.

The studios were frightening in their immensity. I thanked the Lord when the guard found my name on his list and the huge gates swung open. Once inside, the soundstages were tremendous, like football fields, and there were so many. Between the various gates, passes, different stages, mazelike office locations, wardrobe, and makeup appointments, I gave up trying to get things right and enjoyed wandering around the sights.

Nothing was quite as impressive as when I walked into makeup for the first time and saw Mr. Gable in one of the chairs. Clark Gable—in person. I'd seen a few so-called handsome men in my day, but no one who looked like him. Then the makeup artist asked how I liked to be made up.

I looked at Gable. For a second I thought about getting out of the business and becoming a plumber.

"Whatever he's wearing," I mumbled. "Whatever he's wearing. That would be just fine."

I noticed Gable's head shook slightly. He had a bit of palsy in later years. I spotted him sipping from a glass, and I worked up the nerve to ask what it was.

"A little gin, a little coffee," he said. "Keeps my head from ticking."

"Good," I said. "Maybe I should have some."

Slowly, that famous Gable grin came my way. He was thrilled. He thought he'd found someone with a similar shake.

"Do you have—" he started.

"No," I said. "I'm just scared."

When he didn't laugh, I thought either that wasn't as funny as I thought, or maybe he has no sense of humor.

Director Walter Lang had the pretty boy go first. Coe, who turned out to be a real gentleman, had recently generated a buzz in the movie *Peyton Place*. There were all sorts of agent and manager types around him, but his test was just all right, nothing spectacular. In the middle of his test I heard Gable talking to him, but I couldn't make out what the hell he'd said.

So I said to my friend George, "Whatever he tells you, will you tell me after?"

"Fuck you," he said.

A good guy, George. But then it was his turn. In his black turtleneck, he was as subtle about his New York method acting as a taxi speeding down Fifth Avenue. He poured it on, all from the school of Marlon. Every little nuance and trick, but he was very good. And as before, I heard Gable ask him something in the middle of the test, only this time I heard what it was.

"You duck hunt?" Gable asked.

"No, I live in New York," Maharis replied.

I thought, What a putz. I hoped Mr. Gable asked me the same question. I'd come back with something amusing and make him laugh a little.

Of course, when I got out there I could barely talk. I looked up at him and, holy shit, I saw Clark Gable. The king. The only thing I was able to focus on was the collar of his sports shirt. It was up, an affectation of his. Watch any of his films and you'll see that he often had his collar up. For about a month after, I put my collar up like him, and every time I did, somebody would come up and say, "Hey, your collar's up."

It's like tying a necktie around your waist. Fred Astaire did it once at a party I attended and it looked great. I did it at another party after that and somebody remarked, "Here's some money. Buy a belt."

So my turn came. Between setups, Mr. Gable said, "Buddy, you duck hunt?"

"As a matter of fact, I was a stone killer once," I said. "But then my mother took me to see *Bambi*. 'Killer is all gone now.' "

Gable said, "Yeah."

I thought, Maybe I shouldn't have said the punchline with a lisp. Oh, well. After my test, I asked my agent what Coe had said, because he looked too pretty to be a duck hunter.

My agent replied, "Barry said he had a Browning over and under and had just been to the Roosevelt Game Preserve two weeks ago, where he shot thirty-eight ducks and two geese."

I nodded and said, "Well, I guess George and I aren't going to get this job."

And we didn't. Barry got it. My only solace is that he's also Mr. Goodwrench now. But I'm also sure he's still a gentleman.

# CHAPTER
# 1 7

THE LAST LIVE TV SHOW I DID IN NEW YORK WAS A "Robert Montgomery Presents" starring film legend James Cagney and Lee Marvin. What a way to go out. During a break one day I boxed a little with Cagney, who was so wiry and fast he was tough to hit. For some reason, Marvin also took a liking to me and invited me out to lunch every day, which meant we laughed and I watched him get drunk.

On one of these occasions, he uttered the words every young actor wants to hear and is too ignorant not to believe.

"You know what, kid?" he said. "When you're out in Hollywood, look me up."

*When* I was out in Hollywood? My first trip had kind of soured me on the idea. Till then, I didn't know *if* I was going.

Now two people had suggested I go to Hollywood: Josh Logan and Lee Marvin. The idea took about a week to germinate, but finally, I said, "Why not? I'm going." It was 1958. Summer was about to start. If I'd stayed in school, I would've been looking at my senior year. Why not graduate in Hollywood?

Before venturing west, though, I visited Riviera. I wanted to see my mom, and I knew a good dose of my old man would get my competitive juices going. I stayed busy by acting in several local theater plays and coached drama and football at Camp Keystone in Tampa. I also saw my old football teammates at FSU, which made me, for one insane moment, consider a comeback.

"Hey, Buddy's going out to Hollywood to be a movie star," I heard Prinzi tell a bunch of the guys.

None of them snickered.

"You gonna call us when you become a big movie star?" Joe McGee asked.

"I'll call ya'll," I said. "Now ya'll know Vic and I are real close. But I'll still be ya'll's friend, too. Everybody but Bagget. I don't like Bagget."

I was kidding. I loved all those guys. Even Bagget, who would knock your jock off.

About a week later I arrived in L.A. I stayed with a nurse I'd dated in New York who now worked at UCLA. Cookie Knomblach, God bless her generous soul. She gave me a place to live and cooked and cared for me in so many ways. She also let me use her new red MG, essential in navigating the vastness of L.A. We lost touch for ten or fifteen years, then one day I heard that Cookie took her own life. Why, I'll never know. But her kindness in those early times meant so much to me. I know she's in a place where only the very best of us get to go.

My first stop was MCA's Review Studios, in the San Fernando Valley. I'd imagined this for weeks. At the gate, I told the guard I wanted to see my so-called mentor, Lee Marvin. But I might as well have asked to see Charlie Chaplin. The guard shook his head, apologized, said he was sure I was a nice guy, but he wasn't letting me on the lot.

"Sorry, pal," he said.

Suddenly, the anticipation and hope that had fueled my trip across country vanished. In those days, I needed about five minutes to recover from such a setback.

"Never mind Lee Marvin. Your loss," I said to myself. "What next?"

Fortunately, I had another connection: Monique James. Many years before, my influential MCA agent Maynard Morris's assistant was Monique, who had quickly climbed the agency ladder to vice president and transferred to Los Angeles. I called her and got a warm reception.

"Oh, Buddy," she said, "I'm so glad you're out here. Listen, they don't know your work in Hollywood. So get another actor and come in and do a scene for us. Just do something that'll really knock their socks off."

"Okay," I said enthusiastically. "I will."

Although I didn't know any other actors, I learned the most popular actor's hangout was a small bar called The Lamplighter. I went there, scanned the joint, and noticed a guy who obviously was an actor. He had that look—Brando guarding a bowl of free peanuts with his life. I asked if he wanted to do a scene with me for MCA.

"MCA?" he asked with surprise. "Wow." I could see the wheels turning. Many times, when someone goes in for a reading, the other person gets signed instead. "MCA. Really?"

"Yeah."

"Great," he said, and then introduced himself as Ed Thompson. "What do I play?"

I explained we would be doing a scene from *All My Sons,* the moving Arthur Miller wartime drama. "I'm going to do the part Burt Lancaster played in the movie. Ed, you'll play my father."

"Oh, goddamn," he said. "I don't know if I can do that."

"Edward G. Robinson played it in the movie," I said. "It's a great part."

"Oh," Ed said, his eyes once again brightening with hope.

A few days later at MCA, Ed and I walked into Wally Hiller's office. Monique managed to bring in agency head Lew Wasserman and powerhouse Jay Cantor, who represented Brando. The room was small, but very classy. I figured its size would work for us and give the scene maximum effect. If I was on, I knew I had them.

However, as I reached the most dramatic moment, Wally's phone started ringing. Out of the corner of my eye, I saw him move to pick it up.

Dammit, the hell he is, I thought. Not during my scene.

Borrowing a page from Rip's handbook on how to audition and make enemies, I leaped across the room, grabbed the ringing telephone, pulled it out of the wall, and threw it on the ground. Everyone, including Ed, was stunned. But I walked back into the center of the room and finished the scene. Nobody clapped or said thank you. Not a single word. They still hadn't recovered from the phone being pulled out of the wall.

"Screw you, guys. Screw all of you Hollywood bastards," I growled, and then stormed out the door.

On the way out, I heard, "Oh, my name's Ed Thompson."


I walked down the street to a bar called the Little Club and proceeded to get plastered. About 10:00 P.M. I called Cookie and asked her if she could pick me up. In the car, she said the phone had been ringing off the hook since early afternoon.

"Yeah," I said. "I was an asshole."

"You'd better return the call anyway," she said.

I dialed Monique.

"Buddy, we're going to sign you," she said.

And I said, "Really?"

"Yes," she said. "Everybody thought what you did was very exciting. Plus, we've got to pay for Wally's phone somehow."

Two days later Monique took me out to Review Studios. As she gave me the nickel tour, I saw Lee Marvin. It was lunchtime, and I knew what that could mean. Despite my better judgment, I walked up to him and said hi. Lee just looked at me, and I thought, Christ, he's not going to remember me, and I will be mortified. But at the last second I heard that famous voice save me.

"How's Rip?" he asked.

And I said, "Rip's good."

Lee draped his arm around me and said, "Come on, kid, I'll find you something to do."

Monique had another client to see, so I let Lee guide me over to the soundstage where he was working. He introduced me to director Don Medford, better known as "Midnight" Medford. He was good, but he often worked painfully slow, very late into the night, hence the nickname. He loved method actors. As soon as he spotted me, he became excited. He said I looked exactly like Marlon and asked if anybody had seen me yet.

"Nope," I said, smiling.

"God, I can't believe it!" he exclaimed.

"Then use him in your next goddamn show," Lee said.

"Well, I'll try," he said.

"Not try," Lee growled. "Give him the fucking lead."

After I promised I could act "almost" as good as Brando, Medford gave me the lead in an upcoming episode of "M Squad," Lee's hit police series. That week's story, entitled "The Teacher," concerned high school delinquents. I was a kid in a machine shop, and playing opposite me as the heavy was Tom Laughlin, who would go on to widespread fame as Billy Jack. My call sheet said "7 for 7:30," which meant I was supposed to show up at 7:00 and be ready to go at 7:30. I didn't know shit from shineola about call sheets and thought I had a choice. So I chose 7:30.

Well, when I arrived, the assistant director, Carter DeHaven, chewed me out real good. He called me every name in the book and screamed so loud that Marvin came out of his dressing room, slightly hung over, and yelled, "What the fuck's going on?"

By then, a sizable crowd had formed.

"The kid's a half hour late," DeHaven said.

"Fuck, I know that," he yelled. "I was, too. So get the hell away from him."


By late morning, Medford had the first scene set up. As written, Tommy was supposed to approach me and say, "Pete, I heard you was interested in joining our gang." They lingered in the background. My line was the equivalent of "Why don't you get lost, and take these idiots with you." But as soon as Medford said action, Laughlin began improvising: "Petey, Petey, Petey—oh, Petey, Petey!" Not a friggin word he said was printed in the script. And I froze.

"The moment won't hold that long!" Medford screamed. "The scene just won't hold that long before you speak."

Panicked, I called, "Lee! Oh, Lee!"

We walked into a corner.

"Shit, I didn't know you were allowed to improvise," I confessed.

"Just say whatever pops into your head," he said. "Use your instincts."

Take two. Tommy said, "Petey, Petey," and began playing with my shirt collar. "Petey, Petey." Then he looked at me for a response.

Unable to think of anything, I did the first thing that came to mind. I grabbed his shirt, tore it off, lifted him up, and tossed him over the table and right out the door. After the dust settled, I turned around and looked at Medford, who simply said, "Cut! Print it! Loved it!"

Laughlin, a big, strong man himself, and thank God, a good guy, got up with a big smile on his face. He loved the action, and we spent the next few afternoons palling around the studio lot, talking, sight-seeing, and gawking at stars. Ironically, as we mused about the future, I actually saw mine. It happened when we wandered onto the "Mike Hammer" set, a series starring Darren McGavin. After ten seconds of watching McGavin work, I said, "What a putz."

"Yeah, what a putz," Laughlin agreed. "He'd be a nightmare to work with."

Little did I know he'd be *my* nightmare.

# CHAPTER 18

In 1958 I SIGNED A SEVEN-YEAR CONTRACT WITH Universal Studios. In addition to providing an enormous boost to my self-confidence as an actor, there was a certain amount of security even though they could drop my option every six months. Universal's president, Lew Wasserman, personally selected me to test for the co-starring role of the riverboat pilot Ben Frazer on NBC's first color show on TV, "Riverboat," starring and co-produced by Darren McGavin. "Bonanza" would be on with other color shows soon, but "Riverboat" was on first. They were so used to black and white on TV that they hired "Curly" Lindon, who did *Gone With the Wind,* as the director of photography.

My character was supposed to be the co-star—like Chester was to Matt Dillon. However, it only took a short while shooting the test to realize Mr. McGavin had more of a "silent" partner in mind. He ate my lunch in the test. But even though his company was co-producing with NBC, Lew Wasserman outvoted everybody, and I was cast as Ben Frazer.

As the season got under way, I was in for quite a few great lessons on how to steal a scene. In those days, an extra could steal a scene from me. But playing with Mr. McGavin was like learning to play tackle opposite "Mean Joe Green." You learned or you got killed. In the scenes where I had some dialogue, which were rare, in a two shot (which means when both McGavin and I were on camera), I learned that your eye always goes to the action. So Mr. McGavin, as I talked, would slowly remove his jacket or light a cigar. Cute! If I ever had a close-up, no matter if planes, rockets, or whatever flew over and ruined the sound, he would always say, "We got it. Let's move on." If I didn't fall down or faint and get a nose bleed, well, "We got it. Let's move on." As a result, when you watched the show, the cutting would go from a two shot to a close-up of Mr. McGavin, or to a two shot of the two of us, one talking, the other one just busy as a bee. I'm actually grateful to Darren for teaching me so many tricks early in my career. It was really a compliment, because he was a hundred times a better actor. And no matter what, I did three years of "Riverboat"—177 shows (we did thirty-nine one-hour shows a year back then). What a great way to learn your craft. No matter, too, what my personal feelings were toward Darren, he was never dull, which is really the worst sin of all for an actor.

In 1958 when I first got there, Universal was like a big campus. Because I had signed in the waning days of the studio system, contract players had acting classes, a gym, and Miss Universe (no matter if she spoke a word of English, she was signed to a seven-year contract every year of the contest). So you would sometimes see breasts coming around a corner long before you saw Miss Universe of nineteen fifty-whatever following them.

On one side of the street were beautiful apartment dressing rooms for Cary Grant, Kirk Douglas, Tony Curtis, Ray Milland, and Audie Murphy, and on the other side of the street were smaller ones with my old dear friends Doug McClure, Robert Fuller, Robert Horton, the great

Ward Bond, and many other contract players. One night, at 3 A.M., the legendary director John Ford was directing an episode of "Wagon Train" as a favor to his old friend Ward Bond. Well, Doug, Robert Fuller, and myself sat spellbound as Bond and "Pappy" Ford told stories. Then all of a sudden Mr. Ford said, "Why the hell don't you open this place up, Bond?"

"What do you mean, Pappy?" Bond said.

"I mean, you big dumb ass, why don't you tear down these walls so you can talk to these nice boys and have a good breeze, too!"

"Damn good idea, Pappy!" Bond said.

So off we went and scoured the lot for sledge hammers or whatever. We came back and, after a few hours, all the walls were down between the Bond, Fuller, McClure, and Reynolds dressing rooms. Cement blocks were piled up everywhere on the street. By morning, we had one big, long room—a great breeze, too.

I swear to you, not one word was said to us by the studio because the word was out that the great John Ford was behind the stunt. To get away with a prank like this confirmed all of us to some sort of holy status.

Because I was playing "Dum-Dum the Whistle Blower" on "Riverboat," I had lots of free time to wander around the back lot. Especially at night it had a truly magic feeling. It became my own special playground. I was Errol Flynn sword fighting at the castle, and Gary Cooper on the western streets. I walked down the street "Beaver" lived on and thought, Someday I'll be married and have a house like that.

One day I was working out at the gym with our instructor Frankie Vann, an ex–pro fighter. I'd had about twenty amateur fights and had won them all. I was a southpaw as a boxer. Most fighters circled right into your best punch because they very seldom fight left-handers. Anyway, in came Audie Murphy, who always seemed so unaffected by the whole movie star thing, and was a hell of a nice guy. He said, "How about we go a few rounds?"

I could see Frankie Vann shaking his head no, but old Burt couldn't pass up a chance to box the most decorated soldier in W.W.II!

Well he circled to his right like most fighters who haven't fought southpaws, right into my best punch, a left hook. Blam! Down he went. I was laughing trying to help him up when I realized he was anything but amused. In fact, he disappeared into the other room. Frankie said, "Get the hell out of here!"

I said, "Why? We're just having fun."

"Not to Audie. He takes this stuff real serious," Frankie said.

Just about that time I realized what he meant. Audie came around the corner with a .45 in his hand, saying, "Let's try my game." I ran through the door and all the way to the *Psycho* set on the back lot, hiding in one of the motel rooms.

I steered clear of Audie and the gym for almost a year. Great guy, but very serious about not losing.

During that period, they were shooting *Inherit the Wind* with Spencer Tracy and Fredric March. Director Stanley Kramer had closed the set to outsiders. But since all the guards knew me as Dum-Dum the Whistle Blower, I had no trouble sneaking in.

I went as often as possible, sometimes every day, and watched Mr. Tracy and Fredric March go at each other. Mr. Tracy never did anything the same way from rehearsal through whatever number of takes Kramer wanted. He surprised you every time. Fredric March, meanwhile, delivered his lines identically each time. Brilliant but identical. He was like a rock who refused to break. Both were extraordinary to watch. Mr. Tracy wasn't trying to play tricks. God knows he didn't need to. He felt that acting is reacting, so it was great for the other actors to have something new to react to. He never changed the words, only the rhythm.

But the most amazing thing happened each afternoon at five o'-clock: Mr. Tracy would just go home. It was written into his contract. This remarkable act occurred every day, and if the director was busy and the actors distracted, Mr. Tracy's driver would quietly drift into his view, pointing at his watch. At that point, Mr. Tracy would say, "Good afternoon, gentlemen," and—bye-bye.

On his way out, he passed me standing in the back and I took that as my cue to follow. Always a few steps behind, like a shadow—a shadow dressed like a riverboat pilot. One day he asked me to start walking with him rather than behind him. Sometimes he spoke, sometimes he didn't, but he was always kind. He told me to call him "Spence." After hearing

I'd worked on the stage in New York, he reminisced about doing *The Last Mile,* and told me how Gable took over his role when the play went on the road. He also told Louis B. Mayer about Gable and the rest is history.

One time I asked Spence about eating on camera. Unlike most actors, who when they have to eat, always take the smallest amount possible, I'd noticed he ate ravenously. He stuffed his mouth. Food spilled out when he talked. His scenes had so much gusto and life.

"But how do you match scenes?" I asked, referring to the need to duplicate action from take to take so the shots match. "It's impossible."

He said, "That's someone else's job."

Finally, I worked up my nerve and asked for some advice about being an actor. Spence smiled.

"Just don't ever let anybody catch you at it," he said.

Best acting advice I ever got. To survive in Hollywood, you learned the tricks. But you only used them on someone trying to kill you. Like McGavin, who was an expert.

By the second season, though, I changed my attitude. Instead of being charming and shy, I tried and sometimes did everything to him that he did to me. He didn't find it endearing. Everybody realized it was just a matter of time before there was a major explosion.

Unfortunately, of course, I went first. An assistant director, a major ass everybody hated, accused me of always being late (a lie) and unprofessional. He chewed me out real loud. I was on the verge of making it so he'd have to unzip his pants to chew his food when he walked away.

But later that day, I caught this same sack of shit pinning a pretty extra girl up against the wall. I saw she was trying to resist and interceded as would any Southern gentleman. . . . who was asked. She didn't, but I did anyway.

"Fuck you, kid," he said.

I never cared for that phrase. In an instant, I picked the fat blowhard up, held him overhead, and threw him right off the damn riverboat. He landed in the studio's dirty little lake, looking like a drowning a pig.

Universal gave me mixed reviews. They said, "That was very exciting, but you're fired." (To this day, the Universal Studios tour includes a reference to me throwing the A.D. off the riverboat.) Colorful, but not good for selling your work.

That same year the studio also canned two other friends of mine—Clint Eastwood and David Janssen. According to the studio, Clint's Adam's apple stuck out too far, David's ears were too big, and me . . . they said, "You can't act." I told Clint he was in a hell of a lot of trouble. I could always learn to act someday, but he could never get rid of that damn Adam's apple.

# CHAPTER
# 19

$B$Y THE TIME I GOT TOSSED OFF "RIVERBOAT," I'D been dating a very sweet movie actress for about a year. I'll call her Sandi. She was a free-spirited MCA starlet whose all-American prettiness took my breath away. She worked regularly on films, always as some-body's best friend or daughter, and her anecdotes from the set led me to believe movies really were a special, exciting world apart from TV.

The whole time I was enamored of her, almost unable to believe that I was dating someone you saw on the big movie screens. You could actually buy a ticket, sit with a bag of popcorn, and see her larger than life. Maybe for that reason alone we'd gone to-gether a long time before making love. Then we fi-nally became intimate, as they say.

In all honesty, I think it happened because she

had too much champagne, but for whatever reason, I felt like a man who'd experienced something otherworldly. Leaving her apartment at two in the morning, I told myself, "A movie star! A movie star!"

I put the top down on Cookie's MG, which she still let me use two years after breaking up, and started driving down Ventura Boulevard until I couldn't contain my exhilaration any longer. I pulled over by a pay phone and called Prinzi in Tampa.

"Hey, Vic," I said excitedly.

"Buddy?" From the sound of his voice I knew I had just woken him up. "Do you know what time it is?"

"I don't care! Do you know what I just did?"

"What?" he said.

"I just fucked a movie star!"

We broke up soon after that fabulous evening, perhaps because I had such a sophomoric, sexist attitude, and I was still too immature for a woman like Sandi. Then I got my chance to join the ranks of movie actors when I got a strong supporting role in *Angel Baby*. Shooting in Florida, it was done before *Elmer Gantry,* but by the time it was released, it was called a knock-off. It was about a husband and wife evangelist team starring George Hamilton, Salome Jens, Joan Blondell, Mercedes McCambridge, and Henry Jones. George Hamilton was an actor who intrigued the hell out of me.

George was different. When I came to Hollywood, there were 175 Marlon Brandos, 2,000 Jimmy Deans, and a lot of Carroll Bakers. But nobody wanted to be David Niven, except George. He arrived in Hollywood in a borrowed Rolls-Royce where he sat outside the MGM studios smoking cigarettes and looking debonair, until some executive finally said, "Who are you?"

In 1960, the film *Where the Boys Are* catapulted him into movies big-time. We both had graduated from Palm Beach High School, a few years apart. From the moment we first met on location in Florida, he made me laugh a lot. I've always said that if anybody could have gotten him to be that relaxed and self-deprecating on film, he would have been the next Cary Grant. He showed me how to shop for suits. I'd never ordered one custom made before. George made it look so easy "No pleats, and I'd like the pants a quarter inch from the bottom of the heel."

The salesman said, "Yes, Mr. Hamilton," then looked at me and asked, "Will you be picking it up?"

"Yes," I said. The toughest part about *Angel Baby* was doing a fight scene with George. At that time he was a contender for the title of the World's Most Uncoordinated Human Being. Yet he had to beat me up, something that was almost impossible for him to fake. In the dumbest fight scene ever, he sort of lifted me, and I leaped into the bushes, hoping it would look as if I'd been thrown. But it looked as if he'd lifted me and I'd jumped.

His birthday was soon afterwards, and his party included about a hundred of the biggest people in Hollywood. Whenever people asked me what George really looked like I said, "If producer Robert Evans and Tony Perkins had an affair, the result would be George." So my present to him that year was a beautiful chrome picture frame with Tony Perkins's picture on one side and Bob Evans's on the other. The inscription at the bottom read, "Happy Birthday, Love Mom and Dad."

George laughed louder than anybody and passed it around. That was the first time anybody thought I had a sense of humor. Cruel, maybe, but humor nonetheless.

THAT winter I was cast in the World War II spy drama *Armored Command,* one of the first pictures in which Howard Keel had a nonsinging role. He should've sung. We needed all the help we could get.

As in my previous film, I played a rapist again and I was begining to worry about being typecast. The picture also starred Tina Louise, Earl Holliman, Mary Ingels and Brandon Maggers.

The movie, which took three months in Germany to shoot, provided my first overseas adventure. Not long after checking into the hotel in Munich, I developed a real appreciation for German women. They have the greatest legs. Great calves, to be specific. Because of several past relationships, people don't think of me as a leg man. But I love great, muscular calves. Dancer's calves. Athletic legs. All the German women I saw had them—and walking beside them was always a truly ugly dachshund.

Around Christmastime, I started dating a gorgeous German girl who didn't speak a word of English, and I didn't speak a word of German. When you don't speak the language and you're in a relationship, touch becomes very important and laughter is incredible. One night she took me to a bar in Schwabing, the Greenwich Village of Munich. We sat at long, wooden tables, drinking beer with artists and soldiers. But the atmosphere was so festive it didn't matter that we didn't understand a word we said to each other.

I felt a hand in my lap, and I hoped to God it belonged to her and not some infantryman. She gave me one of those long, overripe, Kim Basinger I-want-you-bad-and-I-want-you-right-now looks, and I thought, holy cheese and crackers, I'm in love, and I'm going to have to take a German home and introduce her to my father who still hates them because of the war. Later, I lived with a Japanese girl, and when I brought her home he asked, "What, are you two opening a restaurant?"

After almost three months together, she learned enough English and I managed to understand enough German for us to be able to have a conversation. Of course, you know what happened. I didn't like her. This goddess, with whom I dreamed of spending the rest of my life, turned out to be an absolute fascist.

After returning home, my attitude was more *c'est la vie* than say you're sorry. Everything that had happened to me in Germany, I realized, was part of the fantasy of being on location for twelve weeks with a movie company. Relationships like that—brief, intense fairy tales—happen all the time, and then, once the last scene is shot, mysteriously they go poof under the harsh, unforgiving light of reality.

After two movies, I began to see that. Rules, morality, and work ethics are simply different when you make a film. A group of strangers are thrown together. They sometimes have no past or no future. Every footprint is new. Every kiss an adventure into unexplored territory. You move as if there's no gravity. It's as close as you come to being on another planet.

And I thought I liked it. No, I thought I loved it. I knew it was possibly the most wonderful way in the world to make a living.

And I wanted more.

# CHAPTER
## 20

In the slow early months of 1962 I returned to the theater while waiting for more film offers. After starring in a successful run of *Picnic* in Traverse City, Michigan, I moved into a much-talked-about Broadway production of Hugh Wheeler's *Look, We've Come Through* that allowed me to be directed by the great José Quintero.

At the end of the summer, Quintero held readings for *Look* at The Circle in the Square, the same stage where he'd directed Jason Robards in Eugene O'Neill's masterful *The Iceman Cometh*. That's what I loved about New York theater—that sense of history, that you acted on the same stage as great actors who also bared their souls in front of a live audience. In September, we did three weeks of previews. The cast was young and unknown, and we really caused a buzz after three weeks of previews in September. We opened at the Hudson Theater in October. From backstage I could feel the excitement of the audience out front. My character "Skip," a kind of Stanley Kowalski with laughs, had the actor's perfect entrance. Talked about the whole first act, he opens the second act all alone on stage laughing. Well, the curtains parted and I began my laughter but I also committed a cardinal sin: I broke the fourth wall. As I was bending over laughing, I looked right into the faces on the front row.

Seated as neatly as books on a shelf were Tennessee Williams, William Inge, Natalie Wood, Warren Beatty, and Ben Gazzara. My brain froze. I forgot my line but I kept on laughing. I held onto the laugh as if it was a life preserver and I was stuck in the middle of the ocean. In a sense, I was.

Then the audience began laughing with me. It was contagious.

Finally, after an eternity, God said, "You've suffered enough," and gave me the line.

After the play, I ran to my dressing room, thinking of never coming out. But there was a knock at the door. It was Gazzara. I'd seen him as Jocko DeParis in *End as a Man* and thought he was brilliant. He spread his arms and said, "What a choice! That was the goddamn bravest choice I've ever seen. To hold the laugh that long! What a fucking choice."

He left and then Inge came by and said virtually the same thing, adding that he wanted to write a play for me. A few moments later, Tennessee Williams rapped on the door and said "Buddy, that was quite a choice. You are fascinating to watch, dear boy." After commending my bravery, he also indicated he wanted to write a play for me.

Well, feeling full of myself suddenly, I went down to the next level and told my fellow actor Ralph Wilson that "Tennessee" and "Bill" were going to write me a play. "Oh, shit, they told all the actors that!" Well, I then joined the opening-night party. I flirted with Natalie Wood and envied Warren Beatty. They'd just finished making Inge's *Splendor in the Grass.* The picture hadn't been released yet, but everyone was talking about it.

Several nights later Inge invited me to dinner at his plush apartment on Riverside Drive. He lived in a great building, one like Josh

Logan's, in which the elevator opened directly into the apartment. I stepped out, expecting a small gathering of people, but instead found only Inge and a stunning woman wearing a silk canary yellow blouse with no brassiere underneath. I mention this because this was 1961, and no one at the time dressed like that—at least no one that I knew.

I was near apoplectic. Inge introduced us, but I was deaf. He mentioned that she'd been at the play opening night. I didn't hear that either. All I saw were boobs that pointed straight at me. I half expected to be introduced to them, too. She guided me to the window and said, "Tell me about your life, and what you don't tell me here, you can tell me later . . ."

I then did one of the dumbest things I've ever done in my life. I looked at my watch, at Inge, and then at the lady's boobs, and said, "Excuse me, but I run every night at this time."

"What?" Inge asked.

"Run!" I said and bolted for the elevator.

Ten or fifteen years later, while walking across the MGM lot, I saw Inge and Ralph Meeker heading toward me. I knew Ralph and asked Inge if by chance he remembered me. He laughed.

"Remember you?" he said. "How could I forget the young man who turned down Greta Garbo?"

# CHAPTER
# 21

Critic Richard Watts's review of *LOOK, WE'VE Come Through* said of me, "Please don't let this actor run back to Hollywood." But that's exactly what I did. Away from New York. Away from Broadway. Away from Garbo. And straight to Dodge City.

Having secured a reputation as a pretty tough character, I won a recurring role on the CBS hit "Gunsmoke." After six years of modest but steady work, it was the first job that caused my folks to get excited, especially my dad. He loved westerns and also Jim Arness, who was his idea of a fine sheriff.

"Pretty good, Bud," he said, which might've been the biggest compliment he paid me up to that point. I felt great.

In its seventh year, "Gunsmoke's" producers were trying to find a replacement for Chester. My character, Quint Asper, a half-Indian blacksmith, was thought to be the solution. For $3,000 a week, an unbelievable sum to me, I agreed.

The only hurdle I had to overcome was the sour taste "Riverboat" had left me with for TV, but that disappeared after one day with the remarkable "Gunsmoke" cast. A trivia buff all my life, I remembered being told that prior to Jim Arness, a slew of rugged actors including Robert Stack, Bill Conrad, and Raymond Burr had tested for Matt Dillon.

After them, however, the producers all agreed only one man was right for the part—John Wayne.

Duke said, "No, I'm not going to do television. But I've got a guy under contract. He's six-foot-seven, and he'd be great."

He was talking about Arness, but Jim didn't want to do TV either. So Duke took him out and got him absolutely pissed. Now Duke could pretty well out-drink everybody. Right before Arness lost his motor skills, Duke put a contract in front of him and had him sign it. It looked like a child's scrawl, but it was Arness's signature.

After we became good friends, I asked, "Are you sorry, Jim?"

He replied, "I own the company that does this show, and in the seven years it's been on the air, I've sold it to CBS, bought it back, sold it and bought it back again, and I've made more money than Duke has in his entire motion picture career."

You didn't need to work with a computer to understand that TV could be very good indeed.


BETWEEN takes, Jim, Amanda Blake, and Milburn Stone, who played Doc, sat on director's chairs on that wooden sidewalk and traded some of the best, funniest stories I'd ever heard. Dennis Weaver, a wonderful guy, also did around five episodes that year. But as I was the new kid on the block, I was sent out to promote the show.

Back then, instead of bringing all the big honchos from the CBS stations around the country to L.A. to promote the season's shows, the network chartered a plane and flew the stars of all their new shows, and new actors like myself on old shows, to meet the affiliates in all the different cities. They don't do that anymore, and I think it's ridiculous that they don't. In order to build a strong, lasting loyalty, you have to give of yourself in person in that affiliate's hometown.

I had a great time. I was in a group with four-time Academy Award winner Walter Brennan, whom I peppered nonstop with questions, and Richard Crenna, who was exactly like George Hamilton. Richard is one of the funniest human beings I've ever been around in my life, whether you're with him at dinner or a poker game. Socially, he's brilliant. But so far he hasn't taken it with him to the big screen.

I have a theory about this. Basically, if a man wants to get laughs, he has to come off one of two ways: either he has to give up lots of IQ points, which I'll do willingly for laughs, or he's got to play a guy so in love with himself he's a major asshole. (Nobody played that role better or got more laughs doing it than Jack Cassidy.) But just being handsome and playing it safe won't get you a loud smile.

Anyway, the publicity junket took us to nine cities, enough to disorient everybody on board. During the day, we met the affiliates and gave interviews; at night, we were on our own. After a few nights, Walter had just about told me every story from every movie he'd been in. Every story ended with him saying the same thing:

"You know, Burt, they don't make 'em like they used to."

Every old actor thinks like that. And so do I.

Walter was so talented it was frightening. On camera, he stole your underwear. What right did he have criticizing modern films when he was so damned good in them? Maybe every right. Those who can, do; those who can't, teach; those who can't do either—review.

One day on the plane I noticed this little girl flitting about like Peter Pan. She had short hair, a bright smile, and a cute body. She was too cute for her own good.

Someone said, "She's doing that show 'Fair Exchange,' with Eddie Foy. Her name's Judy Carne."

Judy was an outrageous flirt. With her British accent, every word she uttered sounded adorable to me. Being from the South, I'd never heard a woman say the "f" word, but she said it in every sentence and made it sound as if she'd said "flower." The only other person who could do that was Dan Blocker, who played Hoss on "Bonanza." I once introduced him to my mother, and he said, "Ma'am, it's a fucking pleasure."

My mom smiled and said, "Thank you."

I asked her to dinner, but before we left on our first date, I cornered the sweet little chaperon sent to make sure our behavior didn't embarrass the network, and told her, "We won't be in at eleven. Don't wait up."

The next stop was Chicago, where we had a great time. The English actor who played Judy's father jumped aboard the tour. He was a witty older man who seemed to appear in every English movie that came along. Toward the end of the night, he took me aside and said, "Look here, old boy. I see sparks flying between the two of you."

"Good," I said.

"Just remember the girl is totally amoral," he said.

I had no idea what that meant. But I knew moral was good, and I knew *A* was better than *B*. So it sounded good to me.

My first clue to what that meant came as soon as we returned to L.A. We'd had an incredible time in a few short days. I couldn't imagine not seeing her anymore, and asked if we could keep going out. She looked at me like I was nuts.

"Of course," Judy said. "But first I'll have to break up with my boyfriend."

Boyfriend?

"Oh, I don't want to come between . . ."

She cut me off and chirped, "No, don't worry, love. I like you better."

The first night I picked Judy up I brought her a lithograph of a painting she'd admired in a gallery in Chicago. It was an impressionistic portrait of a sensual-looking young girl. I had it framed and gift-wrapped. Judy was touched and immediately hung it on the wall. Then she turned to her roommate and said, "Look, this girl in the picture has tits just like mine."

Maybe I was old-fashioned, but it shocked me to hear a girl talk like that.

"Burt, look at her tits," Judy said. "They're just like mine, don't you think?"

"I hope so," I retorted.

But we shared a lot of laughs. One night I arranged for "Gunsmoke" 's Milburn Stone, whose father, Fred Stone, had been a vaudeville star, to get together at my house with Eddie Foy, Sr., another great entertainer from that period. Eddie starred on Judy's show. Milburn and Eddie had never met each other, but I knew it would make for a great night.

And it surpassed my expectations. For starters, Judy was a fabulous cook. But nothing equaled Milburn and Eddie, who re-created everything wonderful about this bygone era in my living room. They danced, sang songs, performed classic vaudeville routines, told jokes, and reminisced about Al Jolson, Fanny Brice, and everybody else they'd ever met—till four in the morning. Till we were all sick from laughing.

Afterward, I remember getting into bed next to Judy and saying to myself, "God, show business is great. I have a series. An incredible girl. I'm making three thousand dollars a week. I hope it lasts forever."

# CHAPTER
## 22

Whenever a friend tells me he's getting married, I tell him about this club I belong to: Marriage Anonymous. I say, "Listen, you call me when you think you're going to get married and come over to my house. Then I'll beat the shit out of you and force you to drink until you come to your senses. You can't get married. It's unnatural."

Somehow, though, Judy and I ended up engaged in 1963. I don't remember proposing to her—I swear I don't—but women have a way of doing that to men. We'd been dating for six months. Now, my idea of marriage wasn't very sophisticated or mature. To me, it was more of an exclamation point to this passionate, kooky, whirlwind romance than the type of lifelong commitment my parents made look so easy.

My folks adored Judy. She had so much spunk and enthusiasm, it was impossible to feel any other way about her. Judy could outfit herself on a moment's notice for any event. She was game for anything from moose hunting to car racing, dinner in Europe. Whatever anyone suggested.

That asset also turned out to be one of her major drawbacks. You could say, "Judy, we're going to church Sunday," and she'd reply, "Fine." But between here and the john, if someone else said, "Let's go to Africa and screw alligators," she'd say, "Okay, what time do we leave?"

I had a bull's confidence then. I bought a cozy little nest in the Hollywood Hills for Judy and me, and then I used what was left of my savings to buy a 180-acre ranch outside Jupiter, Florida, a spectacular spread of trees and lakes where I'd played as a boy. I moved my parents into the house, which was reputedly once a hideout for Al Capone's boys who got too hot in Chicago.

Like the impending marriage, taking care of my mom and dad was almost a rite of passage. I had quit trying to prove that I was successful, knowing that I'd be able to take care of them.

Then I went looking for a church where we could hold the ceremony. After turning several down because they wanted too much money, I stumbled upon a tiny church in Burbank with a pastor who had an attitude that was light and fun. His price was fair and he had dates open that worked for everyone.

The happy event brought together friends and family. My mom and dad flew out, as did Prinzi, my best man. Judy's parents traveled from England. Her dad, short and slight, resembled Wally Cox, including his big glasses and sense of humor. Her mother was as big as Roseanne at her heaviest. I looked at them, especially their mismatched features, and then at Judy, and wondered how she ended up looking so good.

"Let me ask you something," I said to her. "Your answer doesn't matter to me, because I love you. But why do your parents have noses longer than Jimmy Durante's and yours is a beautiful little button?"

"Because I had a bob done on it," she said, as if that should have been obvious, and what planet was I living on anyway?

I used to think we'd have a great kid, except he'd look like Danny Thomas. His nose would get in the way whenever he tried to do anything wicked.

"How big did it used to be?" I asked Judy.

"Oh, enormous, love," she said.

From then on nose jobs have amused me. Some years later at a Friar's roast for Paul Anka, I remarked that, prior to his own surgery, Paul's nose had been so friggin big, and he was so immensely talented, that the little piece they took off the end of Paul's nose became Joel Grey.


In early 1964, during my second season on "Gunsmoke," my initial enthusiasm for playing Quint was replaced by a gnawing frustration. It wasn't merely that people constantly remarked, "Oh, you play a half-breed," and I had to say, "No, I play a half-Indian." It was that I really hadn't fulfilled what the show needed, which was someone to take Chester's place. As soon as Ken Curtis guested as "Festus," I knew that was what the show needed.

The bottom line was the job had become boring. Each week Quint got insulted. Then Jim, after spending six days in Hawaii, would show up on the set and beat up the guy who insulted me.

Every week Milburn Stone, who acted as a surrogate father, encouraged me to leave. He told me I was just wasting my time.

"We've been on nine years," he said. "How much longer can this shit go on? When I came on this show I was fifty-seven years old and played an old man. Now I am an old man. Burt, you're a movie star. I know what I'm talking about. You go. It may take a while, but you're going to be a movie star. So get the hell out of Dodge."

I tried letting the producers convince me otherwise. Fond of the money they paid me, I hated the notion of walking away from dependable work. I asked those in charge to let me try some comedy. They thought I was nuts. "The Indian wants to do comedy? Did you hear that? He thinks this is a comedy." They pointed to my fan mail. "They love you with your shirt off—not being funny."

At that point, I took Milburn's advice and quit. Who the hell was going to write comedy for a half-Indian who had two expressions, mad and madder?

It was a difficult period. Judy and I had our problems, and had been having them for some time. Basically, when reality settled over our romance we saw two nice, completely incompatible people. She smoked pot heavily and loved staying out all night with the strangest people I'd ever seen. I drank beer, hated potheads, and loved old movies. She stood poised on the launching pad of the sixties, while I avoided such heights.

Out of work, I watched friends like Clint Eastwood score big on "Rawhide" and then easily shift gears into movies made in Europe. I was thrilled for Clint, one of the last good guys. But, discouraged by Hollywood, which seemed to be a pattern with me, I was on the verge of doing something drastic, like returning to Florida and coaching football or doing construction work, all of which would have been better than my third movie, *Operation CIA,* which was my worst film ever. If it played on a plane, people would be killed trying to jump out.

More than anything, it enabled me to postpone thinking about the payments I had to make on both my home in the hills and the ranch in Florida, and also the fact that my marriage had turned into a thrill a minute for everyone but me.

The piece of shit movie, which looked every bit its $70,000 budget—yes, $70,000—was an action-heavy spy story scheduled to shoot for two months in Vietnam, a remarkable bit of travel planning, considering the war and the fighting were about to escalate. After two weeks, the State Department forced us to relocate to less volatile sites like Bangkok and Laos.

It was still crazy, though. The heavy was played by the hotel bell hop, because he had a deep voice. The prop man screwed up once and used live ammo. I fought a cobra that hadn't been milked of its poison. And near the end I did a fight scene in a river that was contaminated with pollutants. Perhaps it wouldn't have mattered even if I'd had a spleen to purify my blood. As it was, the toxins got into my system and went to town.

The movie finished shooting in mid-March 1965. But instead of flying home I went to Selma, Alabama, to participate in the march with Dr. Martin Luther King, Jr. I had been ashamed for far too long to do nothing. I love the South, and it certainly isn't the only hotbed of prejudice in our country. But it seemed a damn good place to start trying to get things right. People could go on dying for this country, yet not be allowed to eat or play in certain areas because of their color.

I got as far as Birmingham. The next thing I knew I woke up in the hospital; I looked up and saw a woman in a blue hat, indicating she was a nurse's helper. It was Luraline Wallace, the wife of Governor George Wallace. She smiled.

"The governor wants to meet you," she said sweetly. "But first we've got to get you well."

It looked very bad. My lymph glands were the size of softballs. At first the doctors thought I had Hodgkin's disease, but they weren't certain. Later I discovered they didn't know what the hell I had and brought in specialists of all kinds. Talk about God watching over you— again, my lucky star was right on time. As luck had it, the leading hospital in the study of Asian diseases is in Birmingham, Alabama. If I'd passed out in any other city in the U.S., it's doubtful I would have made it. Doctors there diagnosed my illness as schistosomiasis—snail eggs in the bloodstream. Yes, snail eggs that were about to hatch.

A Japanese man took some blood from me and later brought the slides for me to look at. I could actually see tiny snails crawling around in the test tube. The cure had been discovered only two years earlier. I started taking shots immediately and got better. But the coincidences are more than just that. I must do something before I leave this place, I have so much to pay back.

I couldn't wait to get back to L.A. and finish recuperating. But walking into my house was like arriving in the middle of a combination Fourth of July, nudist camp, and New Year's Eve party—in San Francisco. The place was packed. Boys dancing with boys. Girls with girls. A bunch of in betweens. Christ, I'd gone from Asia to Alabama to Fire Island. Hell!

I looked out on the front lawn to see if there was a For Sale sign.

Maybe Judy was having an auction to raise money for freaks. I didn't know a single person, and didn't want to—including my wife, who wasn't anywhere to be found.

I decided to leave and come back later. I found my car keys and went to the garage. We had three cars, but none of them were there. That made me even happier to be back home. I turned around and crawled through the house, intent on finding Judy, who I finally located in the back. She was so high she could have killed birds with a rake. I asked who the hell all these people were and where the hell were the cars.

"I loaned them out," she said. "I met these wonderful people who don't have a car . . ."

"I don't have a car," I said. "Who's got my cars?"

"I don't remember two of them," she confessed. "But darling, you're going to be so proud of who's driving the third."

"Who?"

"Stirling Moss," she said. "The great race-car driver."

"He's staying here?"

"Yes," she said brightly.

"Didn't you used to go with him? Why is he here?"

"I know how you love those sporty types. I just thought it would be lovely," she said.

I was doing well not to have gone ballistic. Half the people were stoned, the other half were homeless. There were drugs everywhere, pot and cocaine. I asked Judy if she wanted to ask people to leave, or did she prefer me putting on my gorilla suit and throwing them out? She said she'd prefer telling them. A lot of them had to be carried out, they were such zombies. I told Judy to just lay them in the middle of the road.

"They'll never feel a thing," I said.

In the midst of this, Stirling Moss came back. Of course, I liked him. He was charming, and I'm sure great fun. But I suggested he drive away—very fast. Despite having a "Leave It to Beaver" house, it seemed I had an untamed beaver for a wife. It just wasn't going to work out.

Finally, after almost three years, the marriage ended. There wasn't a scene, per se. I sort of reiterated everything that I'd already said. I wasn't for her. Although not much older, I felt like Robert Young to her Annie.

I couldn't stand her friends. I saw she was already headed down that dirty road of drug addiction.

And so I said, "I'm leaving. Please try to be good to yourself."

I gave her the house and the cars. I took the basset hound Clyde, the dachsund Festus, and my football trophies. I called Doug McClure to come pick me up.

As we went out the door, she said, "We'll always be friends. You can always jump on my bones, you know."

"Great. What a wonderful thing to say," I said. "I'll always try to remember those tender words."

Knowing Judy, she meant that in a very sincere way. I know she still cares a little about me. She married three giant assholes after me, but they don't get mentioned on the talk shows. Just me. She sometimes claims that I beat her, other times she says I was a saint. Both are entirely untrue. Those things keep popping up only because some scumbags pay her to say things that get her drug money. She is forever showing up on talk shows looking totally zooey.

It's not surprising that she's always failed to mention the money I've given her over the years. Every time, she says she's going to go straight. I won't say how much I've given her, because what does it really matter if she won't face the fact that she's worth saving? Only she can cure herself—when she really wants to. She was born at the wrong time. She can sing, she can act, and she can dance—but no one is making *Singing in the Rain* anymore.

The next time Judy and I saw each other, it was in front of millions of people. Until then I took Clyde, Festus, and my trophies and moved to New York.

# CHAPTER
## 23

Once in New York, I immediately got a movie because of Mr. Eastwood. By then, Clint and I had been friends for years, but like everybody else who knew him, I never asked for his phone number or was asked to his house.

Jump ahead fifteen years. He suddenly asked me to Thanksgiving dinner. Stunned, I said, "Jesus, Clint, you sure we aren't rushing into anything?"

His place was in the hills, but hidden. No mailbox, no numbers, nothing. Nobody would've known anybody lived there. You pushed a button that opened the garage. Inside, I met a guy who asked how long I'd been friends with Clint. I said, "You go first."

"I went to high school with him," he said. "Then I was in the army with him."

"Oh well, I've know him over fifteen years," I said.

"Gosh," he said. "Nobody's ever been invited here in only fifteen years."

That's Clint. There's not a selfish bone in his body. But he's extraordinarily private and shy. What many don't realize is Clint's also very funny. He's got a great sense of humor.

From the start, he had the same pebble-kicking, star quality as Henry Fonda or Gary Cooper. By "Rawhide," Clint was just waiting for the explosion. I think everyone was. Though likable, he exuded a sense of danger. You only had to watch actresses like Julie Harris, Jessica Walter, or Gloria Talbot react when they worked with him. Some were already great, but he made them all better.

I spent enough time over the years with Clint to know he wasn't dying to be accepted as a great actor. But he had a raging desire to be a respected director. He had ideas and vision, and people were scared to death of him, qualities all good directors possess. The only time I saw him lose his patience in the "Rawhide" days was with directors who didn't know what the hell they were doing and just phoned it in. They didn't appreciate the privilege of being in control of an eighty-person crew. It drove him nuts.

One day while I was still on "Gunsmoke," Clint had me meet him at a small screening room at Review Studios. He had recently come back from Italy, where he'd filmed *A Fistful of Dollars,* and he wanted to know what I thought. It was just Clint and me in the room, and as those corny little titles came up and that (at the time) strange music played, I wondered how in the hell I was going to tell him the picture was very, very strange. Then all of a sudden came that opening shot, a long, long lens shot of someone, then suddenly a super tight shot of Clint. The look was totally unique, the music suddenly was like nothing I'd ever heard before, and I was in love with it.

At the end, I said, "This guy Sergio Leone is brilliant. He gives every actor the greatest introduction of any director I've ever seen. And he's not afraid to stay or go in, way in, and I love that. The guy has big *cojones.*"

So after I arrived in New York, Clint called me. He'd heard about my split from Judy, but that wasn't as important as introducing me to

Dino de Laurentiis, who was in town searching for an American leading man who could star in his next spaghetti western. Dino and Clint became friends when he made *A Fistful of Dollars,* and Clint was on his way back to make *For a Few Dollars More.*

"You know, they'll love you in Italy," Clint said. "You're a quarter Indian. You can ride a damn horse like nobody I know, and you like to hug people."

"You're right," I said.

So I met Dino, who kept saying "He's *simpatico,"* and signed me to do *Navajo Joe.*

Dino gushed, "Burt-a, this-a picture, it's going to be-a so big-a. I tell you-a, in order for *Fistful of Dollars* to make-a the money it made in Italy, the average Italian had to see it thirty-five times-a. But Burt-a, we're going to be bigger. Clint killed a hundred people. You're going to kill 245 people. We'll-a be-a two times as big-a!"

Here was a thinking man, I thought, and then said, "Great-a."

MEANWHILE, I met with Renée Valente, a Screen Gems vice president who was also one of the first women in our industry to have a position of power. She took one look at me and asked, "What in the hell are you so angry about?" I explained about the divorce I was in the middle of, and then asked what business was it of hers anyway.

"Hey, it's your dime," she snapped. "Check out anytime you want."

Renée wanted me to test for the lead in the ABC pilot "Hawk," a gritty police drama whose principal character was an Iroquois Indian detective, NYPD Lieutenant John Hawk. I asked if the test would be seen by the network president Tom Moore.

"Yes," she said.

"Let me tell you something," I said peevishly. "I tested for *The Long Hot Summer.* I'm Southern, and there was nobody more right for that picture than me. But Tom Moore saw it and said, 'He ain't pretty enough.' So screw him and the horse he came in on."

Somehow Renée convinced me to go have some lunch. We went to a fancy restaurant where we had artichokes and vodka, the kind they set aflame. I'd never had either before and felt my level of sophistication going up two notches. By dessert, she convinced me I had to do the test.

I did a scene with Louise Sorrell playing a psychiatrist and Gene Hackman, who'd been in two films nobody had ever seen, as the heavy. For the personality part, Renée climbed up on a ladder so I'd have to look up. You can't believe how hard my eyes are to light, because of my Neanderthal head. She suddenly said, "I bet you can't name five William Lundigan pictures." I gave her three and then began to laugh so hard I sounded like Yma Sumac in the shower.

"Is Tom Moore going to see this?" I managed to ask. "Because if he is, I want him to know I ain't any prettier now than I was before, you son of a bitch."

Moore screened the test the next day and loved it. He said the mix of anger and humor were the kind of eruptive qualities he imagined in John Hawk. A short time later the pilot was shot with an unbelievable cast that included Sorrell, Hackman, and Robert Duvall. On 16mm it looked so real while running amok at night on New York City streets that a couple of actual NYPD cops joined in one scene and billy-clubbed three extras they mistook for fleeing thieves.

It was wild. But the network needed until the end of June to decide if the series would be part of their new fall schedule. Which was perfect. If it went, shooting would begin at the end of June. That afforded me three months—plenty of time for *Navajo Joe* in Italy.

"TELL me, Burt, why-a is a TV series so *importante?*" Dino asked.

I'd been in Rome five weeks and had done nothing except drink *molto vino* at the sidewalk cafés and wait for the script to be completely rewritten. I'd planned on spending eight weeks in Italy and couldn't see why we'd need more, given the script I'd read on the plane trip over. But each week, as we prepared to start filming, Dino would at the last minute reject the script and order a rewrite.

"Don't-a worry," he told me the first week. "You got to have a perfect wardrobe. Go to-a your hotel. Stay there. Relax. I see you with-a the wardrobe man tomorrow at ten o'clock."

Sure he would, that's ten Italian time. Eleven, twelve, and one o'-

clock came and went. Around three the wardrobe man arrived. He was about 150 years old. He opened up a big book so old it was falling apart and pointed to an Indian, the sort of Indian Columbus saw when he landed. This Indian had feathers down to his feet and a little tiny jock-strap.

"Indiano?" he asked.

"No," I said.

"Si."

"No!"

"Americano Indiano," he said.

We did that every day for the first month. I finally took the damn book and thumbed through it, looking for a picture that resembled a Native American warrior. But I couldn't find a single photo that didn't look like a guy in a turkey outfit. Dino rescued me from killing the old guy by saying he wanted to see how well I rode a horse.

Thanks to the cameraman, Silvano Ippoliti, one of the great Italian cinematographers, and a great horse, I looked tremendous in the test. Black hair flying, fringed leather vest. I could always ride, and this horse let me do whatever I wanted. Dino told me he'd never seen an actor who could ride like that and invited me to his house to watch the test.

His house was no house—it was a damn castle, the biggest place I'd ever seen that people actually lived in. Upon entering, the first person I saw was one of the sexiest women in the world—actress Silvana Mangano. I hadn't thought of her for years, but suddenly, with this dark beauty standing in front of me, I recalled every seductive frame of her in *Bitter Rice*. Nylons rolled down, dress hiked up.

Dino ushered us to a screening room downstairs, where several other people waited. After we screened the test, they applauded.

"You're going to be a big-a star," Dino gushed. "You're going to get your brains fucked out everyplace."

"I hope not everyplace," I said. "Maybe different countries. But not everyplace."

Silvana Mangano added, "You are very sexy. Very, very sexy." Her girlfriend, who also watched the test closely, was not pleased. To her, I was not "very, very sexy." But she and she alone did not like the test, and this was quite a group.

Dino hosted a fabulous dinner. I sat between Claudia Cardinale and Clint. Anthony Quinn and Joseph Mankiewicz sat across from us. Italian actors filled up the other spots. It was incredible, festive, loud, great fun, and everything you'd imagine dinner to be like in an Italian castle.

I told Clint that I'd been there six weeks and Dino had just approved the script. It felt as if I'd been there forever. Parties followed parties. I lived rent-free. I wondered if I wouldn't soon be too old and fat to play Joe.

"It'll get done," Clint said. "And if they really like you in the picture, when it's finished they give you an envelope with three or four hundred thousand inside. Do what you want with it. Give it back. Declare it. Or don't. I just wanted to warn you."

As I said goodbye, Dino hugged me over and over like somebody practicing the Heimlich maneuver. Finally, he declared with enthusiasm, our movie was soon to begin shooting. Clint was going off to do his picture. I'd start mine. The world was a wonderful place, no?

"Dino, one question," I said. "I got Sergio for this picture, right?"

"Of course, Sergio's directing," he said.

"Leone?" I asked.

"Leone? No. You got Sergio Corbucci."

"Corbucci?" I asked.

"Yes, my friend. But he's-a almost as-a good as Leone."

# CHAPTER
# 24

THOSE DAYS EVERYBODY WENT TO ALMERÍA, A LIT-
tle outpost located in the arid plains of Spain, to do
westerns. But in May 1966, it seemed like the end of
the world, especially in temperatures that routinely
soared past a hundred degrees. I couldn't believe I'd
traveled so far and waited for five rewrites to film
what was now the worst script I'd ever read, other
than *Operation CIA*.

As far as plots went, *Navajo Joe*'s was barely visible. A renegade Indian seeks to revenge his mur-
dered wife by cutting down the band of killers.
Corbucci, a wonderful director who actually was very
talented, salivated over the opportunity. I wanted a
strong horse that would carry me through the nonstop action.

A handsome gypsy named Mahan was in charge

of all the horses used in films in Spain. A great horseman himself, he had some beautiful animals. But they had no Pintos, only all blacks or whites. Every time he went to get another horse for me to look at, he jumped on an old horse with no reins, not even a hackamore. He just grabbed what was left of an old mane and rode off bareback to bring down another horse. I asked him who this horse was that he was riding. He said, "This my horse. This horse Destaphanado."

I asked if I could ride him. He said, "I would be honored." In those days, I could jump flatfooted onto a horse. Now I can't jump over a coffeetable. I leapt on Destaphanado. If you're a horseman, you know in twenty-five yards what you're onto. This was some animal. But old—and, God love him, plug ugly! He had no mane, no tail, and was sort of dirty gray. Well, in Italian, makeup is *mokeakee*. I screamed, *"mokeeakee!"*

Makeup people came running over from everywhere. I told them I wanted this horse to be beautiful. I said, "Put a spot on him here and here, and a blaze on his forehead, and give him a great mane and long tail. Also perfect socks. Tomorrow I want to see the most beautiful Pinto in all of Spain."

For some reason, I swear, Destaphanado knew what I was saying. He gave me a look like no leading lady ever has.

By the time I arrived at six the next morning, Destaphanado had been transformed from a twenty-three-year-old plug-ugly horse into Ricardo Montalban. He stood so proud and beautiful as I drove up. From the very first scene, he did things for me that Trigger didn't do for Roy Rogers. On him, I could do anything; and most of the time I had to. Since the script was so bad, Corbucci substituted stunts for bad dialogue. On Destaphanado, I could do a transfer onto a train, fall down a mountain, make him rear up on command—he did it all without hesitation.

By the time we changed locations to Castille, the stuntmen, all gypsies, were so impressed with my horsemanship (and believe me, you only think you can ride until you see a gypsy ride) and courage they asked me to stay with them at night in the mountains. It was a great honor, which I accepted. They always slept with their horses, so I did too. They played flamenco guitar and we drank wine and danced by the moonlight. It was a night to remember. Although I had to pass the guitar when it got to me, I did get up and dance. With all the lovely gypsy women singing and clapping, how could I not? I knew all I had to do was look over my shoulder, clap, and pretend I was in love with my ass. It worked for me.

In the midst of shooting, I received a telegram from Valente informing me that "Hawk" was picked up and was scheduled to start shooting at the end of June. If I wanted to be the Hawk, I had better be there.

Corbucci, who appeared to be warming up after three weeks, had four or five weeks to go. I pleaded with him to do something to speed it up. Now, this was a funny man. He'd lost one eye after getting shot in an action movie he directed. A great actor's director, he knew the business, and we liked each other a lot.

"Sergio, I've got to leave," I said.

"What? What-a you mean, you have to-a leave?" he asked. "We have-a hundred more people to kill. We have to kill more than Clint."

"It's in my contract," I argued. "If the series sells, I have to go. It's not my fault it took two months to get this picture off the ground."

"Stronso," he said. "You're just like Cameron Mitchell."

I had no idea what he meant by that, and still don't. But he walked off in a snit. Then, all of a sudden, he turned around, beaming like a big happy kid. He ran up and gave me a big hug.

"Dynamite!" he said.

"Dynamite?"

"Yeah," he said. "With dynamite we can kill hundreds of people."

I'd already shot, choked, speared, and stabbed innumerable bad guys, but the whole next day Corbucci shot me throwing dynamite. I killed them riding down the street, then climbing up a building, and then I killed more while on the roof. Four cameras rolled as if stuck on fast forward, capturing the bloodbath until the dust settled and the blood dried under the hot sun. At the end of the day, Corbucci bid me farewell.

"We'll keep shooting," he laughed. "We have to kill many, many more."

And he did. He shot six more weeks, blowing up everything and everyone he could find.

The night before I left, Dino called me to his house and gave me an envelope of money. Just as Clint had warned. It was as thick as a telephone book. As Dino told me what a fantastic job I'd done and how much everybody loved me, I could only imagine how much money was inside the envelope. My God, it was bursting through the paper! I didn't dare ask him how much, which would've been rude. So we hugged and I left.

Back at the hotel, I decided it wasn't worth the U.S. customs rate, and I mailed it to Mahan, to keep Destaphanado in the style he should be kept, like Sophia on her best days.

# CHAPTER

# 2 5

I STARTED "HAWK," AND IT WAS THE MOST INSANE and daring TV experience anyone could have. Before Steven Bochco ever dreamed of creating "Hill Street Blues"—he was still in college—we were doing an hour show in five days, shooting in 16mm fast film, with available light. Since Lt. John Hawk worked nights, we shot after darkness blanketed the city, and 90 percent was done on the streets of New York. People were always calling the cops, reporting robberies, shootouts, chases. Boy, did we get away with murder. But that was why it was so damn much fun.

My salary was $6,000 a week, but with the hours I put in they probably still owe me about a million. I never made them pay for my overtime. If I had, they never could have afforded the show. The last three days of each week I went around-the-clock. Up all night with one crew, then another twelve hours with a second crew. I also got involved in directing, writing, and casting a lot of the episodes. I already knew how much I wanted to work behind the camera eventually.

After shooting all night, we did interiors during the day at a studio in Harlem. I drove a Pontiac, which I parked on the street in front of the Biltmore Studios. Nobody parked on the street in that neighborhood. But on the first day I pulled up, I saw these two black guys staring at me. If nothing else, being a cop's son has made me pretty street smart. So I called them over.

"Look, I'm Burt. I'm playing the Hawk, and that's my car," I said, taking out my wallet and removing two fifty-dollar bills, one for each. "Will you guys watch my car?"

"Don't worry, nobody's going to touch the Hawk's car," one of them said.

And nobody ever did. My business manager came up once, parked on the street, and when he returned all four tires and most of his engine were gone. Probably took about five minutes. Everybody else parked across the street in this place with a big iron gate, a guard, and rigmarole that took about twenty minutes to get your car. But my guys, whom I took care of, took care of me. Every other week, they asked if I wanted a TV, washing machine, or some other appliance one of them happened to have. No charge for the Hawk.

Wayne Grice, the black actor who played my assistant, laughingly said that I was helping the local economy. Wayne was a gentle, agreeable young man who wore glasses and kept to himself, but he had a wonderful sense of humor. I always regretted not knowing him better. After work one day, he asked me for a lift. I said, "Sure, where to?" "The Muslim mosque in Harlem," he said.

I knew it was Malcolm X's headquarters and ignorantly asked why he was going there.

"I'm a Muslim, Burt," he said.

"You are?" I stupidly said. "All this time I never knew."

"It's okay. We're friends, you know," he smiled.

Years passed. One day I asked my friend Ossie Davis if he knew whatever happened to Wayne. Ossie turned to stone.

"Where do you know Wayne from?" he asked.

"From 'Hawk.' Wayne was my guy on the show," I said. "We were buddies."

"Wayne," Ossie said solemnly, "was killed when they shot Malcolm."

Drawing from the wealth of actors in theater looking to pick up a few extra dollars, the series served as a springboard for future superstars like Jon Voight, Louise Sorrell, Gene Hackman, Robert Duvall, and Richie Castellano. Billy Dee Williams uttered a single word on one show. Bert Convy guested once. And my close friend Charles Durning showed up as an extra in a police uniform on several episodes.

Voight once invited me to a play he was doing in the Village. The theater, he explained, was across from Jack Warden's apartment, one of those rent-controlled shoe boxes that he'd had for years and loaned to everybody, which made it a true landmark. The theater, which seated about fifty people, was staging *A View From the Bridge*. Directed by Ulu Grosbard, it starred Voight, Dustin Hoffman, Richie Castellano and Bobby Duvall.

Like an asshole, I thought, Boy, these actors are pretty damn good. I didn't know I was looking at perhaps four of the best actors in the world. But that's what made living and working in New York so damn exciting. You never knew.

It was like that on the show. Forget that I'd worked my way up by doing theater, I had so much testosterone in those days the crew thought I was invincible. They had seen me do some impossible stunts, including hanging off the side of the *John Brown*, a ship harbored at the waterfront, while fighting at the very top, then dropping into the water. Once I knocked a guy out cold while trading punches as we dangled off a rope rigging on the side of a ship at the docks. It wasn't my fault; there was a real shortage of good stuntmen in New York then, and this guy just forgot the routine.

After that incident, they brought new guys to fight me. One guy looked very familiar. I said, "What pictures have you done?"

"None. But he eats glass," the assistant director said.

"He eats glass?" I said. "You think he can do a fight scene because he eats glass? Bring me some stuntmen, some guys who really know how to fight."

Big mistake. They brought in a hairdresser and explained that "I know it sounds a little strange, but he's a great fighter." I laughed. A bigger mistake. This hairdresser turned out to be boxing champion Emile Griffith. We did a few gags together, and he was a terrific fighter, but he taught me a great lesson: you never fight a professional fighter. If he sees an opening, he *will* hit you. It's instinct; too many years to unlearn.

I sat ringside the night Emile killed boxer Benny Perett in a bout at Madison Square Garden. During the weigh-in, Perett had called Emile a fairy. That night Perett got caught in the ropes and Emile unloaded on him. He got off at least two unanswered punches. The barrage stunned everybody who witnessed it. I turned to Lee Warren, an actor who was with me, and said, "We just saw a man get killed."

It was true. Perett was half-dead before they got him out of the ring. He died that night.

If I was wild on screen, I can't even begin to describe what I was like off it. Divorced from Judy, I was like an uncaged animal. My apartment was on East 68th Street, and with some money in my pocket I was free to roam. Thank God almighty, free, free free at last! I met women everyplace I went, but mostly in the bars around my place and on the show. Women on any set are always warned about the leading men.

"Watch out, he's going to hit on you."

But I never hit on women, that wasn't my style. I always waited, and after I didn't make a move for a few days, they wanted to know what was wrong.

My regular haunt was a little restaurant-bar where they loved actors. Back then, I could drink about a fifth of vodka and not even blink—a great accomplishment, eh? So you can imagine how much they liked me. I also discovered the Carlyle Hotel bar, where Bobby Short, the master interpreter of George Gershwin and Cole Porter songs, started playing. Since I'm a jazz nut, I was crazed for the place.

Everybody was. One night I met Peter Jennings there. We became very good friends, and we watched each other do fairly well in our respective fields. When he became ABC's anchorman, he said, "I guess I have to change my ties."

"You've got to change everything, pal," I replied. "The suit, and get rid of the lisp." He laughed, thank God.

A great guy, all Peter really needed was a lot of air time. Obviously, he's done just great. In fact, today he's my favorite newscaster.

Another Carlyle regular was Ed Sullivan. Although I saw him there a lot, it took him awhile to know me, but when he did he blurted out, "Hey, Hawk!" Now, Ed never pronounced anything correctly, so how he got that out I'll never know.

"Sir?" I turned around.

"You're the Hawk, aren't you?" he asked.

"Yes, sir," I said.

He asked if I wanted to sit in the audience one night and he'd introduce me. After saying no, thank you, I moved to the other side of the room. All night Ed stared at me like a hurt child. I happened to sit down next to actor Robert Webber, who was a brilliant actor, especially at playing pricks. We became friends and I discovered he was crazier, sexually, than anyone I had met up until then. But I didn't know that many people yet.

He always seemed to have wild women around. This one night he had two of them, which I thought wasn't fair. Somehow I weaseled into his party, and he asked if I wanted to go to his house with them. I said, "Sure, I wasn't doing anything anyway. Can we go *now?*" (What the hell, was he crazy?)

As soon as we got in the door, the two girls leaped on each other. Webber shrugged, offered me a drink, and then took a shower. Left alone, I watched the girls roll around and grind awhile. A few minutes later I said to myself, I'm not ready for this. So I grabbed the prettiest one, the one who had the best legs, and ran with her out the door, explaining, "Bob will be just as pleased with your friend."

As it turned out, "Hawk" got critical raves, but pulled up short in the ratings against the top-rated "Dean Martin Show" and the "CBS Thursday Night Movie," but the girl stayed with me through almost the rest of the series. However, way too fast for me, she ended up leaving me and took up with an English band, a group called the Rolling Stones.

But I'd gotten tangled up with a creature who was even wilder.

She had a small part on one of the last shows. I was supposed to save her from being raped by tackling a guy as he sped through Times Square on a motorcycle. It was kind of an insane stunt. If it backfired, the biker would've killed a few people. As we rehearsed, this girl approached me and whispered, "I'm supposed to be raped, but I want them to *really* do it. Can you fix me up?"

"We'll have to talk to the DP about that," I said. "In the meantime, want to have lunch?"

We went to a German restaurant on West 46th Street, by the Hudson Theater. The place was packed, but the maître d' got us a nice table. This girl started groping me under the table. I fell in love before the waiter brought the bread sticks. Over drinks and appetizers she suddenly unbuttoned her blouse and showed me her potatoes. She said she loved doing stuff like that in the middle of a busy restaurant. This wasn't good.

Well, it was but it wasn't.

Later that night she fulfilled every expectation I had, and some I would never have given a thought to. Strangely, though, she wouldn't stay overnight. I couldn't imagine where at that hour she was going and asked her if she was going to be all right.

"I'm living with Bob Evans," she explained.

"Bob Evans, the clothing guy?" I asked.

"Yeah. He loves to screw me on the fire escape with all the people watching. And I love that, too."

"Swell," I said. "Sorry, I don't have a fire escape."

# CHAPTER 26

WITH SOME MONEY IN THE BANK, I COMMITTED myself to films and went back to L.A., where I moved into an incredible house on Miller Drive up in the hills. For a thirty-two-year-old who felt a decade younger, it was the ultimate bachelor pad. It was called a "bird house" because the architect was a rather famous man named Bird. His houses were all wood and bricks. It had a view of the city as it unfolded from the nighttime glitz of Sunset Strip to the golden hue of Beverly Hills and beyond—the sandy beaches and glittery blue of the Pacific Ocean. If a lady didn't feel romantic there, it was a good possibility that she was going to be a nun.

I barely had time to test the headboards. My schedule had revved up. In succession, I worked in

Sam Fuller's underwater action picture *Shark,* and then made *Fade-In,* a sweet, artsy, movie-within-a-movie love story, with Kazan's wife, Barbara Loden. Paramount execs thought it was such a bomb they never released the film to theaters. I was then offered a film for United Artists called *Impasse,* a good word for where my career was. Annie Francis, a great gal, was my leading lady, and I was going to the Philippines for the film. The pay was the pits, but I figured I was discovering a new part of the world—which sometimes helps you discover new parts of yourself.

On the way to location, I convinced a stuntman friend, Bill Catching, to go three weeks early so we could visit Japan. I figured if we didn't like it there, we could move on to Hong Kong. I didn't tell Bill, but secretly I had always been fascinated with Kabuki theater. I figured Bill would prefer a geisha house on the Ginza, but we could both soak up our own type of culture.

Well, that's exactly what happened. He lasted for one visit at a Kabuki theater, then I didn't see him again until we arrived in Manila three weeks later to start the movie.

Kabuki was everything I had hoped it would be, and more. You have to remember that in 1969 in Japan, there wasn't the widespread dislike for Americans that is everywhere today. Also, it didn't cost three hundred dollars for breakfast. As an American actor, I was treated as a fellow artist.

While on a trip to an older theater on the outskirts of Tokyo, I saw a young actress who absolutely stunned me. She took over my senses; I was possessed by her beauty. Her hair was long and down below her rear—a rear that you could deliver drinks on. And, amazingly, while you usually think of Asian woman as small-busted, she had gorgeous, gigantic breasts and the most beautiful, shapely, athletic legs I had ever seen. Her voice, too, was a surprise. Not high or shrill but sweet, yet husky. She was in her early twenties and had come to the theater at the age of nine. She only left to visit her mother in Osaka on special occasions. Her last visit had been over a year ago.

All this information was gathered for me by my Japanese actor friend, Fuji Kasai, who was assigned to me by the department of the arts through the American Embassy. Her name was Miko Mayama, and we were to have high tea together as arranged by the manager of the theater.

It was a wonderful tea. Fuji was great at somehow making me very amusing. Miko had a terrific laugh, was very animated, and moved like a cat. I asked about her family, saying I would love to visit Osaka before going back to the United States. Since I'd heard it had been over a year since she had seen her mother, perhaps she would be my guide if I could arrange for her to be off long enough to go there? I told Fuji to tell Miko that I was so fascinated when I first saw her that I could draw her face with my eyes closed.

Fuji was sure this was our ticket to Osaka, and possibly beyond. He talked, and I watched Miko watch me. Her hand went to her mouth as she smiled and then dropped across mine, slowly caressing it. She said (and he translated), "Could we go to Osaka this coming weekend as it is my brother's birthday? Also, the dogwood blossoms are pink and more full now than at any other time of the year."

That weekend, we took the bullet train—Miko, Fuji, and me—to try to talk a little Japanese lady into letting her daughter go away for a few years to the United States. Well, she let her go, not only to America but first to Manila to watch me make a bad movie. Miko wound up getting a role in the film. She wasn't bad in it, especially since she learned her lines phonetically.

After the film we returned to Los Angeles. It was a new experience to have someone waiting at home to rub my feet after work. She'd say her only full sentence in English, which she'd learned from television: "What's up, doc?"

While Miko improved her English, I devised what I thought were little ways of testing her, when actually I was testing my own level of commitment. For instance, I stayed out till all hours of the night on a pretty regular basis, drinking and bullshitting with the guys. Most women would've demanded to know where the hell I'd been till four A.M., prohibited such selfish pleasures, kicked me out of the bedroom, or perhaps the house, and probably told me to take a flying hike. Not Miko. She greeted me each morning with a smile and asked, "What's up, doc?"

Over time Miko became proficient in English, adept in the ways of

American culture, and developed a great sense of humor, but the basis of her personality remained unchanged. She showed nary a trace of jealousy when I made the offbeat western *Sam Whiskey* and had to do my first nude love scene with Angie Dickinson. Most women, I believe, even if they didn't say anything, would be a tad concerned if their man was anywhere near Angie. But nude, in bed with her? Again, not Miko.

But the ironic part is that it scared the shit out of me, and I was the one doing it. I mean, for all the ego, braggadocio, boldness, and derring-do that most people thought was Burt, I was petrified. I admitted this to Angie.

Now Angie Dickinson is a rare woman. You can take this lady to an expensive restaurant or the fights, give her diamonds or a pair of boxing tickets, escort her to a black-tie ball or lay around the house in blue jeans, and she is absolutely perfect in every situation. She loves men, adores women, is smart, funny, quick. In a word, why didn't I marry her? She never asked!

"How are we going to do this nude scene?" I said.

"Burt, it's simple," she said. "They get used to you being in the altogether. It's like a marriage. The thing to do is come right out of your dressing room nude and act normal. Say, 'Good morning, Bob. Hi, Bill'—or whatever. Just be yourself. They'll get used to you, and you'll forget you don't have any clothes on."

"Right, thanks a lot," I said, and then started walking back to my dressing room. I thought Angie was out of her mind. The day anybody gets used to seeing Angie nude, will be the day they're half-dead.

The next day, as Angie was about to come out of her trailer, I opened my dressing room door a minute crack and peeked out. Damn, if she didn't live up to her word, and liven up a few other things in the process. She strolled out of her dressing room stark naked, wearing only satin slippers and a smile. The sight literally caused a meltdown of atomic proportions. The whole crew gasped while pretending not to notice.

Then it was my turn. Brave soul that I am, I ran out wearing my ratty old terry-cloth robe and underneath that I wore one of those Japanese slingshots. I set a new hundred-yard dash record streaking between my door and the bed sheets. Then and only then did I remove my robe.

Angie came over after saying "Hi, Bill; hi, Bob" a lot, kicked off her slippers, and hopped into bed.

Up in the rafters, or the grid, as they call it, there are usually one or two guys operating some piece of equipment. But when we looked up, there were about 150 guys hanging on the beams, ropes, and ladders. The casts from "Wagon Train," "Laramie," and other shows were hanging around leaning against the wall.

Ain't nobody ever gonna get used to seeing people in the buff—particularly when that person happens to be Angie Dickinson.

# CHAPTER 27

By THE END OF 1968, I HAD GOTTEN PRETTY HOT playing the third guy from the left. It got me that very role—third "half-breed" from the left—in *100 Rifles,* a gritty Southwestern war saga starring Raquel Welch and Hall of Fame football star-turned-actor Jim Brown. Forget story, acting, drama, and all the other components that make a movie. Both of these people were animals, supercharged sexual creatures, whose mere presence generated major heat before the first frame was even shot.

The film was shot on location in Granada, Plopos, and Almería, Spain, where I'd made *Navajo Joe* and all my gypsy friends lived. I flew to Madrid, where I planned to catch a little flier to Almería. But Raquel's husband, Patrick Curtis, somehow heard I needed a ride and asked if I wanted a lift on their private plane.

"Yeah, great," I said, appreciative of the convenience as well as the chance to meet Raquel a little sooner.

The plane, a twin-engine Cessna or something similar, idled on the Tarmac, surrounded by reporters and paparazzi. I cut through the crowd and struggled to climb up the stairs. Stepping into the plane, I heard Raquel, agitated by the commotion, say, "Look, Patrick, they're trying to get inside. They're everywhere." Then to me, she snapped, "Just go in the back."

As I stepped in, the corner of my eye caught a photographer climbing on the wing. He swung into the open door, stuck a camera right into Raquel's face, and snapped several frames. With catlike reflexes, she twisted around and air-mailed a crisp smack across the side of his head. The sharp blow caused him to lose his balance and fall to the ground. It was a sizable drop for a professional stuntman. But this guy had about thirty pounds of camera equipment around his neck. He landed on his back and stayed there, aired out and motionless.

Almost immediately, the plane started backing up. Raquel wasn't even breathing hard. Perfectly composed, she sat down, buckled up, and said, "So Burt, what were we talking about?" This was going to be some movie. And I still hadn't met Jim Brown.


JIM knew I'd played a little football, but I was smart enough to understand that college football is a laugh compared to the pros, and that making all-State in high school is slightly different from making the Hall of Fame. As soon as I walked into the hotel, I spotted him in the lobby. In bell bottoms and a loud print shirt, he was hard to miss.

We traded smiles. I went over and shook his hand and said, "I bet you can't swim worth a shit."

As those words left my mouth, I thought this might be the wrong joke. But, thank God, he laughed. This man owned an incredible physique—huge chest, small waist, and long, powerful legs. My legs. The legs God forgot to give me. You could've chiseled another me from one of Jim's legs and he wouldn't have missed a step.

In the picture, Jim and I were enemies, which meant we had to fight each other. It was a big, important fight scene. In those days, I choreographed all the fights I did in films. As the moment approached, Tom Gries, my first really good writer-director, wanted to know how I planned to do it.

"You know, Jim's got a few pounds on you," he said, smiling.

"He's also got a few muscles on me. If I don't have my shit together, we're all going down the tubes. But I'll come up with something."

"Okay, let me know what you work out," he said.

I failed to mention that I'd already started working on Jim. I had to find some physical activity in which I could at least compete with him, and maybe even win. The ocean came to mind. In terms of competitiveness, Jim and I stood on equal ground. Both of us were crazed, and hated to lose. Having been raised in the ocean, I knew I had an edge on him then. The bigger the waves, the better I swim.

"Want to take a swim?" I asked the first day.

We waded out in the water, talking and joking. Without him realizing it, I inched farther and farther out, until I asked, "Want to race?" and took off for shore.

I heard this whop-whop slapping in the water behind me. It was Jim. Every day he would say, "Ocean?" and each time I beat him. Jim hated to lose. He never said anything, but every day he found me and said, "Ocean?" That announced the start of another race. Well, guess what, folks—every day he narrowed the gap between us in the water, and on the last day we raced, he beat me.

But things were going well. One day I asked if there was anything that frightened him. Frightened, no, but . . .

"There are two things I don't care for," he said. "Heights and horses."

Those were the magic words I was waiting for. I found the director and told him I was fighting Jim on horseback, on top of a mountain. "And just to make it real interesting, we'll be handcuffed together hanging off a cliff."

"Great idea," he said.

Actually, Jim gave me immeasurable insight into racism, and the subtle things black people deal with every single day. He told me about growing up in Georgia, about going to Syracuse and playing pro ball. Each story made me angry.

One night he showed me his hands. They were massive, but the interesting thing was how scarred they were. "That's Butkus, that's Nitschke, and that's Huff. All of them stepped on my hands. They tried to break them, to put me out of the game." The most incredible thing about Jim is that he never missed a game in his entire career.

"Were there racial slurs when you came up?" I asked.

He laughed. "I know it's a stupid question," I said.

"The first time I played against Huff," Jim said, talking about his famous feud with Hall of Fame linebacker Sam Huff, "he came up to me and said, 'Nigger, you smell like shit.' The next time I got the ball I blew past him. I ran something like sixty yards, straight into the end zone. Then I yelled back at him, 'How do I smell from here?' "

I remember he surprised me one night by saying he'd rather have dinner with two rednecks than two Yankees.

"I hope you're not talking about me," I laughed.

"If I was, we wouldn't be here," he answered.

Then he explained that if a white, so-called liberal asked him to dinner, he didn't know where he stood with the man. But, if a redneck asked him out, he knew the amount of shit the guy was going to have to take from his friends.

"Forgive me, Jim," I said. "But I sense anger in this statement."

"Forgive me, Burt," he shot back. "But you aren't black."

"Checkmate," I said.

As our fight scene neared, I guess I did something considered drastic in those days. Chuck Robeson, who was John Wayne's longtime stuntman, a great guy, was supposed to double for Jim on the riskier parts. The director planned to put blackface on him. As soon as I heard about that, I knew it wasn't just improper, it was stupid and an insult.

"If you put blackface on Chuck, Jim will take your head off," I said to the director. "You'd better get a black stuntman here right now."

"Fox will never go for it," he said of the production manager. "It's not in the budget."

I reached in my pocket and peeled out $500.

"You put in five hundred and get another five hundred, because I'm not working with anyone in blackface. Those days are over."

"But I don't know a black stuntman," he said.

"I do," I said. "I'll get him over here tomorrow."

Jim never said anything about it, but I'm sure he knew. Our fight scene resembled a struggle between equals, but I wasn't fooled for one moment. In one exchange, I threw three punches and then tried to get away. But Jim grabbed me and held me in a bearhug. It felt like a grizzly had gotten ahold of me. I couldn't move and all the air came out of me like a balloon.

Even when I had the advantage, I couldn't escape my place. At one point, we were handcuffed together, dangling over a cliff that dropped off three hundred feet into a tiny creekbed. A safety cable ran up my arm, through Jim's sleeve and down the back of his pants leg. Three guys held the other end. It took forever to set up the camera.

"You telling me they couldn't have put stand-ins here?" he winced.

"Do you have something better to do than hang around?" I said.

"But why am I the one who has to look down?" he asked. "I don't like this shit."

"Well, close your eyes," I said. "I won't tell anybody."

"You're a funny man," he replied.

"You're a funny man, too," I said. "But you want to know what's really funny?"

"What?"

"If the cable breaks, we're both going together. But I'm pissed, because the headlines will say, 'Jim Brown and unknown actor die in fall.'" This time, he really laughed.

By comparison, our carefully staged fight scene paled next to the one Jim and Raquel had off camera. Till that point, they'd gotten along famously, like two chemicals that give off tremendous heat when mixed. Their interracial love scene generated more publicity than anything I'd ever seen. A photo of them topless, in a tight embrace, became a best-selling poster.

Fernando Lamas, who was also in the movie, told the director that he should have both of them take off their tops and let him say all the lines.

Then the heat exploded. One extremely hot afternoon Raquel, Jim, Fernando, Hans Gudegast, and myself were riding to the set in an open-topped Land Rover. The temperature soared way above one hundred. The dust stuck to your skin. It was more than just uncomfortable. While bouncing over the unpaved road, we saw the black stuntman walking to the set. Jim patted the driver.

"Come on, get in," he said.

"He's not getting in anywhere," Raquel said. "There's no room."

"What?" Jim asked, amazed.

"He's not getting in," she repeated. I thought, Oh, shit.

With that, Jim picked Raquel up and very gently set her down outside the car. Then he helped the other guy in, sat him in Raquel's spot, and told the driver to go. The driver then looked at me, uncertain about what to do.

"You'd better go," I said.

I remember the sight of Raquel disappearing in the distance as we drove off down the dirt road, spewing clouds of sticky dust behind us. And that ended what could have been one of the hottest love affairs in screen history. From then on, Raquel would've preferred to have worked with another cast, or been someplace else, and I can't say that I blame her.


AFTER that, Raquel and I had our own little altercation. It happened as we prepared to shoot the first scene in which we had any dialogue together. We were on the very top of a mountain. Both of us sat atop my horse, the same gorgeous half-Arabian Yul Brynner had ridden in *The Magnificent Seven*. Gries was using a 500mm lens, so the crew was a half-mile away.

For the first time in the picture, Raquel and I found ourselves alone. I had no idea if she was attracted to me. Miko had flown over. Jim had gone berserk over her. All of us whooped it up with my gypsy pals and had a great time. Raquel stayed by herself, though apparently she watched from afar. She told me recently that she knew I was going to be hot and was very attracted to me.

Anyway, as we sat by ourselves on my horse, no one else around us, she said, "Let me ask you a question."

"Sure, go ahead," I said.

"Why haven't you made a pass at me?"

Without the slightest pause, I replied, "Because I'm positive that I'd pull up your dress, pull down your panties, and find an eight-by-ten glossy of your cunt." What an asshole I was. She had every right to never speak to me again.

Needless to say, she refused to go anyplace near me, though three years later, in 1972, we ended up starring together in the movie *Fuzz*. Raquel signed to do the picture only after the producers and the director agreed she didn't have to appear in any scenes with me.

Although we had four scenes together in this movie, we never exchanged one word. Never even saw each other. Her double stood in the wide shots with me, and after I did my close-up, I got in my car and drove off the lot. When I was good and gone, they called her, she drove on and my double repeated the same shenanigans with her.

We would've remained foes if Raquel hadn't sued the producers of the 1982 film *Cannery Row*. The producers had fired her from the lead, claiming she was unprofessional, and then replaced her with Debra Winger. Well, I knew Raquel wasn't unprofessional. She's anything but that. In reality, they'd begun rehearsals and somebody thought she wasn't good or right for the part.

At the time, I was the number-one box office star in the world and wielded some influence, so I testified on her behalf. Although Raquel and I didn't like each other, I told the lawyers at my deposition that she was always on time, well prepared, and thoroughly professional. They just wanted somebody else for the part. But calling her unprofessional was bullshit, and she deserved all the money promised to her.

Well, she won $5 or $6 million. Years later, I had the pleasure of directing her on "Evening Shade." And I mean pleasure. After that week, I realized I could've fallen in love with her. She has a good heart, which she hides under beautiful boobs and a tough exterior. I wanted to tell her what a damn shame it was that we wasted so much time.

The moral of this story concerns the mistakes all of us make by judging people too quickly. I only have to remember the dignitary-filled premier of *100 Rifles* in Washington, D.C. A White House official hosted a private party, where every congressman, senator, and bigwig greeted me the same way. "Burt Reynolds. You're part Indian, right? 'Riverboat.' 'Gunsmoke.' You're a helluva actor. Keep it up."

They didn't know me from Clu Gulager, but they'd all read the same bio. Jim Brown laughed hysterically. He'd been through it before, and told me exactly what was going to happen, only I didn't believe him. While everybody proceeded to get falling down drunk—embarrassingly, commode-hugging drunk—Jim and I slipped out the back and wandered over to the Lincoln Memorial.

I don't care who you are, the sight of that man in that great big chair and the words printed on the wall behind him puts a lump in your throat. It was late at night. As we stood reading and talking, a police car pulled up. The cop leaned out the window, shined his light, and asked, "What are you guys doing here?"

We turned around. The cop saw Jim and asked if it was really him. Jim glared at the officer for a minute and then responded, "Does it make a difference?"

# CHAPTER 28

IT'S IMPOSSIBLE TO EXPLAIN WHAT IT TAKES TO BE A star, but by 1969 I'd been around for a decade and still hadn't climbed into that rarefied air at the top of the mountain. With three series under my belt, people recognized my face. I was the only actor who had been fired by all three networks, made a dozen films, and worked on Broadway.

But my career seemed to have settled into cruise control three notches below mattering, and that annoyed the hell out of me. Ambition is funny. Some people have it, some don't and some struggle against it. For me, each day was like third and goal. I wanted the ball; I didn't just want to score, I wanted to win.

The only thing I knew for sure was that to become a very hot actor, you had to be different, break through that thin, invisible layer. It's like the earth's atmosphere; you have to soar right through it to get into outer space. Yet I seemed stuck.

On January 1, 1969, I sent my agent a memo: "The only Indian I haven't played is Pocahontas. I'm tired of shaving my arms—it's easy to get the left, but when you shave the right with your left, you cut yourself to ribbons." It sounded lighthearted, but I was deadly serious. Dammit, get me a project and let me shine!

For me, that meant finding a feature script containing action, drama, romance, and, most important, comedy. Kinda like asking God to let you win the lottery. But instead of waiting for it to materialize, which is like waiting for Godot, I went to Quinn Martin, the classiest producer on TV ("The Untouchables," "The Fugitive"), and told him I wanted to do a series. Anything but a cop. Quinn's cops were as funny as Jack Webb.

However, he did have in a mind the hardboiled detective series "Dan August." ABC had given him twenty-six guaranteed episodes on the air. With his reputation, the offer looked attractive. But it really wasn't what I wanted.

"He's a tough, no bullshit cop," I said. "There're no jokes."

"You're not funny, Burt," Quinn answered.

"I beg your pardon?" I said. "I am funny."

"Oh, you're funny, all right, but you won't be funny in this," he explained. "You'll be sexy, exciting, and wonderful, and ABC is crazed for you right now."

"I don't want to play 'Book 'em, Dano,' " I said. "I don't want to do that."

"Let's change subjects," Quinn said. "Who's the highest-paid actor on television?"

"I don't know," I replied. "By now, I guess maybe one of the guys on 'Bonanza.' Maybe Michael Landon."

Quinn picked up the phone and made some calls. I heard him ask someone about Landon's salary.

"Okay, Landon's top pay is $25,000 a week."

I got a little sick for a moment.

"I'll pay you $26,000," he said.

"You know something," I said. "I love this friggin cop."

Mom and Dad, reunited after he returned from WWII and about to leave on a second honeymoon.
BURT REYNOLDS COLLECTION

Sister, Nancy Ann, Mom, Pop, and me, heading for Florida.
BURT REYNOLDS COLLECTION

Pop, the Chief of Riviera Beach, was tough as he looked and I'm proof.
BURT REYNOLDS COLLECTION

Football let me become a winner, and that
face shows my determination.

Darren McGavin and "Dumb-Dumb the Whistle Blower" on the set of *Riverboat*, 1959–1960. PHOTO COURTESY OF THE NATIONAL BROADCASTING COMPANY, INC.

A struggling New York actor in 1958, the critics said I had a touch of Brando, but the Miller lips were all mine. BURT REYNOLDS COLLECTION

Me and "Astor" filming *Fade In*, in Moab, Utah, 1968. BURT REYNOLDS COLLECTION

Navajo Joe (Native American by Italy) and Destaphanado—two great wigs—in 1967.
BURT REYNOLDS COLLECTION

With some of the wonderful gang on *Gunsmoke*—Jim Arness, Milburn Stone, "Quint," and Ken Curtis.
BURT REYNOLDS COLLECTION

Jon Voight and I listen to director John Boorman on the riverbank while shooting *Deliverance*.
COPYRIGHT © 1972 WARNER BROS. INC.

*Deliverance*, maybe the best film I made, was a picture that threw audiences against the rocks, and us actors, too. COPYRIGHT © 1972 WARNER BROS. INC.

My first nude scene, and I was lucky enough to have Angie Dickinson there with me, in *Sam Whiskey*.

In my lucky No. 22 for *Semi-Tough*, I played against the pros—and lived to tell about it.

At a 1981 Friars Club roast, my dear friend Johnny Carson gave me an award. Though not an Oscar, I gave a speech anyway.
BURT REYNOLDS COLLECTION

In action with Jim Brown and Raquel Welch, two of the best, on the set of *100 Rifles*. COPYRIGHT © 1969 TWENTIETH CENTURY FOX FILM CORP. ALL RIGHTS RESERVED.

I put my "little feet and hands" alongside some big names at Grauman's Chinese Theater.

Clint and I finally got together for *City Heat*, though I was seriously injured on the first day.

And that was it. In addition to the money, my deal included the option of doing all my own stunts, script approval, and the chance to direct all the stunts and B-roll footage. As the 1970 season got under way, it seemed like a dream come true. But the show was competing against ratings powerhouses "Hawaii Five-O" and "McCloud." Although this was frustrating, I was suddenly asked onto the talk-show circuit, which changed my entire life.

After warming up with Mike Douglas, I went on "The Merv Griffin Show." Long before "Oprah" or "Donahue," Merv had theme shows. The evening I appeared the show focused on bachelors. I joined Caesar Romero, Hugh O'Brien, guys like that. God bless them, these bachelors told Merv they loved their movies, loved every actor, loved Mexico, loved having the runs, loved dirty children, loved shitting their pants . . . these guys loved everything.

My turn came, and I criticized every film I had ever made—hopefully with humor—which nobody had ever done before. I made fun of everything. Made fun of my whole career. The movies, TV shows, and my off-screen relationships. And the audience became hysterical. I got huge, huge laughs. Before the show finished, Merv asked me to return the next night, which was another theme show—all women, plus me. And things got even hotter.

Afterward, Merv wanted me for the following Monday with Sophia Loren and Gina Lollobrigida. On that show, I sat between these two beautiful women like a twelve-year-old boy noticing bosoms for the first time. At the end, Sophia finally grabbed my face and planted a kiss that caused a tear to roll down my cheek. The place went nuts and so did Merv, who leaned over and said, "You've got to come back tomorrow."

Well, I ended up doing twelve nights in a row, which must be some kind of record. Each night I knew I had to top myself. People were flabbergasted. Judging from my work, they had no reason to suspect I had a sense of humor. After two weeks on Merv, the best joke in Hollywood was that I'd gotten a personality transplant. Quinn Martin even sent me a telegram that said, "See, I told you that you weren't funny." Quinn was one of the last of the great class acts in Hollywood.

My favorite appearance came the day after I learned "Dan August" had been canceled. It hadn't been announced publicly, but I'd heard from the producer. When Merv opened by asking how my career was going I surprised him with the truth.

"I'll tell you how good my career's going," I said. "I came back from lunch yesterday and there was no set."

"Really?" he asked, scooting to the edge of his seat. "What happened?"

"I'm off the air. Canceled. Kaput. Finito."

"You're joking."

"I don't joke about my life turning to shit."

When Merv and his audience realized I wasn't joking, they laughed uproariously. They had to. Because rather than say I hated life because my series was axed, I went on the air and said I was happy. Deliriously so. I had purchased an enormous house with a gated driveway on Carolwood in Holmby Hills, a Mercedes large enough to rent out as an apartment, and movie offers of all sorts piled up.

I never told anyone, but just after "Dan August" was over, Cubby Broccoli asked to see me. He was having problems with Sean Connery, and felt I should be the next James Bond. I was flattered, but felt no one would accept an American as Bond. They were very kind, thanked me, and cast George Lazenby. I think I was right, but who knows what would have happened had I taken that road well traveled!

More important than all of the above, I'd also quietly fallen madly in love with a very famous woman. Thanks to Merv, my life was indeed changing.

# CHAPTER
# 29

I HAD NO IDEA THERE WAS A CLUB—OKAY, AN UNOF-
ficial club—of women who met to watch me on Merv
and laugh. The club's membership included Dinah
Shore. Apparently Dinah thought I was funny and
wanted me as a guest on her talk show. Her staff contacted my office, but at the time I was too busy taping
the final episodes of "Dan August" to accept.

But they kept inviting me. Since I didn't know
what the hell I could possibly do on a cooking show, I
turned them down. I turned them down so often her
staff made it a running gag. They'd tell her I was
scheduled for the next day and then say I canceled at
the last minute. They warned her not to be shocked if
she opened the closet one day and I stepped out.
Then Dick Martin would emerge. This went on for
months.

Then one day I went on a game show about movie trivia—a subject on which Earl Holliman, Roddy McDowall, and I shared reputations for being experts—and bumped into Dinah's producer. He laughingly explained how this minor scheduling problem had mushroomed into a campy backstage drama. He also mentioned that in real life Dinah thought I hung the moon.

"Why that is, I don't know," I said. "But even if you're putting me on, it's very flattering. Even though I've never met her, I think she's great."

"Let me ask you, is there any way you could possibly sneak on the show?" he asked. "She might literally pass out."

We worked up a plan where I'd hide in the closet, exactly what they'd been telling her for months. I also asked them to replace Dinah's regular kitchen table with a breakaway one. I had an idea that would at least ensure that mine was not your regular guest spot.

As they snuck me into the closet before the show, I reminded myself that Dinah had been a star at seventeen on Eddie Cantor's radio show and worked with every big name in the business. I also knew she was probably the most beloved person in town, the closest any single person came to sainthood in a business where backstabbing, treachery, and deceit is routine behavior. Beyond that, she was a mystery.

Then came the point during the show when she opened the closet and instead of finding the ingredient she needed, she found me. Her mouth dropped as I stepped out, smiling. She started to laugh and then I laughed, neither of us able to control it. We hugged. Between guffaws, she said, "Oh, my God. I can't believe this. It's been how long? I can't believe you're really here."

It was a wonderful, warm, engaging moment. Great television. After Dinah recovered, we chatted for a few minutes. The conversation, even for a talk show, flowed as if we were two old friends reunited. Of course, Dinah made everyone feel as if she was their best friend. You couldn't help but be drawn to the warmth of her Southern soul. She was like the sun—nourishing and life-giving. I felt a pull on my heart immediately.

Then it was time for some fun. As I exited, I propositioned Dinah. Right on the air, I asked if she wanted to go to Palm Springs that weekend. While I knew it was in jest, my heart could think of nothing better.

It caught Dinah completely off-guard. She did that wonderful stuttering thing, "Uh, um, ah . . . you're crazy," and finally said, "No."

"Look, I'm going to ask you one more time," I said, looking as serious as possible, "and then that's it. Will you come to Palm Springs with me this weekend?"

Again, she answered, "Uh . . . no!"

"Okay, that's it," I said and started to walk off the set. By the door, I shouted, "If you don't want to go, the heck with you. I'll just kill myself." Abruptly, I turned, ran back into the kitchen, and dove over the counter. I landed on top of her cooking table. The table collapsed. The food, pots and pans, various ingredients, bowls, utensils flew every which way. It made a huge noise, an unbelievable mess, and scared Dinah half to death.

They cut to a commercial. Dinah, slightly rattled, bent over and asked if I was okay. I heard the concern in her voice. Slowly, I turned over, pretending for a brief moment that I was hurt.

"Now I'm really serious," I said, staring into those twinkling blue eyes of hers. "Would you come to Palm Springs with me this weekend?"

"You're insane," she laughed.

After the show, Dinah and I talked for hours. I'd never met anyone quite like her. No one with her combination of intelligence, humor, warmth, inquisitiveness, and wisdom. When Dinah asked, "How are you," she really meant it. That afternoon I left the studio knowing I'd been rattlesnake-bit. Blissfully charmed. Scratched behind my ears. My tummy rubbed. It was like a first love all over.

Until then, Miko and I had been perfectly happy, but I knew I wanted to try and make something happen with Dinah and I didn't want to cheat on Miko. She had too much class for that. I had to tell her. So when I got home I said that I felt our relationship was over.

Miko accepted the rather abrupt news exactly as she had been raised to handle such things: with grace and not a trace of emotion. She didn't cry, nor did she argue. In a strange way, that convinced me my decision was the right one. After four years of Miko's total acceptance, her lack of possessiveness and jealousy, I craved a woman who'd show me a whole sweep of emotions. I wanted Dinah's passion.

Long before attorney Marvin Mitchelson created palimony suits, I wanted to be fair to Miko. I'd taken her from her Japanese home, brought her to America. She put up with me, God knows. She deserved to be free of worry while deciding which way her life was going.

"I'm making pretty good money," I said. "What do you want? What do you think you need?"

Without a second's hesitation, she said, "I want an apartment at beach, I want a Cadillac convertible, and I want five hundred dollar a week for two years." I was a little taken aback, but I said, "You got it."

"After that, if you want to go back to Japan, I'll buy you a ticket," I said. "Or you can stay here. But you'll be on your own."

She understood. Exactly one day before the two-year deadline was up, Miko married Barbra Streisand's manager. They had a son together, but it ended in divorce. She got a lot of money. The next time I saw Miko I was in my car, stopped at a red light. A Rolls-Royce pulled up beside me. I glanced over and saw a woman with long, black hair in wraparound sunglasses. She pushed her glasses up, smiled, and said,

"What's up, doc?"

AFTER an exciting weekend together in Palm Springs, where all we did was trade stories about our lives, Dinah and I realized exactly where fate was leading us, and we put up only mild resistance. It was one of those cases when you have to constantly remind yourself to put your foot on the brake—not because you're going too fast but because you want to enjoy the scenery.

There were a few small fears. I think some of Dinah's friends thought I might be using her. Others couldn't understand the attraction. They told her she was nuts. And everybody, it seemed, glommed onto the difference in our ages. Suddenly, all talk concerned older woman–younger man relationships. The press made it sound taboo. Which was bullshit.

I was thirty-five years old then, and to this day I swear to God I don't know Dinah's age. I didn't know it when we started dating, nor did I care. If someone asked about it, I jumped on them like a bad cold. Like somebody's skin color, I have no time for that.

Besides, Dinah was ageless. She had wisdom and the eyes of a child.

I've always felt age is a state of mind, a desire to embrace life. Dinah's sense of discovery reminded me of the first time Miko saw the Empire State Building. Or when I visited St. Peter's in Rome. I don't care if you're the biggest atheist in the world, you can't walk through that front door without feeling the holiness of the place.

And that was Dinah. I remember taking her to a friend's ranch to go horseback riding. After getting on her horse, she said, "This is the most beautiful horse I've seen in my life."

"Then you haven't seen a lot of horses," I chuckled. "I mean, it's nice, but not beautiful."

It made no difference to Dinah. By then, her attention was on the walnut trees, birds, mountains, clouds . . . I marveled at that ability of hers to see. But I wasn't alone. Edward G. Robinson, who amassed one of the most impressive private art collections in the world, and did it well before collecting art was trendy, once told me Dinah had the only good eye for art in L.A.

And she loved people. We missed more planes, and spent more time waiting in airline terminals, simply because someone would ask for an autograph and then Dinah would ask them how they were. An hour later, I'd have to interrupt and say either we caught the next plane or invited this person home with us.

Although Dinah and I fell in love quickly, our courtship moved cautiously. This was not a lady who jumps into the sack with you a half-hour into the first date. I followed Dinah around the country, meeting her in various cities while she did promotions. Then I went off to Chicago to star in a Neil Simon play, and one night, at the end of the first act, I looked out and there she was.

She invited me to her hotel and ordered champagne. Later that evening, we made love for the first time. For me, it was the discovery of how different sex is when your heart is full of real love and your body aches for life to be full. I realized I was in a whole other league with Dinah.

Soon after that, we visited my parents in Florida. It was so cute. Dinah insisted on sleeping in what we called the treehouse, which is actually a cabin on the ranch that I had built on tall stilts. It sits high in the branches of huge Australian pines, overlooking all 180 acres of lakes and trees. It's a place where you close the door and shut out everything but the glory of Mother Nature. I slept in the big house.

Every night I snuck back and forth between the two places, wearing a pretty good track out in the backyard. This charade continued for four or five days. Finally, over breakfast, my dad said, "Who the hell do you kids think you're kidding?"

I felt like I was seventeen again. Dinah laughed. She called my dad every Sunday without fail for the rest of her life.

"Now ya'll just get comfortable back there," Mom added. "And Buddy, take some clean clothes with you."


ABOUT that time Johnny Carson, the High Lama of late-night television, asked me if I wanted to guest host the "Tonight Show" while he took a night off. In my world, this was tantamount to the President of the United States asking if you could take over a meeting in the Oval Office.

I would never have had the same career without Johnny. From my first appearance on the "Tonight Show" in the late sixties, we were captivated by each other. I was still pre-Dinah then, and I think I was doing everything Johnny would've liked to be doing. I think he saw me as his alter ego.

"So what are you doing after the show?" he asked.

"I'm going to walk up and down Broadway," I said, "and try to be recognized."

I studied Johnny like a premed student taking basic anatomy. Damn, he was the best. If he laughed at you, America laughed, too. If he liked you, America liked you. You were a great guy. And Johnny liked me a lot. Not only did I know how to set him up thirty-eight different ways, I created a character for myself who was super-cocky: a wise-cracking, carefree, outlandish, daredevil womanizer. It was one of several suits in every man's closet. This might have been a tough man for a woman to live with, but it played great on television.

The public loved this wise-cracking guy, especially as it started to see the fun he was having. They saw him winking at the camera and saying, "I'm having a great time, and being rich and famous is not a bad thing!"

Johnny loved him, too. During my first show, they cut away to a commercial and I started talking to Ed McMahon. I'd been told not to bother Johnny. He didn't talk to anyone during commercials. But then Johnny leaned over and asked if I wanted to be a guest host sometime. I said sure. No actor had ever sat in for Johnny before; only comedians. But I was too dumb to be scared.

Prior to me hosting, they asked if I wanted anyone particular on the show. I told them to book my ex-wife, Judy Carne. We hadn't spoken for six years. Everyone thought I was crazy. She called me the day before and asked why I wanted her. The problems we'd had still weren't resolved. There was still a lot of tension and antagonism between us; of course, I knew that could make for sensational TV.

"I don't need to talk to you now," I said. "I'll just see you on the show. We'll have fun."

We did, and then some. Judy was on for thirty minutes, and each moment crackled with electricity. Everything she said was a straight line, beginning when she sat down in the chair and said hello.

"God, you look good," she said.

"I'm sorry to say, so do you."

"What are you doing now?" she asked.

"Oh, you know, hanging out on the corner, selling old Burt and Judy towels. They're tough to get rid of."

The audience ate it up. They laughed, cheered, and sensed the sparks we still generated. It was like watching high school sweethearts reunite after a dozen years. She'd recently married again but confessed there were already problems. I described how I'd grown up in the years since our divorce. If the audience could've had their way, we would've hugged, kissed, and gotten back together. But then Judy made a terrible mistake.

"Are you dating again?" she asked.

"As a matter of fact, yes," I said. "A very nice woman."

"Oh, yeah, I forgot," she said. "I heard you like older women now."

I always can sense an audience's reaction, and at that instant they left her. I mean, certain things are sacred: Mom, apple pie, the American flag, and Dinah Shore. You do not insult them. But Judy committed a sin. I knew as host I had to get the audience back in sync, balanced between me and her, but before I did that... well, what the hell. I had to slap her wrist.

"No, Judy," I said. "Not older. Just classier."

The audience cheered. Judy, aware she'd done wrong, teared up, and apologized. At that point, it was my job to bail her out.

"You love Dinah, don't you?"

"Yes, I love her," Judy replied.

"You own all her records, don't you?"

"Yes," she said.

"You're lying," I said. "But that's okay. The crowd still loves you too, don't you?"

They applauded, and once again all was right in the world.

# CHAPTER
# 30

T HE NEXT DAY DIRECTOR JOHN BOORMAN CALLED
me at my hotel and said he wanted me to read for a
part in his next movie.

"It's *Deliverance,*" he said.

"Oh, I read the book," I answered.

"You read the book?" The sound of his voice
told me that he was surprised.

"Yeah," I said. "I know it's strange, an actor who
reads. But I've read a lot of Dickey's poetry; he's a
brilliant writer."

"I agree. Can you do a Southern accent?"

"When do you want me to come in?" I said, sti-
fling whatever sarcastic thought popped into my
mind before I blew the job.

A few days later I returned to L.A. and met Boorman in his office at Warner Bros. It was a little odd

hearing Boorman discuss this intensely Southern novel in his British accent, but he had tremendous feeling for this story about four Atlanta businessmen who set out on a weekend canoe trip and end up fighting for their lives against a treacherous river and murderous rednecks.

"What made you think I'd be right for this part?" I asked. "What movie did you see me in?"

"I know you do all your own stunts," Boorman replied.

"Yeah, but what movie did you see me in? I'm interested. Was it *Navajo Joe?*"

I named off these pieces of shit that I'd done. But I figured Boorman was so smart and insightful, he saw something.

"Actually," he said, "I saw you host the 'Tonight Show.' "

"The 'Tonight Show'?" I said.

"Yes," he said. "I have to have a guy who's in control of three men. Total control. And that night I watched you control five people. You're absolutely fearless, aren't you?"

"No, I'm dumb," I said, laughing. "I'm too dumb to be scared."

I knew the script was flawless, a once-in-a-lifetime chance to establish myself as a serious actor. For three months' work, I accepted $50,000, much less than I got for "Dan August," but worth one hundred times that in credibility. At some point, Boorman mentioned he'd cast Jon Voight as Ed, an even-tempered man who'd never challenged himself. Compared to my character, Lewis, who lived to confront danger, he was the big question mark. I adored Jon's work. He'd just been nominated for an Oscar for his role in *Midnight Cowboy.*

Boorman asked if I'd read with him. As soon as I agreed, Jon suddenly appeared. He'd been hiding in an adjoining office. I wasn't surprised. Jon, a soft-spoken man, has flawless timing. And I knew Boorman was testing my reaction. Jon and I improvised for about an hour, until we had each other in stitches and Boorman was satisfied.

Then our shrewd director asked us to help pick the other two guys. I'd heard Boorman loved actors; this told me it was true. He knew the chemistry on the picture had to be perfect, and wanted us involved in the selection process.

"I hear there're two wonderful stage actors doing *The Pueblo Inci-*

*dent* at the Arena Theater in Washington, D.C.," he said.

All of us flew there and saw these two sensational actors, Ned Beatty and Ronny Cox. After the play, we went backstage and told them they were in the movie. Neither had done a movie before and they were thrilled. Boorman, Voight, and I were equally excited. It was really quite moving to walk into a room and be a part of handing two guys a dream role, something you know will change their lives.

All of us bonded immediately. But it grew exponentially as soon as we began six weeks of rehearsal in Clayton, Georgia. If I'd scribbled my wildest dreams in a calendar at the start of 1971, I couldn't have imagined a better way to start the summer. The weather was perfect. The air carried the fresh, invigorating scent of possibilities. It was like the book: nary a clue of the hazards and fury that awaited us once the journey began.

Once there I learned the original cast had included Marlon Brando, Jimmy Stewart, and Henry Fonda, but then they were informed about the Chattooga, fifty miles of white-water hell and deadly waterfalls running from South Carolina to Georgia. On a danger scale of one to six, the river is rated a five—the second most dangerous river in the U.S. You aren't supposed to go down in a canoe unless you're an expert. Those big stars wisely got the hell out.

Every day from six A.M. to one, we trained with experts hired to teach us to canoe, climb up the sides of cliffs, hike through untracked woods, and shoot bows and arrow. It was like being plucked off the street and going to training camp with the navy S.E.A.L.S. The physical pain was grueling. Then after lunch, we rehearsed till midnight. At the end of each day, the four of us crashed and burned. But we grew stronger.

At night we would go to this great bar at the country club. At first no one but Jon, Ned, Ronny, and me were there. However, Dickey, all six feet seven of him, started coming there every night too. Well, I just couldn't handle his act—his Jim Bowie knife on his belt, cowboy hat, and fringed jacket. He would corner Jon, Ned, and Ronny every night and tell them stories about the real people the novel was based on. However, he insisted on calling everyone by their names in the film. One night I was sitting way over at the other end of the bar, talking to my favorite cocktail waitress, and I heard: "Lewis! Lewis, I'm talking to you, boy."

The waitress whispered, "Mr. Dickey's calling you."

"He ain't calling me. My name's Burt," I said.

"Lewis, goddammit, I'm calling ya, boy. Come over here!"

I didn't move. I saw this mountain moving over toward me. Soon he was standing above me.

"Lewis, I'm talking to you, son. Now why aren't you answering me?"

I said, "Because I'm not Lewis. Tomorrow morning at six-thirty A.M. I'll be Lewis, but, goddammit, right now I'm Burt, so get your big ugly face out of my way. If you want Lewis, talk to him in the morning!"

It got real quiet. Then he knelt down close to me and said, "By God, that's exactly what Lewis would have said!"

Dickey had adapted his own novel brilliantly, but interfered with the task of making the picture in the sense that we all needed time alone. He walked around telling stories, talking about motivation, and in general competing with Boorman. I understood. The man's blood was on the page. But like it or not, Boorman was captain of this ship.

One day midway through rehearsals, we were all on the floor of this wonderful old house, splayed out and thoroughly exhausted after a day on the water, and the door opened. A cold, foreboding shadow filled the room. Dickey followed it inside.

"I understand that my presence would be more advantageous by my absence," he intoned.

I looked around.

"What the fuck did he just say?" I asked.

"I think," Jon piped up, "Mr. Dickey is saying that he's going to go home and allow us the honor of taking care of his picture. He'll be back to play the sheriff, and we love him for it. At least I think that's what he said."

"That's what I said," Dickey added.

Before leaving, Dickey addressed each of us in character. He went to Ned first and whispered, "Bobby, save my picture. You're the only one I can trust." He said the same thing to Ronny. Then he went to Jon, who I heard respond, "I don't think . . . see, I . . . well, I'll try." I finally interrupted and said, "Shut up, Jon, he's going to talk to me now." Then Dickey grabbed the back of my head with hands as big as ham-hocks and asked, "Are you Lewis now?"

"Yeah, I'm Lewis," I said.

"Lewis," he whispered. "Lewis, save my picture. You're the only one I can trust."

"Don't worry," I said. "I will."

I watched Jon work with true amazement. I thought he was an incredibly intellectual person. Before each shot, he talked everything through. He analyzed every word and nuance, phrase, and gesture. I'd never seen anybody do that. Later, of course, I realized he didn't always know what the hell he was talking about. Acting is reacting. As Spencer Tracy said, "Just don't bump into the furniture."

But Jon did forty-five takes because Boorman would always ask if he wanted another one. Finally, I took Boorman aside and said, "Dammit, don't ask if he wants another one. He's going to say *yes* every time until you reach take one hundred. For chrissakes, let's get on down the river."

Although I had trouble finding my character at the beginning, Boorman straightened me out with the book called *Zen and the Art of Archery*. The point was that when you pull the arrow back, the arrow releases you, you don't release it. It leaves your hand only when it's time to hit the bullseye, and not before or after.

Well, I came to believe this. The movie opens with the men driving into the woods, but their conversation was actually recorded during a scene at an archery range in Atlanta that was supposed to run over the titles. It was edited out, so we used the sound track. One day when we were shooting at the range, I took the arrow back using a sixty-five-pound pull and shot four straight bulls-eyes. This was when I was in char-acter as Lewis. When Boorman broke for lunch, I stayed to shoot more. I thought, "This archery stuff is easy." But I was no longer Lewis, and my first shot went into the woods. The next went into my foot. As Lewis, though, I was a perfect shot. As Lewis, I was invincible.

I felt the same way on the river. Since *Deliverance,* there've been about twenty fatalities because people tried to canoe that river without helmets or safety gear. For some strange reason, though, I never gave the danger a second thought. I felt immortal. But in case I wasn't, Boorman shot in chronological order. If one of us got hurt or drowned, he could write it in: "Lewis drowned the other day."

Every day we set out down the river—Boorman, the remarkable cinematographer Vilmos Zsigmond, and about ten crew guys. We ate lunch out of paper bags on the riverbank, because once you started down you couldn't go back. And every day, no kidding, one of us was saved by the others. All of us got tossed in the water, bumped against the rocks, gripped by the current. Two of Voight's canoes splintered beneath him. When you talk about closeness among a cast, this was staggering.

I came the closest to biting it, but it was my own fault. We reached the scene where Lewis was supposed to go over a waterfall. It showed Lewis's true mettle, his willingness to spit in the face of death. The falls, about ninety feet high, were the largest on the Chattooga. After my double, an expert riverman, refused to go over, Boorman and Zsigmond shot it with a cloth dummy the costumer rigged up. But it didn't look right on film.

"How'd it look?" Vilmos asked.

"Like a dummy going over a waterfall," Boorman said.

"Let me do it," I said. "Hell, I can do it."

Boorman gave me a look, a real studied assessment of me as a man as opposed to an actor. And rather than argue against the stunt, rather than say it was too dangerous, rather than ask if I was out of my mind, he announced to the assembled crew, "Burt says he can do this. Burt *can* do this." Then he turned to me. "How are you going to do this, Burt?" It wasn't just Boorman; the whole crew had that kind of crazy respect for me.

Like a dummy, I said, "When I go over I'm going to go down there, turn left, hit the rock, I'll bounce over there, do a quick slide, and then flip into the water. But I won't be able to hear anything. So my hand will go up and then I'll go."

There was a control dam behind the falls, which they shut off. Then they pounded a mountain-climbing spike into the center rock. A rope was connected to that. I wrapped it around my hand as I walked out wearing my wetsuit with the cutoff sleeves, tight army pants, and boots. Everything felt right. Then they unlocked the dam, turning the water back on. Suddenly, I heard this noise, a rumble that I will never forget. It grew louder and louder. I glanced over my shoulder and saw a wall of water coming at me.

My options were all gone. The hell with it. I raised my arm and went for it.

The first rock I hit cracked my tailbone like an egg. Somehow I made it to the surface and gulped some air before getting pulled again through the racing falls. I turned several flips, hit something, doubled up, landed on my neck, and entered the hydrofoil at the bottom where the falls plunge back into the river.

I had never been in a hydrofoil before, but I remembered this guy rescuing me from heavy surf when I was a youngster. He explained all about waves and tides and he happened to mention that you can't swim out of a hydrofoil. It spins you around like a washing machine. If you try swimming out, it pulls you back in and eventually drowns you.

"What you do is go to the bottom and it'll shoot you out," he said. "It sounds crazy. But trust me."

God made his voice come back to me. "Go down to the bottom. Trust me."

I dove down. But what the guy neglected to tell me was that it shoots you out, all right, but it's like being shot out of a torpedo tube. You rocket through the water at about 180 miles an hour. I'd come over the falls a thirty-five-year-old daredevil in perfect shape. When I surfaced, about two hundred yards downriver, I was a nude seventy-five-year-old man—yes sir—without a stitch of clothes on. The boots, pants, wetsuit I had on were gone. Disintegrated. I rose slowly and literally crawled out of the water. It was pretty obvious I was hurt. The next thing I knew I was in the hospital being X-rayed. But I got out in time to see rushes.

"How'd it look?" I asked.

"Like a dummy going over a waterfall," Boorman said.

● ● ●

ALTHOUGH that wasn't the most perilous stunt in a picture where everyone from actors to crew jeopardized their personal safety every single day, there was no more difficult, traumatic, or disturbing scene than when Ned's character gets raped by the two deranged scoundrels who come out of the woods to haunt the adventure. By this time we had all become as close as family, but Ned had to go over these falls himself.

In the wake of mounting tension, Boorman confessed to me that he couldn't find an actor who would pull his two front teeth out. The two villains had to resemble the lowest form of human life, a half-step up from animals, who've spent their whole lives in the woods. I commiserated, but understood why actors wouldn't want to pull out their teeth.·

"I don't want them to pull all of them," Boorman said. "I only need about two here in front."

"John, that's still a lot to ask," I said.

"But they've got to look real. They have to have the accent. They have to look like the devil himself in blue jeans."

He brightened a bit when I told him about Cowboy Coward, a guy with whom I'd done a few stunts many years earlier at a tourist place called Ghost Town in Maggie Valley, North Carolina. We had re-created the gunfight at the O.K. Corral; he played the Walter Brennan part. He stuttered a bit, but was a wonderful actor. Boorman had me call him.

Turned out Cowboy still worked the wild west show at Maggie Valley and ran moonshine during the off-season. I started to explain the part, but the money interested him more. Then one day a truck drove up with a passel of kids in back and Cowboy got out. He wore bib overalls without a shirt and long clodhopper shoes. He couldn't have looked more right if Central Casting had flown him over first class. Boorman was floored.

"Did you tell him what to wear?" he asked.

"John, I'm telling you, it's the real thing here," I said.

Boorman immediately put the fear of God into Cowboy by asking him to read a bit from the rape scene. Christ, I immediately realized I'd forgotten to do the one thing Cowboy had asked of me: to tell Boorman he couldn't read. Snatching the script, I suggested improvising. I'd feed him the line, then he could say it any way he wanted to. I read Cowboy's first line: "Go over by the tree and pull down your pants."

Cowboy said, "Get over by that sa-a-a-pling and take your p-p-p-panties down."

Boorman lit up.

"You've got the job," he said.

Nonplussed, Cowboy got up and walked toward the door. Before he left, Boorman stopped him.

"I want to know something, Cowboy," Boorman said. "You play the friend of a guy who fucks another guy in the ass. An accessory, in a way, to a horrible attack. How do you feel about that?"

After thinking a moment, Cowboy said, "That's all right. I've done a lot w-w-w-worse things than that."

I thought the other guy, Bill McKinney, was a little bent. I used to get up at five in the morning and see him running nude through the golf course while the sprinklers watered the grass. A strange dude, he moved to L.A. after *Deliverance* and worked in a lot of Clint's pictures. He always played sickos, but he played them well. With my dark sense of humor, I was kind of amused by him. But as we got closer to the rape scene, I caught him staring at Ned in an odd, unnerving way. Ned would see it, and look away.

The day before we shot the scene I noticed him hovering beside Ned and sat down between them. I wanted him to see I was Ned's friend. No different than in the script. Then I asked him how he planned to handle the rape scene.

McKinney turned out to be a pretty good guy who just took the method way too far.

Staring straight at Ned, he whispered, "I've always wanted to try that. Always have."

Ned shouted, "John! Oh, John!"

In his brilliance, Boorman reassured Ned but also brought in several additional cameras, knowing Ned wasn't going to give him a second, third, or fourth take. Ned was only going to do the brutal scene once.

When it came down to shooting it, Cowboy and McKinney were hands-down brilliant. Scared the shit out of everybody who saw the movie. People crawled out of the theater. None of that creepy "Squeal, piggy, piggy" stuff was in the script. But McKinney, I swear to God, really wanted to hump Ned. And I think he was going to. He had it up and he was going to bang him. It's the first and only time I have ever seen camera operators turn their heads away.

Finally, I couldn't stand it anymore. I ran into the scene, dove on McKinney, and pulled him off. Boorman, hot on my tracks, helped hold him down. Ned, who was crying from both rage and fear, found a big stick and started beating him on the head. Half a dozen guys grabbed Ned and pulled him away. We separated the two of them and let things cool off.

"Damn you, John!" I said to Boorman. "Why'd you take so long?"

"I was waiting for you to run in," he explained. "I knew when you ran in that I'd taken the audience to the breaking point."

Which he did. Right after Ned's character is buggered, Lewis kills the bastard with an arrow.

After fourteen weeks of filming, all of us were completely spent. We didn't have an ounce more to give. It had been a long, emotionally and physically grueling picture. Like the characters we played, we had the sense of surviving something hellish, something extraordinary, something we might not ever repeat in our lives. But we did it that once and we knew it was special.

Somewhere deep down inside, I know no other film may ever equal *Deliverance.*

# CHAPTER
## 3 1

IF I HAVE ANY CLASS, ANY DIGNITY, THE TINIEST shred of upper-crust respectability, it came from Dinah. In terms of preparing for the rest of my life, I was so damn lucky to have been with her. She didn't gossip. She wasn't judgmental. Her sense of decency, of right and wrong, was impeccable. Her insight into people was as sharp as anyone's and her advice always on target.

She once showed me a copy of an old *Hollywood Confidential,* an early scandal rag. In it was a story that she was half black. I became livid, even though the thing was ancient history. Dinah laughed and calmed me down. She said that when the press asked her, she replied, "Gosh, I wish it were true."

"Lies sink straight to the bottom like a rock in a

pond," she said. "The truth is like cream. It rises to the top."

God, her voice alone had the effect of good medicine. It was warm and soothing, like a favorite blanket.

Almost a year passed between the end of *Deliverance* and its release to theaters. During that time I made two pictures, *Fuzz* and *Everything You Always Wanted to Know About Sex*.

I told Dinah about my turning down the James Bond role. I could've played the hell out of it. Whenever I chided myself for making such a poor decision, Dinah reminded me that a singer always learned more from singing a bad song than a good one.

"If that's the case, then I'm a much better actor than Robert Redford," I said.

"I think you are," she smiled.

Dinah lived on Oxford Drive in Beverly Hills, across the street from Glenn Ford and behind the pink Beverly Hills Hotel. She adored being in the kitchen, as anyone who saw her show knows, and prepared dinner for us almost every night. The meals tasted wonderful. They should've been photographed. She could whip up hush puppies and filet mignon with equal aplomb.

The rest of her home was magnificent. Such taste. She bought Chagalls when they cost nothing. Yet when I moved in, she redid everything to make it more *our* house. The couches were reupholstered in leather and she acquired Southwestern paintings, which she wasn't too crazy about. Dinah's taste, not surprisingly, was much more sophisticated than mine. I didn't appreciate Impressionism at the time, but she wanted me to fall in love with art in the same way she had.

I already showed an interest. Years earlier I'd purchased my first painting, a small oil by Olaf Wieghorst. Wieghorst was considered by western art experts to be the Charles Russell of our day. When we met, he told me how he'd ridden with Pancho Villa, and I told him my dad's battle stories. He then said he wanted me to own one of his paintings.

"I can't afford one, sir," I said.

"What's the most you can afford to pay?" he asked.

Not wanting to embarrass myself, I thought of the biggest sum I could part with. Two thousand dollars.

"Just paint me a tiny little Indian," I said, jokingly, "and don't charge me for the clouds."

A few weeks later Wieghorst delivered a sparse landscape, with big, white clouds floating in a light blue sky. Beneath the clouds, so small you have to look hard to notice, is an Indian. Wieghorst, bless him, titled the piece, "No Charge for the Clouds." It's one of my most cherished possessions.

Clint, among other things, owned a Charles Russell. I saw it and decided if I was going to envy a piece of art, that was the piece. Art collecting is not a competition sport, but I decided to buy a Remington and invite Clint over. I found one at the best gallery in Beverly Hills. Remington is famous for both his use of color and the sense of movement of his horses. The piece I saw in the gallery was unbelievable. I loved it immediately.

"How much is it?" I asked.

"A million two," the dealer replied.

"I don't like it," I said.

Two years later the gallery found me a Remington I could afford. I happened to be on location but I asked how big it was. The man said, "Huge." That was all I cared about. I had them deliver the painting to my house and asked my right hand, Clarence, to hang "my Remington" over the living room fireplace.

"And get a light installed over it," I said. "When I come home, have all the lights off, except the one on my Remington."

I came home excited to see "my Remington." It was night. I walked inside and saw the single light shining. As I set my luggage down, I couldn't wait to set eyes on the painting. I imagined the colors, the horses, the expressions on the cowboys. Then I finally walked into the room and saw *it*—a black and white painting of goats with a few sheep in the background, and the skinniest Indian I had ever seen. He looked like Gandhi.

Okay, the painting was at least a Remington. I overcame the disappointment. But what irked me was Eastwood's reaction. He came over, studied it for a moment and asked, "Who the hell painted that?"

Art can be a funny thing. I fell in love with a painter who signed his works G. Harvey. He did great, dramatic nocturnal renderings of cities in the past. Like Washington in 1814 or Houston in 1812. When I met him he was struggling to stay afloat. Dinah suggested helping him by throwing an auction.

"What people will come?" I asked.

"I'll give you a list of people here who might be interested," she said. "I also know a few others from out of town."

We sent cards to the biggest ranches in Texas, and the night of the auction there were so many Lear jets flying into L.A. it looked like a convention for private jet owners. We set up in my backyard, which was the size of a football field. Except for the paintings, the scene resembled a wedding. On one side were a sea of cowboy hats. The other side was filled by the likes of Mel Brooks, Dom DeLuise, David Steinberg, Ed McMahon. G. Harvey took one look, went behind the house and threw up.

The auction was fantastic. G. Harveys normally sold for around $3,000, but his first painting that night went for $60,000. Those cowboy hats bought everything. Nobody from the show business side bid, and I felt a tad embarrassed. I admitted as much to Mel Brooks.

"Somebody's got to bid from over here," I said. "We're looking real bad."

"You're right," he agreed.

Mel went up to Steinberg. David wasn't the best choice in the world. He still has money from his bar mitzvah. But he had such respect for Mel that he would say yes to anything Mel asked. The next painting was the largest thus far offered.

"Bid $40,000, David," Mel said.

"Yeah, b-b-but," David stammered.

"Don't worry. Everything's been going for sixty or more."

"Yeah, but—"

"Do it, dammit!"

The painting was held up. David did as told, and in a very timid voice bid $40,000, expecting to be topped immediately. But a great big Texan stood and hollered, "Let the little Jew have it." An unbelievable quiet followed. You could've heard the grass bend. David got down on his hands and knees and crawled across the yard to the big oilman and pleaded, "Please, let's make this competitive."

"Don't look so sad, little man," the Texan said. "You won."

Ed McMahon might've gotten the best deal that night, depending on . . . well, just depending. At the time, he was married to an ex-airline stewardess who transformed herself into Miss Bel Air. I kidded her, saying it's a dead giveaway when you ask your guests if they want a "beverage."

"You should ask if they want a drink. And don't give us the almonds in a bag."

During the evening, a cowboy had fallen in love with her, and gave her a beautiful painting he'd paid over $60,000 for. Ed and I walked into my pool room and saw this drunken cowboy shoving her over the table. He had his hand up the back of her dress and was saying something about how her skin was the softest thing he had felt other than ostrich skin. Ed is an ex-Marine, and I go ape shit when I see this stuff. I got ready to pounce and looked at Ed.

"Come on, Ed," I said. "I'm taking this son of a bitch out."

Ed quickly grabbed my arm.

"No," he said, "I want that painting."


JUST as she opened my eyes, Dinah opened doors. She took me into worlds and introduced me to people I might have met under different circumstances but never would have had the relationship I did by knowing her. One night I took Dinah to Nicky Blair's Club, a restaurant on Sunset Boulevard. The place was packed and as soon as we walked in, as always people stared at Dinah.

Frank Sinatra, seated at a corner table, waved to us. He was eating with Harry Guardino, two bodyguards—Poochie East and Poochie West—and his sidekick Jilly Rizzo, who owned a joint in New York and had an eye like Marty Feldman's. It was an interesting group. Dinah and I waved back. He motioned again.

"I think Frank wants us to come over," Dinah said.

"So what," I said. "We don't work here. Let's have something to eat first, then visit."

As we ordered, I saw actor Harry Guardino get up from Mr. S.'s table and come toward us. He said hello and extended a personal invitation to join Frank for drinks. I said thanks, but to tell Mr. S. we'd come after dessert.

"You want me to tell him that?" Harry asked.

"That's what I said, wasn't it?"

When we finally stopped by Mr. Sinatra was charming, as everybody was with Dinah. He was charming to me, too. He called me "Pally." I liked being called Pally. It reminded me of the movies, Damon Runyon and a lot of great stuff.

"Pally, want to play a little poker?" Sinatra asked me.

I'm not a bad poker player. I said sure.

"Where are we playing?" I asked.

"In the kitchen," he said. "Right now."

I started to back out of the game, excusing myself because I had to take Dinah back home. But Dinah being Dinah insisted on taking a cab. She wanted me to play cards with Sinatra. She knew invitations like that didn't come along every night.

All of us moved from the dining room to the kitchen, where a huge table was set up amid the cooks, waiters, and dishwashers. Sinatra named the game. Five-card stud. And we played for a while until one of the busboys, a young Latino, dropped a tray full of dirty glasses. The startling crash of breaking glass was followed by silence. Nicky Blair rushed in and stood over the busboy.

"You're fired," he screamed.

"Just a minute, Nicky," Sinatra interrupted. "How much do those glasses cost?"

"I don't know, Mr. S.," he said. "Ten, twenty dollars apiece, why?"

Sinatra nodded to Poochie East. He took out a roll of $100 bills and started counting. When he reached $4,500 he handed the stack to the boss.

"Bring me $4,500 worth of glasses," Sinatra said.

"I beg your pardon?" Nicky asked.

"I said bring me $4,500 worth of glasses," he repeated louder.

Nicky shrugged but didn't argue. Suddenly, the kitchen buzzed with activity. Guys ran everywhere. It looked like somebody had yelled "Immigration." After ten minutes, we were surrounded by this army of busboys holding trays of glasses. Sinatra then looked at the young guy who had dropped the tray and started this.

"What's your name, son?" he asked.

"Hector," he said.

"Mexican, Hector?"

"*Sí,* " he answered.

"Hector, do you see all these glasses?"

"*Sí.* "

"Good. Now break 'em."

Hector said, *"Que?"*

"Break 'em," Mr. S. ordered.

Glass was breaking all around us. A sea of glass surrounded us by the time Hector finished the job. It was crazy. I don't know who looked more bewildered, Hector or Nicky. The other busboys struggled to contain their smiles. God knows what the people eating in the restaurant thought or what they drank with. But the Chairman of the Board wasn't finished yet. He looked at Nicky.

"Everytime I come in here I want to see Hector working for you," he said. "Understand what I'm saying?"

Without missing a beat, Nicky said, "I always loved Hector."

All of a sudden, Poochie West shuffled the cards. Sinatra and the guys returned their attention to the card game. In the meantime, I'd gotten up and started crunching my way across the floor.

"Where the hell are you going?" Sinatra asked.

"Home," I said. "I got my Sinatra story."


It seemed every weekened we had dinner with the Hollywood royalty, the crème de la crème—Jack and Mary Benny, George and Gracie Burns, Groucho Marks, David Niven, and so on. In awe of these people, I hid my sweaty palms and told myself not to be nervous or intimidated, because I was with the First Lady and her radiance was enough to get me through. All I had to do was stand in her light.

Dinah taught me how to dress when more than blue jeans were required. As you all know, I'm still not a major clothes horse, but she got the pants to match the jacket. She also taught me how to fold a handkerchief for the front pocket. In addition, she showed me how to set a table, how to serve properly, explained the use of different sized forks and spoons, and then I began my education in fine wines.

I more than held my own in the conversation department, thank you. Even though these people were the best comedians and story tellers in the world, I was from the South, where we treasured our storytellers. I had learned from my Uncle Deeley and I was too dumb to be scared. The first line I ever said to Jack Benny put him on the floor.

We arrived at the Bennys'. Dinah asked if I knew Jack. No, I didn't. But for some reason he warmed to me immediately and squired me off to a corner where we could talk and watch. George Jessel, the old toastmaster, sauntered by with all his friggin medals pinned to his jacket, with a uniform from some strange army we'd never heard of, and a hairpiece that was sometimes there, sometimes here. At times it looked like a golf divot that was upside down. His date looked maybe seventeen, prompting one of Benny's famous looks.

"Burt," he said, his chin held in his right hand, "do you think George . . . still does it?"

"Oh, I know for a fact he does," I said.

"You do?" He sounded surprised.

"I know that girl," I said. "She told me George was terrific, but when he comes, it's dust."

Mr. Benny crumpled to the floor. From then on, the whole evening he'd say, "Burt, tell a story." You had to have major "prairie oysters" to tell any story in front of Groucho and Niven, but I was enough of a schmuck to try.

I don't think anybody enjoyed himself more than I did. And why not? When the party was at either Dinah's or my house, the evenings all ended unbelievably. Edward G. Robinson discussed art. Dinah sang. Peggy Lee sang. Mel Tormé sang. Ella sang. Orson Welles told wonderful stories. Groucho sang, but not until he did twenty minutes of standup. Otherwise we wouldn't let him sing. The same with George Burns.

Eventually I had a sign painted with the House Rules: George Burns must do twenty minutes before he sings. Groucho Marx must do twenty-two minutes before he sings. Ella Fitzgerald can sing anytime, anyplace, anywhere.

It was a remarkable period in my life. If I learned anything about show business from spending time with these giants, it was the importance of thinking about a career in terms of the long haul. Everyone had ups and downs, periods of being flavor-of-the-week. The trick was sticking around. Given the precariousness of the business, changing fads and the fickle public, the true test was if you were still around after many years.

"Oh, you're never going to have to worry, honey," Dinah said. "The camera is like an X-ray machine. It looks right straight inside you. People make up their mind whether they like you or they don't, and there's nothing you can do short of murdering a child that can change their mind. In your case, they've already made up their mind.

"They love you."

(I hoped it was true.)

# CHAPTER
# 32

Boorman, who tinkered endlessly with *Deliverance* and then let it sit in the can for a while, finally screened a long version in early 1972, over a year after we finished the film. Invites to the private screening at Warner Bros. went out to cast members and a very small group of Hollywood insiders. The film was watched by this jaded little audience with great respect and reverence. My best scene was a nearly four-page soliloquy that I delivered to Voight, where I convinced him to climb the mountain to kill the second guy.

"It's time to play the game, Ed," I said in the film. "Now's the time to play the game."

When the scene ended, the group applauded. I couldn't believe it. As I watched, in all honesty, I did feel that that particular scene was the best thing I'd ever done as an actor. I remembered how Boorman had taken me aside just before the first frame was ever shot and confided, "The only way this film will work is if you take the first half for yourself and then let Jon take it during the second half."

"Don't worry. Jon's such a generous actor," I said.

"Bullshit," Boorman said. "The first half you have to take it. You've got to take the son of a bitch."

After the screening, we all congratulated each other. Dinah gave me a big hug. My old hero Lee Marvin shook my hand and warned me the picture would make me a movie star.

"Don't let it kill you, kid," he said.

The acerbic British critic Malcolm Muggeridge shook his head as if a tragedy had befallen us and said I was a shoo-in for an Oscar.

"Sir?" I said.

"You're going to win an Academy Award," he said. "And if you're smart, you'll tell them to stick it up their ass."

It was a heady moment. I literally floated outside and stood in the alley behind the theater, the same alley I'd walk down a decade later with Goldie Hawn in *Best Friends*. To this day I have flashbacks of standing there as Boorman came up and asked me to take a walk with him. People continued to mill about. Dinah, who'd been standing next to me, disappeared as soon as Boorman entered the picture. She sensed it was men time. It was amazing that a star of her magnitude could so quickly take the light off herself. But Orson Welles once explained that if you don't want to be recognized, you simply won't be, and I've always believed that.

As Boorman and I walked down this dark alley by ourselves, he didn't say anything for a long time. Then we stopped.

"I'm going to cut it," he said. "I have to take it out."

"What?" I asked, understanding but not really.

"Your scene with Jon," he said. "I have to take it out."

"Okay," I said softly.

Perhaps I should've fought with Boorman to leave it in, but I didn't. I believed in him as a director, as an artist. John was the painter. He had the right to choose the colors, and if not for him I never would have been in the film in the first place. I also believed that I'd be offered other movies as good as *Deliverance,* and other parts with equally strong speeches. It turned out I was wrong. I have never been given a scene that powerful again in all my years as an actor.

Even if I'd known that, I had to be loyal to Boorman for taking someone like me, a guy whose biggest picture till then was *100 Rifles,* and putting him in *Deliverance.* God knows, he could've had the Jimmy Caans of the world. He could've had all those guys who smelled of New York. He could have had anybody. But he went with me.

And Boorman—this is why I love him—could've told me a whole bunch of chocolate pudding and crap, but he didn't. He told me the truth.

"I know it's your best scene," he said. "But it has to come out because if not, the movie's over at that point. For the movie to succeed, Voight has to take the picture right then. But if he gets all his courage from you, the film doesn't work. We won't have a movie. He has to do it by himself. He has to find it inside."

We walked back and Dinah and I got into the car. I drove up to Mulholland Drive and parked at a spot overlooking the city. Dinah knew from my silence that I had something either real good or real bad on my mind. I think she thought I had an engagement ring. I wish I'd had one.

"Honey, it's bad," I said.

"What?" she asked. "Are we breaking up?"

"You mean because I'm such a big star now?" I smiled. "No, not at all. Boorman told me the best scene I've got in the picture is coming out."

As I explained why, she started to cry. I calmed her down.

"It's okay," I said. "I'll get other parts."

We talked for hours. By the time we started back, both of us felt a lot better.

"It's tragic because you're brilliant," Dinah said. "But you will come out of this bigger than anybody. Someday you'll get another chance to cross all the *t*'s and dot all the *i*'s. I'm certain of that."

When we got home there was a message from Voight. He'd heard about Boorman's decision and asked what I wanted everybody to do. Both Dinah and I were touched. Then I laughed as I realized we were imitating the movie. Voight and the others looked to Lewis to decide. I called back and told him to do nothing.

"Jon, it's for the good of the picture," I explained. "If we can get in the end zone with me blocking and you carrying the ball, I'll block."

"You're sure you're okay?"

"Don't worry, I'm great," I said.

# CHAPTER 33

Ever since I posed as the centerfold for *Cosmopolitan* magazine, people have praised it as one of the great media stunts of all time. It's always amazed me how many so-called brilliant people in the industry figured that's how I got *Deliverance*, unaware it was already finished and in the can for one year. Some critics even pointed to it as the turning point in my popularity. Others interpreted the photo as a glib bit of political satire. Theories abounded.

If only life was that calculated. The truth is that it hurt my career much more than it helped. Despite all the worldwide publicity, I've always regretted I told *Cosmo*'s editor in chief Helen Gurley Brown that I'd do it.

We were on the "Tonight" show together in early 1972, just after Boorman screened *Deliverance*. It was like fire and gasoline. Both on the air and during commercials, Helen and I got into fairly heated debates. She scoffed at me for playfully saying that men bought *Playboy* for the articles. I made a silly argument that there was no comparison between Norman Mailer writing in *Playboy* and one of *Cosmo*'s pieces, something like "Why He Doesn't Have to Stay the Night to Love You."

"Are you a sexist?" she said.

"I bet in ten years that word will be very tired and so dated that you'll sound like a dipshit to ask," I said.

Time has proven me almost correct. The term is as passé as mood rings. But Helen flipped out after I swore. She called me impossible. I'm sure to her my views were half a step above a Neanderthal's. But Johnny loved the sparks, and so did the audience.

"You know what?" I said. "I want to go back to fighting my way through crinolines in the backseat of a car. It was a hell of a lot sexier. Painful, but sexier."

We traded volleys until the conversation resembled a fireworks display. Then crafty old Helen switched gears. She asked me to become the first male nude centerfold in *Cosmo*. The crowd went nuts. I was speechless. Only one thought popped into my mind.

"Why?"

"Because you're the only one who could do it with a twinkle in your eye," Helen said.

I tried to make light of the offer by saying *Cosmo* could show a leg one month, an arm the next, half my chest the following month, and so on, but Helen didn't bite. The next day she called the hotel. She kept at me until I finally said yes. Why did I give in? Well, somewhere in the back of my brain I thought, Well, I've got *Deliverance* in the can, who gives a crap. Also, I did truly feel that it would be amusing to give women an alternative to the silicone pinups they had tolerated their husbands hanging on the refrigerator and over the tool bench for ages.

My agent, manager, and others argued against it. They said it would hurt my career as a serious actor. At this point, I had great buzz; moviemakers knew about my performance in *Deliverance*. Why, they asked, did I want to detract from that? In all honesty, I thought people could separate the two. They'd get the joke *and* my filmwork would prevail.

On the back of the foldout, I told them I wanted to underscore the *Playboy* takeoff with a photograph of me pushing a grocery cart. I'd list my favorite colors, hobbies, books, and be quoted saying, "I'm looking forward to becoming an actress." But I got screwed.

My PR man David Gershenson drove me to the photo session. On the way over, I told him to stop at a liquor store. I bought several bottles of vodka; one was gone before we even got to the studio, which was cold as the Arctic. I emphasize the cold, as men don't hold up real well nude in very cold air. The photographer had two guys assisting. Each one seemed so gay his hair was on fire. I asked for a glass and some ice, locked the dressing room door, and started on my second fifth.

The session lasted several hours, but like most actors I knew when the guy got the shot. I always know. It's like being a director. I don't have to do forty takes to know when I've got the take I want. I've caught the butterfly. I can feel it flapping around on my finger. I don't have to open my hand to see if it's there.

So I knew when I had that smiling, I-don't-give-a-shit-smile and wink that was required to pull this stunt off. But we probably did another hour after that. Needless to say, during that time I was acting very silly, cracking jokes and doing some pretty funny but kind of lewd things to the bear rug. Anything to take my mind off the embarrassment of lying there totally naked while the photographer purred, "Oh, that's so nice, so beautiful. Uhhh that's good too!"

*Oy vay!*

The day the photo was chosen, Dinah accompanied me to the *Cosmo* offices, where she and Helen and about eleven really attractive editors looked at the proofs with magnifying glasses. I never understood why it required eleven editors. They talked about my smile, my hair, where my hands were, how much pubic hair showed—stuff like that. Jesus, it was humiliating and terribly disconcerting. Finally, I slipped out the door and got a drink. I was turning into an alcoholic.

The centerfold appeared in *Cosmo*'s April issue and literally flew off newsstands. All 1.5 million copies published sold out instantly. Helen described public reaction as "gonzo." The night it hit the stands I sat in for Johnny on the "Tonight" show and immediately started to backpedal. Gut instinct told me I had to play it down. I did my whole monologue as if Don Rickles had written it about me. Every line was a put-down of my bod, and blasted my ego.

"If I was trying to prove something," I said, "why would I cover it up with my hands? I have very small hands."

For about five weeks I was red hot. But not as an actor. I couldn't go anyplace without hearing the same joke, "Hey, I didn't recognize you with your clothes on." That's as funny as "How's the weather up there?" Criticism trickled in, including a statement from the Catholic Church, but the centerfold generated overwhelmingly positive mail from women—and some of the filthiest letters and photos I'd ever seen. I received probably five hundred Polaroids of naked women. I also got snapshots from men, couples, groups, and some I couldn't tell what they were. A lady in Nova Scotia sent me pubic hair in wax paper regularly for three years—I guess till there was none left. I worried about her in that cold weather.

Shit, although I didn't get paid a dime for posing, cottage industries sprang up all over the world. I checked into a hotel someplace, pulled back the bedclothes, and saw my whole body imprinted on the sheets. When I called downstairs, the manager said he bought them at Robinson's. My picture ended up from L.A. to Hong Kong on key chains, floor mats, coasters, pillow cases, wallpaper, T-shirts, and panties. Even worse, five months later, while I was in Denmark promoting *Deliverance* on a world tour, a woman showed me a porno magazine with a photo of me on the cover pretending to hump the bear rug.

Of course it was one of my acting silly outtakes, which wasn't supposed to exist. I'd been given "all" the negatives, positively "all" the negatives. That was the agreement. All the negatives! I've always thought that little putz photographer sold me down the river. I eventually sued him, but to win I had to show financial harm, and I couldn't do that. Because of *Deliverance*, my salary took a sizable leap that year, but money was the least of my concerns.

The problem was perception. When the magazine came out I was starring in *The Rainmaker* in Arlington Park, Chicago. We were sold out—before anyone knew I was the centerfold. The run started a week before the magazine came out. After *Cosmo* hit the stands, the audience's behavior changed overnight from polite to boisterous; standing ovations turned into burlesque show hoots and catcalls. They cared more about my pubes than they did about the play. I apologized to the cast every night.

Actors asked if *Cosmo* had gotten me *Deliverance*. If that had been true, there would've been a line from Hollywood to Europe to pose nude in *Cosmo*. Jim Brown posed for *Cosmo*, so did John Davidson. Davidson actually stopped me in a parking lot and said, "Listen, my spread's about to come out. Should I do a *Deliverance* kind of thing or a romantic comedy? You know, Steve McQueen or Cary Grant?"

"Oh, *Deliverance*, definitely," I said. "I'd stay with that macho thing you've got going, John."

# CHAPTER 34

WHENEVER MY HEAD BEGAN EXPANDING, GOD ALways had a way of tapping me on the shoulder and saying, "Hey, Buddy, remember the word *humility?*" It happened on the football field when I tore up my knee. It happened in another way when I made *Shamus,* a gritty New York detective story co-starring Dyan Cannon.

As Dyan and I walked down Broadway one afternoon a guy stopped us and asked for a picture. A camera dangled around his neck.

"Well, okay," I said.

Grinning broadly, he put his arm around Dyan and handed me the camera.

I took it in the way the big guy upstairs intended. I had a great laugh. That sort of thing happened all the time when I was with Dinah. But at no time in my life did I want to disappear into the background of anonymity more than after the shit hit the fan during the filming of *The Man Who Loved Cat Dancing* in early 1973.

The trouble broke out in the remote desert town of Gila Bend, Arizona, toward the end of shooting on this spooky romantic western set in the late 1800s. I played a train robber, beset by nightmares of his slain Indian wife, who falls for the wealthy woman he kidnaps. British actress Sarah Miles starred opposite me. The cast also included Lee J. Cobb, Jack Warden, George Hamilton, and old friends Jim Hampton and Jay Silverheels.

Sarah, one of the most underrated actresses in the world, was one of those great dames, too. She could sit a wild horse or pour on the English accent and literally ooze class and refinement. She never complained, and I think she'd die for you if she loved you. She told me that Robert Mitchum had warned her about me.

"You're going to fall in love with the son of a bitch," he'd said. "He's funnier than hell, sweet, and he's gallant to women. But you know he wears a hairpiece."

I thought that comment was beneath Mitch, so I said, "Ask him about his false teeth."

Sarah had slept with a few of her leading men, I'd heard, for what she reasoned was the betterment of the picture. It didn't work that way with me. It wasn't because I wasn't attracted to her; it was, thank God, too important to me that I be faithful to Dinah. There was definite chemistry between me and Sarah, though. I loved her craziness; she admired mine. The attraction was real basic.

Yet she, too, was involved with someone—David Whiting, a *Time* magazine journalist, who had followed her around for two years. Their relationship was a mess. She told me that after David had found out about an affair she had with actor Robert Shaw, he traveled to Ireland, where Shaw lived, and waited for months to "accidentally" meet Shaw's wife in the market. He courted her for months, finally got her in the sack, taped it on a small tape recorder, and mailed it to the hard-living actor.

Although I did nothing to provoke him, he was insanely jealous of me. And to me he was a sick, sick man.

On the night of my thirty-seventh birthday, the crew had a big blow-out at a restaurant in town. Lee J. Cobb, who I absolutely adored, and I drove together in his Maserati Citron, hit about 130 miles per hour on the flat desert straightaways, and returned before everyone else. I went straight to bed. About two A.M. I was awakened by a pounding on my door. It was Sarah. She had a bloody nose and was crying. A sixth sense told me what had happened, but I asked anyway.

"David beat me up," she said.

I stupidly took my chivalrous Southern self outside and looked for him, but I couldn't find him anyplace. Not in his room. Not in her room. Nowhere. Back in my room, Sarah asked if she could spend the night. As God is my witness, there was nothing going on between us. She just wanted to feel safe. No problem. But I woke up very early and told her to get her ass back to her own room before anyone saw her. A minute later she knocked on my door again.

"He's lying on the floor," she cried. "Dead."

"What?" I asked.

The only smart thing I did was rustle up a teamster and have him go with me to the room. We walked in and found him on the floor. If you've ever seen a dead body, you know you don't have to take his pulse to know he's dead. There's a certain look. People turn a weird, waxen color; everything literally drains out of the body and you can just tell the ride's over. Mr. Whiting was definitely dead.

Word spread. Before I knew it, somebody called the local authorities and somebody else said they'd seen Sarah leaving my room. In this microscopic dot of civilization, the plumber was the judge, the hardware store owner served as sheriff, and so on. The place got real stuffy real quick. Lee J. Cobb took me to his room and said, "Get the fuck outta here."

"Where?" I asked, confused but not disagreeing.

By coincidence, Merv Griffin had flown in on his private plane to do some location interviews for his show.

Lee said, "I'll tell them you just drove out of here. Meanwhile, Merv said he'll fly you to Flagstaff."

"Okay," I said.

Well, Merv flew me to Flagstaff, where Wayne Newton picked me up in his plane and hid me at his Nevada ranch for a week. Absolutely nobody knew where I was. Not even Dinah, whom I called. She reassured me that the truth would rise to the top. Watching the news, I wondered. I watched Huntley and Brinkley; reports mentioned a gash on the back of Whiting's head. It seemed everybody was convinced I'd killed him. The press convicted me before there was a trial, never mind an investigation. Being a cop's son, it made me sick.

It also made me wary. Wayne understood when I explained that sitting in one spot made me paranoid. I needed to move.

For some reason, I longed to be in Utah, where my father had grown up. No problem. Wayne flew me to St. Cloud, where I checked into a motel under my agent's name. The second day the phone rang. The operator said I had a call from Glenn Ford.

"Those bastards," I muttered, figuring the press had me, and getting mad at myself for not having the presence of mind to say, "He's not here."

"All right, goddammit," I said. "Who is this?"

Then I heard that voice and knew it was really Glenn Ford. I hadn't ever met Glenn before, though years earlier I'd been at a party where some guy had a boa constrictor in the middle of the room. For entertainment, he tossed in a rat. Everybody except Glenn and me was amused. Glenn took the rat out of the snake's mouth, put it in his pocket, and then left. I thought it was gallant.

On the phone, he said quietly, "I'm going to tell you a story. Then I'm going to ask you a question. And then I'm going to hang up. Can I do that?"

"Yes, sir," I replied.

Glenn then told me how, many years earlier, he and Rita Hayworth reteamed following *Gilda* to make a movie for Columbia. The studio's notoriously mean and vindictive chief Harry Cohn shaped the movie in such a way that Hayworth didn't realize the script paralleled her marriage to Prince Aly Kahn. By the time the film ended, she knew what was going on. Distraught, the last night of the filming she asked Ford to have a drink with her. He took her to his dressing room. After talking awhile, she went to the bathroom but never came out.

Concerned, Ford knocked the door down and found her nude

body passed out with dozens of sleeping pills scattered on the floor. His telephone went to a central switchboard. He frantically told the operator to get an ambulance but to keep it quiet. At that moment, there was a knock on the door. Before he could answer, Harry Cohn busted in with four cameramen who snapped photos of Ford and Hayworth.

"Then in a moment of stupidity I dove on top of her so they couldn't photograph her nude body," he said. "It wasn't the greatest of choices. As soon as they got that shot, next day, headlines everywhere. My career and my marriage were over. I was married to Eleanor Powell at the time, and we were Mr. and Mrs. America. It was over."

So was his story. He paused to let it sink in. "I'm telling you, Burt, everyone said I would never work again."

Then he said, "Now my question to you is this: Do you remember any of that story?"

"No, sir," I said. "I don't."

"That's all I wanted to say. Goodbye."

His point, like Dinah always said, is that after some time, the lie dies away. Never in my life was I so overcome with emotion. I sat on the bed and wept. Later, I tried calling him back but couldn't get through. All these years I've never been able to repay him. But because of that call, I went to the airport, flew to Flagstaff, and drove back to Gila Bend right into the lion's den—but thank God it turned out okay. Lawyers delayed the hearing for a month, allowing us to complete filming. When it finally got to court, where David Whiting's mother looked at me and screamed "Murderer!," the coroner testified that Whiting had ingested a large number of Quaaludes. He speculated that David had fallen and struck his head, perhaps on the nightstand, causing the gash. His pillow was bloodied when he laid down.

Fine, the ordeal had been extremely emotional, but no charges were filed. Years later, though, I learned what really happened. Apparently, when I'd gone out to look for Whiting, Sarah had gone back to her room to get the nanny. I'd already been there and found nothing. But then he walked in and started attacking Sarah again.

Just like in the movies, the nanny grabbed a lamp and hit him over the head. It stunned him long enough for them to flee in separate directions. Who knows what shape Whiting was in then, but he returned to his room, lay down, (which is where the blood in the pillow was found), then came back to Sarah's bathroom with over one hundred Quaaludes, and somehow swallowed them all.

I believe the movie had one of my best performances, but unfortunately, the negative publicity ruined the picture. People stayed away in droves. I never saw Sarah again either. Our paths almost crossed in Canada fifteen or so years later. She sent a letter to my hotel, which basically apologized for everything. Her life, she said, really was destroyed.

"I'm an old woman now and you still look fairly young," she concluded. "You'll always have a place in my heart. Love, Sarah."

I tried to find her in London once. I just wanted to hold her and tell her I loved her, too. But it's stayed one of those unresolved things between friends.

Many, many stories were written based on whatever crap people wanted to believe. But the most evil was by Bruce Jay Friedman, the author of the play *Steambath*. The piece was in *Playboy*, and it was titled "The Dirty Little Deed in Gila Bend, or Burt Reynolds Puts His Pants on One Leg at a Time Just Like Me." He was witty, clever, and ruthless, and he put me away. Years later, in the Russian Tea Room, I saw him and walked over to his table. I bent down and quietly asked him how he could live with himself after writing such a filthy, lying story. It had deeply hurt everyone in my family and my friends. He answered, "I was never very proud of that story."

As for the story itself, it surfaces periodically. Not long after he retired from the "Tonight" show, Johnny Carson and his wife Alex had a dinner party at their house in Malibu. Loni and I were skidding to an end, but it was us, Sidney Poitier and his wife Joanna, and Merv Griffin and Eva Gabor.

After several drinks, Merv went on a wickedly funny roll, but carried it too far when he said, "All right Burt, just admit it. You killed that guy."

It was as if someone pushed freeze frame on their VCR. Dinner stopped. Given how protective Merv had been of me when the whole incident happened, I was stunned, confused. I didn't know what to say.

"What difference does it make?" he continued. "Everybody knows you killed him."

Unable to speak, I just looked at Merv. Fortunately, Johnny was equally offended.

"You know, Merv," he said, "if you'd been that amusing on your show, you'd still be on the air. Now shut up or get out."

If only we could have cut to a commercial. Everyone stared into their coffee, until Sidney, who's so classy, said, "You know, Merv, being judged by your friends is man's greatest sin," he said. "You'll realize this tomorrow, but by then it will be too late."

# CHAPTER
# 35

In 1974, LESS THAN A YEAR AFTER IMAGINING MY-self in prison for manslaughter, I was actually in several of the toughest lock-up facilities in the country, scouting locations for *The Longest Yard*. The movie itself was probably the most fun I've ever had on a film, other than *Smokey and the Bandit,* because I got paid for playing football, which had been my dream since junior high school. But prison life was a real eye-opener.

Producer Al Ruddy, director Bob Aldrich, and I first visited Oklahoma State Prison. The conditions there were horrific but perfect for what we wanted. However, about a week after we got back to L.A., the inmates rioted and burned the prison to the ground. We finally settled on the Georgia State Prison in

Reidsville, so we went to see Governor Jimmy Carter about using it.

Carter, a wonderful, gracious man, said, "That's a maximum security prison, it's a pretty tough place."

"We know," I said.

"They're rough physically, too," he added. "But I'll tell you what, Burt. If you're taken hostage, I'll personally come down and replace you."

Although I have no doubt Carter meant it, I turned to Aldrich and said, "This guy's going to be president because he lies so damn well." Everyone laughed, including Governor Carter.

I had no doubt *The Longest Yard* was going to be one helluva picture, if for no other reason than you could describe it in a single sentence. The prisoners form a football team and play the guards. Who's not going to want to see that?

Having shot films in prisons before, I sent down a bunch of movies in which I played a badass and had them screened for the prison population. These guys didn't get to see many of the new movies, but they ran mine every night until we got there. By that time, they thought I was okay.

Thanks to Jimmy Carter, we had complete run of the place, but that didn't necessarily make it the safest spot in the world. The prisoners worked, and, in their free time, had nothing to do all day except lift weights, which is always nice for our criminals. When they get out, they look as if they've eaten steroids their whole lives. Anyway, in addition to constructing a football field on the prison grounds, I had our guys build six basketball courts.

Several of the really badass prisoners were transferred out before we arrived, but I asked to see the "man." In every joint somebody really runs the place besides the warden. In Reidsville, it was Ringo, a white guy with glasses and a build like a Brahma bull. He was in for double manslaughter and kidnapping, and was serving ninety-nine years. I'm sure he stepped into the warden's office thinking he was about to be sent to another joint. But I said, "Mr. Ringo, you're my stand-in."

"So," he said.

"Well, see, what that means is—"

"I don't care," he interrupted. "Do I get paid?"

We paid him, as well as nearly one thousand other prisoners and officers who worked as extras. (I insisted they be paid—if not money, then cigarettes, etc.) In return, I hoped Ringo would watch my back. When we started the picture, I walked among the prisoners and not a single one ever grabbed, stabbed, or made a move toward me. After the movie finished, though, I heard Ringo had killed someone who'd razzed him about brown-nosing the actors. Yes, he was a bad guy; good to me, but then I never razzed him.

I'm convinced nobody was as hard-nosed and tough a director as Bob Aldrich. I was crazy about Aldrich's pictures, which included *The Dirty Dozen* and *Baby Jane,* and so many other great films. I was flattered that he wanted me, battered knees and all. The first time I met him, over drinks at Chasen's, I noticed both of us wore neckties. But his wasn't tied; it was draped around his neck. I later learned that that was part of his signature.

Seated at the bar, we got along great from the get-go. But as we talked, Aldrich told me how he regarded actors.

"There'll come a time when they let you down," he said.

"Isn't that kind of a generalization?" I said.

"Look, I've heard nice things about you," he said. "But I'll be waiting for the other shoe to drop."

The first day of shooting in Reidsville, Aldrich made a speech to the entire cast and crew. It was the same speech he gave on every picture; it could have been a Marine sergeant on the first day of basic training.

"One of you is an asshole," he said. "I don't know which one, but one of you is. And when you rear your ugly head, I'll chop it off. Good luck, gentlemen."

Toward the end of production one such asshole did emerge, and Aldrich chopped his head off. But the incident that's etched indelibly in my mind concerned Eddie Albert, who played the heinous warden right to the hilt. In real life, Eddie's a sweet, charming man, besides being a total pro. When not working, he sat in his little camper and played the guitar. But one sweltering day, with the mercury above one hundred, he tired of sitting in the stadium grandstand as the sun beat down while Aldrich and the cameramen, who seemed a mile away, struggled to set up a certain shot. The wait was long, which is what a lot of moviemaking is like. He asked an assistant director if they could use a double in the shot, as the camera was so far away.

Somehow Aldrich, from across the field, heard Eddie's question. Well, in front of a stadium full of prisoners and crew he picked up a bullhorn and shouted, "You candy-ass son of a bitch! You'll sit there until the sun goes down, if that's how long this goddamn thing takes."

Eddie didn't say a word. He appeared unfazed. But later on, I knocked on his camper door just to make sure.

"Are you all right?" I asked.

"Oh, yeah," he said. "I've done five pictures with Bob. I love the man."

Aldrich was the only man who could've directed a picture like *The Longest Yard*. He looked like a football coach or a warden. His brilliance surfaced in full when it came time to stage the football game that takes up the film's final forty-five minutes. We tried running plays that were rehearsed, but they looked rehearsed. That's the problem with most football pictures.

Consequently, he took advantage of my football background and let me call a play in the huddle every other down; one rehearsed, one not. On the plays I called, the camera department would also be told who would be carrying the ball. That's how he got the great stuff. On one play, I called a tackle eligible, dropped back to pass, and thought I overthrew. But the tackle was Ernie Wheelwright, a professional with the Atlanta Falcons. He reached up with hands as big as hamhocks, nabbed the ball, and rumbled down the field with three semipro players on his back, falling at the one-yard line—the longest yard. Accidents like that happen all the time on good pictures.

Now, there are some unwritten rules when you do action movies. When a wrangler asks if you can ride a horse, never say that you ride like the wind; I did once, and the wrangler yelled, "Bring fireball out here!" And when you make a football film with pro ballplayers, don't ever talk about making all-state in high school or college. Generally it's the off-season and these guys miss hitting people . . . a lot.

Both of our offense and defense had NFL ringers such as Mike Henry, Joe Kapp, Ernie Wheelwright, Pervis Atkins, Ray Ogden, Sonny

Sixkiller, Dino Washington, and Hall-of-Fame linebacker Ray Nitschke. But when I stared across the line of scrimmage, there was always one man looking back more intently than any of the others. Nitschke, the Green Bay Packers' old linebacker, was a gentle, lovely man—until he put a football helmet on. Then he thought he was in the Super Bowl. He was intent on making every man on the other team cry.

Every day Ray played a little game. It was called Kill the Movie Star. I'd been hit lots of times, but never by Mr. Nitschke. He hit you so hard your body went into shock. It shouted and screamed at you to please leave the area. I was honored to be hit so hard by Mr. Nitschke every single play from eight o'clock in the morning until six o'clock at night. I never, ever complained, just got up and somehow made it through the day.

During one set of plays, which had been scripted to set up a bit of dialogue, I pitched the ball to a back and he drop-kicked it. As written, it surprises the hell out of the defense, and Nitschke ran up to me, livid, and said his line: "What the hell was that?"

"A drop kick, you stupid son of a bitch," I said and started walking back to the huddle as we'd rehearsed it the first time.

But Ray didn't care for the dialogue. He grabbed my shoulder pad and said, "Don't say that."

"But Ray, it's in the script," I said.

"I don't care," he replied. "My kids will see this."

"Oh Bob, Bob," I said, "You know, Bob, I was just talking to Ray and there's really no reason to call him a stupid son of a bitch, don't you think? I mean, why don't I just say, 'Don't be silly, you silly man'?"

Aldrich looked at me as if I was having a nervous breakdown. "No, goddammit," he said. "Call him a stupid son of a bitch, and then run like hell."

Well, the next play I tried it. I honestly tried. I said the line, then ran as fast as my legs could go. But Mr. Nitschke reached out and caught me. Then he squeezed, pulled, and twisted the front of my jersey off. I looked up from the turf, where he'd thrown me, and saw the bottom half of my number 22 in his hands—which is the way you see it in the film.

"Thank God, you missed," I said, smiling. I smiled a lot at Ray.

Later that day three of the semipro guys decided to prove how tough they were. From the Augusta semi-pro team that had won the division championship, they were too small or too slow or too fat to make it, or so mean they had been kicked off every team in the pros. But they loved hitting people. They decided they really loved hitting me. They slammed into me on every play, whether or not I had the ball. They wanted me to cry, or go out and use a double, or just be carried off and buried somewhere.

Finally, on one particular play, the three of them tackled me out of bounds. As they brought me down, they drove my head into the sideline bench, and through it. Getting up slowly, I cleaned the dirt from my facemask so the camera could see it was me, then looked around for those assholes. As I turned, I saw Nitschke holding all three of them up in the air by the jersey. I sort of tiptoed by and heard him say, "Don't anybody hurt him."

Ah, thanks, I thought.

"If you hurt him, I'll kill you," Ray continued. "Only I get to hurt him."

I turned to Ray.

"Thank you, Ray," I said. "I think."

*The Longest Yard* was among the highest grossing films of 1974. Audiences loved it, and so did the critics. The *Los Angeles Times* described the picture as "almost perfect entertainment." Reviewers called it my best role to date. *Variety* said, "It became obvious more than a year ago that Reynolds has finally reached merited stardom." But what I treasured most, besides the friendships I made, was a picture Nitschke signed for me. He said, "To a tough son of a bitch." It was like Cary Grant saying you had class. I wouldn't trade that for anything.

The other shoe never dropped with Aldrich. He became like a surrogate father, and I miss him every day, especially when I have to work with these new young film-school wunderkinds.

# CHAPTER
# 36

In winter 1974, I was outside Nashville making *W.W. and the Dixie Dancekings,* an enjoyable and underrated little tale about a slick conman who ducks the law by managing a country-western band. My popularity had jumped to the point where I needed state troopers around for crowd control. One day one of them knocked on my camper door.

"A friend of yours is here," he said. "Said to tell you it's Ringo."

At first I asked, "Who?" But a second later the name clicked—Holy shit—and Ringo, the toughest inmate at Reidsville State Prison and my stand-in on *The Longest Yard,* walked in.

"Hey, you got out!" I said. "That's great."

"Yeah, I'm taking a little vacation," he smiled.

I thought, Dear God. He'd skipped out of prison

and there were three state troopers six feet away, outside my door. I saw the headlines: Burt Reynolds Arrested for Harboring Fugitive. I heard the judge read the crime: aiding and abetting.

"You remember Jimmy?" I said, referring to my friend, actor Jimmy Hampton. "Boy, he's gonna love seeing you again. He's right across the street." Then I loaned him twenty bucks. (I know that's aiding and abetting.) "Why don't you go play a little pool and see ol' Jim."

Ringo said, "Great!" He walked out the door, and I never saw him again.

*Dancekings* was directed by John Avildsen, who later won an Oscar for *Rocky*. He was a picky, arrogant little man, with an entourage of pot-smoking film-school eggheads. But I had no idea what kind of guy he was, so I made the mistake of asking Jack Lemmon about him. Avildsen had directed *Save the Tiger*, for which Jack won an Academy Award in 1973.

Well, I didn't know that Jack doesn't and couldn't say a bad word about anybody! A year later when I saw Jack, I said, "That John Avildsen is very talented, but he's a real prick."

Jack replied, "I guess you could say that."

And a lot more. It's always a shock when you work for one of those legends and realize they are not real nice people. It's like discovering the emperor is nude. Avildsen walked onto the set the first night surrounded by admiring pupils and holding the most complicated storyboard I'd ever seen. Not only was each scene sketched, there were sketches of sketches. The damn thing was the size of a *Superman* comic book.

"You know what, John?" I said. "Why don't I just do a voice-over for those little cartoons and we can release it with Disney."

"I've worked it all out," he said.

"John, how the hell do you know where I'm going? Where I'm going to stand? Or what anyone else is going to do?" I said. "It's so unfair to handcuff me until you see what I have to offer you. If you hate it, so be it, you're the boss.

"But how do you know you'll hate it? You just might like it.

"I have to follow what that cartoon character in your little picture book wants me to do—no instincts, no sudden magic we can do together? What's the use of any spontaneity any of the actors might have?''

Needless to say, the picture didn't start off well—and it only got worse. I found out very early that Avildsen hadn't done a penny's worth of homework about Nashville. He never listened to one minute of country music. We were doing a scene at a tiny gas station on a night that was colder than Minnesota. Mel Tillis, playing the attendant, came up to my car and asked, ''You w-w-w-ant r-r-r-reg-r-regular or d-d-do—''

''Hold it! Hold it!'' Avildsen yelled, interrupting the scene. ''Cut the stuttering. It doesn't work.''

Jaws dropped with a collective thud. Everybody in the cast and crew gave Avildsen a what-the-hell-did-you-say look. I stepped out of the car and asked the esteemed little director if I could have a word with him around back. It seemed I was always taking a director around back, lately. My new protective role in life, I suppose. Once we got behind the filling station, I grabbed Avildsen, literally grabbed him, and hoisted him off the ground.

''You insensitive sonuvabitch!'' I snarled. ''The man has a speech impediment. Anyone who has the least bit of knowledge about country music knows Mel Tillis stutters. He has for his whole life. But in spite of that he has become a major recording star!''

Now Mel didn't stutter when he sang, something else everybody knew. But what few people were aware of, including me, was that he didn't stutter when he was drunk. So while I debated whether or not to put Avildsen into orbit, Mel got ahold of a fifth of something and chugalugged it. When we returned, a newly sensitized Avildsen said, ''Oh, never mind, Tillis, say whatever. Just go ahead and roll it.''

Well, the camera rolled, John said ''Action,'' and Mel said his lines perfectly, no trace of a stutter whatsoever. Not even a pause. Since I'd almost strangled the director, I looked like the world's biggest asshole. But the crew already knew Mel was gassed and Avildsen already had his opinion of me. I never ever work harder than when I'm inspired by anger.


IN reality, while Avildsen was off with his toady disciples, probably working on his storyboard, I was whooping it up with my new and special musical friends like Mel, Jerry Reed, Don Williams, and blues giant Furry Lewis. I've always been enamored of country people. You just put a guitar in front of them and they play a song and pass it around. Everybody sings.

Nobody ever says, "I get paid for this. Not now." They play guitar and sing; that's what they do. I think the cast was shocked at how much I knew about country music. I grew up with Eddie Arnold, Hank Williams, and Ernest Tubbs. I feel that America has only a few things we really invented. One for sure is country music; also jazz and maybe baseball. The English might debate us about football, and the American Indians about basketball.

Anyway, the cast took every opportunity to leave the set and go into my camper, where there was always a tuned guitar and something to drink. Jerry, Don, and Mel traded songs. Furry, at eighty-two, sipped bourbon and played amazing licks that used to dumbfound Jerry, who's considered one of America's three best guitar players. But the most magical—and for me most memorable—session took place when Dinah came to see me.

Any visit from her was an event, but Dinah in Nashville was an experience. It was a homecoming. She'd attended Hume Fog High, had been a cheerleader and all that. She still kept in touch with everyone in town. One day she took me to her old stomping grounds, including the house where she was born in, in Winchester.

I got shivers when she sang with Jerry, Don and the guys, trading lead and harmonizing the way she had in her early childhood. The most unpretentious person in the world, Dinah knew every one of those classic country tunes by Hank Williams and others. I couldn't believe it. That was Dinah, though. After almost four years together, she still surprised me.

I've never had a closer friend than her. We debated where we wanted to make our permanent home, Hollywood or Florida. We dreamed of building a house in Hawaii and spent countless nights sketching plans. We couldn't have been more intimate. Our sex life was never boring. She knew, of course, how badly I wanted children, even back then.

Dinah had two grown children from her marriage to George Montgomery—one she had naturally, the other adopted. There was no difference, she told me. She loved both as soon as she laid eyes on them. For several years we talked seriously about adopting. Dinah was willing but wary. Believing that most men preferred to pass on the bloodline—or at least try—she cautioned, "You have to be realistic about children."

As always, she knew me better than I knew myself. Deep down, I felt that way at the time. At thirty-eight, I'd just entered the fast lane. Although adoption was a possibility, I thought of it as a surrender of sorts, an attitude I look back on now as so damn self-centered and despicable. I admit my ignorance. Children are children. If you're lucky enough to get one of those little sacks of oatmeal, boy or girl, you fall in love instantly and count your blessings.

Still, a seed had been planted that worked subconsciously to taint my relationship with Dinah. On the verge of proposing—what my heart urged me to do—my doctor, of all people, warned me to think twice, and then think again. In his seventies, he was a wonderful man, one of those doctors who was also concerned about his patient's personal life. One day he brought up Dinah and me.

"You know, it's going to end tragically because of the age difference," he said.

"I don't even know her age," I said.

"Well, I do," he replied. "Like everyone else, I love her, too. But there's going to come a time when you're not sexually attracted to her, and then what are you going to do? Think about that before you marry. That's all." I was so angry I changed doctors.

I pushed aside what he said, and went back to what was an extremely passionate romance. Neither of us mentioned the M word. Dinah was too smart and I was too frightened of any lifelong commitment. But I meant every word when I told Dinah, "I want to be with you the rest of my life."

Unfortunately, I had no idea of the effect temptation and the old killer fame would have on me. But if you've ever looked in those funhouse mirrors, the kind that skew reality, well, that's the kind of distortion that gradually crept into my vision. I do not truly know myself, and God forbid that I ever should.

*W.W.* did very well. Not a huge hit, but it still has a cult following. It introduced Jerry Reed to acting, which he was born to do. Also I got Don Williams to R.C.A., and he is now considered one of the giants of country music.

The L.A. *Times* said of the film, "*W.W.* is tailored perfectly for Reynolds, but also is a very funny and surprisingly touching film. By now, Reynolds is a master at portraying a self-mocking hustler."

# CHAPTER
# 37

$D$RIVEN AND UNABLE TO RELAX, I AVERAGED TWO
to two and a half pictures a year. The twin laurels of
respect and box-office clout were within reach of my
type A+ workaholic's grasp. But I still needed a big
picture with a serious director. John Avildsen was
going to go on and make brilliant films, but obviously
not with me. During *Dancekings,* I thought that might
happen when Milos Forman flew all the way to Nashville to meet me for breakfast. He was about to begin
a new film, "a very special project," he explained.

"I know what you're doing," I said, having done
my homework. "I saw *One Flew Over the Cuckoo's Nest*
on opening night off-Broadway."

For almost two hours, we talked about Ken
Kesey's brilliant novel, what it said about the human
spirit and life in general. We waxed as philosophic as

two people can over eggs, toast, and coffee. Although against my principles, I did something I've done only twice in my career. I told a director straight out I could knock a particular role out of the park. But this time I knew it was important.

"I believe you. Otherwise I wouldn't be here," Milos said. "It's between you and one other actor."

"Oh, shit," I said. "Would this other actor happened to have been nominated for an Academy Award?" I alluded to Jack Nicholson.

"Yes."

Damn.

"In spite of the fact that I could do it as well as Jack; in spite of the fact that I would turn in an Oscar-caliber performance; and in spite of the fact that you and I like each other, I think this man, who's one of my generation's finest actors is going to win an Academy Award this year, and then it's going to be all over," I said. "Everyone will pressure you to go with the Academy winner—not that you wouldn't anyway. And you know what, Milos? Jack will win another Academy Award for playing McMurphy."

Well, Jack ended up giving a career performance as Randall McMurphy and deservedly walked off with one of *Cuckoo's Nest*'s five Oscars. Meanwhile, Peter Bogdanovich came to see me about starring in his next film, the musical *At Long Last Love*. Dear God—from Ken Kesey to a musical that's going to be done live.

After his tremendous success with *Paper Moon* and *The Last Picture Show*, Peter was one of the hottest directors. He brought Cybill Shepherd, his girlfriend at the time, with him, but she wasn't the delightful Cybill I know now. Then, she was so under his spell she thought everything he said was so brilliant. She was young and he was the boy genius who was going to do this musical come hell or high water.

"And I want you to do it, Burt," he said.

I couldn't believe it. Why the hell did he think I was right for this?

"Why?" I asked, perplexed. "I don't sing."

"Sure you do," he said. "Look at Dean Martin."

"Dean Martin sings," I argued.

"Yeah, but it's an easy, kind of fun sort of singing, and you can do that."

"Sure. You think because he makes it look easy, anyone can do it. Bing and Perry also make it look easy, but nobody is ever going to sell more records than those two old cats."

If nothing else, Peter was passionate about this $6 million tribute to Cole Porter. He was equally excited about utilizing a newfangled technology that would put tiny receivers in our ears, enabling us to hear an orchestra performing live on the same soundstage. In other words, no dubbing or juicing up in a studio. We would sing live, and we'd have to get it right in front of the camera.

"Why?" I asked.

"Because Lelouch did that," he said.

"Lelouch? Claude Lelouch?" I said.

"That's right," Peter nodded excitedly.

"But he had Rose Marie and Maurice Chevalier."

"Yes, he did. By the way, can you dance?"

"No."

"But you're supposed to be a great athlete—you can learn!"

"Sure, call me a great athlete and you own me," I said.

Now I admit the temptation of playing a Cary Grant–type role was flattering. You know, tuxedos, champagne cocktails, sophisticated witty quips, Cole Porter tunes. "Damn you," I said, "I'm flattered. I'll give it a go."

Every day for two months before the picture started, I had a singing lesson in the morning and a dance lesson in the afternoon.

The time step was the hardest thing I'd ever tried to learn in my life. Don't ask why—I know every kid of five can do it, but I couldn't. One day, as I tried to do my best little time step with my instructor, I had a feeling I was being watched. Looking up, I saw William Holden and Steve McQueen standing in the doorway. Both were holding little ballet slippers, waving them and laughing hysterically. I ran at them and they took off down the street, splitting up so I couldn't catch either one. They were doing *The Towering Inferno* on the 20th lot. I would get them back somehow.

But McQueen was a piece of work. A few weeks later I met him under less embarrassing circumstances during a fitting at Western Costume. He came into the room and said, "It's all yours, kid."

"What?" I asked.

"Number one, kid, it's yours. Take it. I'm stepping down." Then he looked out the window. "They're out there. Damn it."

"Who?"

"The CIA."

"Oh, really?" I said, "That's interesting. Want to have a drink?"

We walked to a bar. He had me looking for anyone who seemed to be following us. We talked about motorcycles, had some laughs; and he said he was racing the next weekend. I accepted an offer to ride on one of his extra dirt bikes. I was leading for a minute or two, but fell out early; Steve then led the entire race until his bike broke down. But instead of giving up, he waited till the guy in second place came over the hill, tackled him, took his bike from him, and won the race.

Needless to say, Steve McQueen hated to lose even more than I did. He was a complicated but fascinating man. And now of course since his death everyone talks about what an actor he was.

Dinah showered me with encouragement about my singing all the time, but Madeline Kahn, thank God, pulled me through the movie. She kept it from becoming an agonizing experience.

Madeline was one of the great crushes of my life. But like a few wonderful ladies, she was a ship that passed in the night because of bad timing. She was a lady who could always make me laugh, and yet was one of the most sexy women I have ever been around. Both of us read under and between the lines and words, both knowing the subtext. We had a secret that I will take to my grave, but let me just say this: she is so damn smart, so damn aware of what men are all about. I truly love her. We seldom talk any more, yet . . . Bambi's father is still (especially lately) standing alone on a high cliff and thinking of white skin, brown freckles, and ships that pass in the night.

Madeline confessed to me that she couldn't sing herself. I laughed at such bullshit.

"You sang on Broadway," I said.

"Yes," she explained. "But I was playing the part of someone who could sing. And the guy you're playing can sing. Get it?"

On the first day of rehearsal, the entire cast gathered around the piano. When it came my turn to sing, Madeline held my hand, winked, nudged my leg, cheered me, and somehow I made it through. But that was just rehearsal. As for the rest of the movie, let's just say it was the beginning and the end of my being smashed through an entire film. I mean pissed from around ten A.M. until we wrapped. I drank screwdrivers in makeup and went on from there. Because Peter was so in love with Cybill, if she was right on in a scene I could fall down and have a nosebleed and it was a print.

I knew early on that *At Long Last Love* wasn't going to make me into the next Fred Astaire; I just wanted to get out before I started dancing like Fred Flintstone. It was insane to do it live; no one knew, and even if they did, why would they care? Reviewers were kinder to me than they were to Peter and Cybill.

*At Long Last Love* was attacked viciously. Peter's greatest sin was that he did something every "serious" movie critic dreams of doing: He left his colleagues and directed *The Last Picture Show*, and, even worse, it was a wonderful film. On top of that, he heaped more pain on the critics by leaving his very talented but middle-aged wife for his beautiful leading lady—who was just a girl, or at best a young lady. This was just torture to all the bored nice people.

Then when Peter directed another commercial hit with Barbra Streisand and Ryan O'Neal, *What's Up, Doc?*, everyone said, "Well, you know, he just steals everyone's shots." Sure, like that's all you have to do, just watch some great French or Japanese film and copy all their best shots. Why didn't anybody else think of that? By the way, I know he steals shots. But how do all those people like Ben Johnson and Tatum O'Neal win Oscars? "Oh, he watched John Ford a lot."

My problem was that I was in two of his flops. And, dear God, when he flops, the sky falls in on everybody. All those untalented people who review hate him so. They become brilliant at reviewing, because all of a sudden they are filled with something new. It's called passion—even though it comes from hate. They write like never before, because of this new talent they have. It's a talent for hating successful, pretty people. They almost killed Peter, just as they killed others.

I feel great affection for Peter. I wish we had been successful together. I'm sure he will again write or direct something that will pass the test of time. I'm still here, as the saying goes, and so is Mr. Bogdanovich.

• • •

As my salary sailed well past $1 million, a tremendous amount of money back then, the air got thinner. The higher the mountain, the thinner the air. It was hard to breathe, harder to think clearly. Popularity and money make for a dangerous combination. You think everyone loves you. Everyone doesn't love you. If I'd had any guidance at all, my people would've taken me to Canada, shut me in a friggin room, and kept me there until some really serious filmmakers called and asked them to let me out.

Celebrity scared them. Some thought I was a joke. Realizing that serious scripts weren't coming to me, I decided to make things happen myself. I found the script for what became *Hustle* and took it to Bob Aldrich, as serious a filmmaker as I knew. And Steve Shagan was surely a serious writer. He liked the hard-edged story of a disillusioned detective who dreams of escaping his sleazy world, while deeply in love with the highest paid hooker in L.A. Bob also loved my idea of French beauty Catherine Deneuve as the high-class call girl.

Catherine took my breath away. She had a way of laughing and looking at a man that was big league, and she had one of the best built-in bullshit detectors I ever saw. Bob and I met her in Paris and convinced her to come to Hollywood. On the first day of shooting, I noticed that about twenty-five secretaries came out to watch. I thought, boy, I must be having a great day. Then someone informed me they'd come to see her.

Women and men were fascinated by Catherine. Without carrying a banner, she lived very independently. She'd had two children without marrying, long before that sort of thing was done. She had a career. She set styles and conducted herself with true elegance and class, no matter what.

We got along *très fantastique*. From what I could tell, there was nothing not to love about Catherine. She looked more spectacular in person than on film, and she lent a sympathetic ear to my concern about troubles I was giving Dinah. Dinah and I never fought. Not once. But the seed that had been planted by my physician caused doubts to sprout in my head. I gave Dinah these bullshit excuses like, "We're growing apart."

We hadn't split yet, but I sensed the future from being around Catherine. She was the sort of woman who brought out the boy in any man. I wanted to impress her by walking a picket fence, turning cartwheels, and making her laugh. Every day she said, "Please, tell me a joke. But don't tell it too fast."

One day Catherine and I decided to have lunch together. Quietly slipping off the set, I went to Ma Maison, the trendiest French bistro in L.A., and asked owner Patrick Terrail to prepare two boxed lunches and to throw in his best bottle of French wine. Later in the day, I drove Catherine up to the giant Hollywood sign, a landmark in the hills. She had no idea where we were.

"We're going to have lunch," I said.

"But there's no restaurant."

"No," I said, but then I unfurled a blanket and took out two gorgeous picnic baskets, flowers, and wine. Catherine was surprised and thrilled. It was one of those rare smog-free days, and we admired a view that spanned from downtown to the Pacific Ocean. I knew I had scored a lot of points.

We were truly smitten with each other. I used to go to sleep at night imagining what it would be like to live with Catherine in Paris. Later I read an interview in which she admitted the only actor with whom she could've had a serious romance wasn't interested in her. Was that me? I doubt it, but if it was, it wasn't quite true. I was still attached to Dinah. But also, to be perfectly honest, I thought Mme. Deneuve was too much woman for me to handle.

We made a big mistake on that picture. My character, having beaten the odds to retirement, dies at the end. Bob had adapted the twist from a real incident. After his last day of work, a retired police officer stops at a liquor store to buy a bottle of champagne. At that moment, a kid robs the place. The cop can't help but try to stop him, and he is killed. I begged Aldrich not to leave it that way, or to shoot two endings and see how it played in front of test audiences. No deal.

Well, the movie bolted out of the box, making something like $2 million a day for ten days. Then it stopped. It did no business. That's how long it took for people to say, "It's good, but he dies at the end." John Wayne chewed me out for that one. "Never play a rapist and never die in a picture," he said. "People don't want to see guys like you die."

Duke died in two films, *The Cowboys* and *The Shootist*. In the latter he was dying of cancer. Both lost money and I think both, ironically, are his best work, next to *The Searchers*.

*Hustle* got some wonderful reviews. "Reynolds' enigmatic smile keeps the audience guessing. Is he really so relaxed about his girlfriend being a hooker—or is he kidding, a defense mechanism? He is superb," said Molly Haskell.

# CHAPTER
## 38

BREAKING UP WITH DINAH WAS THE HARDEST thing I'd done in my life. I'd tell myself to be a man, to be straight with this remarkable woman. Then I'd back down. Wracked with doubt and pain, I'd wonder if I was making the right decision. I was at war with myself, but I couldn't see a winning side.

I rationalized the conflict until I was too tired to think. I wanted a child of my own, of that I was certain. Dinah knew where I stood. I was also on a rocketship ride, traveling so high and so fast my brain ceased to function normally. If I wanted, three people would pull up my zipper.

I'd been there before. During "Hawk" I had a bodyguard, more like an assistant; actually I think I could have taken him. But I loved him. He was an ex-fighter, a sweetheart. He massaged my neck, told jokes. One hot afternoon I turned around to give him my jacket and for some reason he wasn't there. "Tony!" I started to yell, but then caught myself. Everything stopped. I realized the other shoe had dropped. When I saw him later, I gave him a $100 raise. He asked, "Why?"

"Because your boss is a major asshole," I told him.

I could resist the corrupting nature of power. That was like playing with pain. But ego was a whole other matter. All of a sudden you start to think you're Secretariat. People tell you that you're fast, strong, handsome, virile. They tell you it's your duty to spread some of that wonderful bloodline around.

I loved Dinah. My parents loved her. But I couldn't help myself. I was surrounded by demands, offers, enticements, and temptations of all sorts. The London Philharmonic Orchestra that played every time I opened our door had dwindled to a jazz trio. I wanted to exit while Chet Baker was still singing.

I talked to Dinah at her house. She sat on the couch holding a hankie. I paced, then sat beside her. We didn't have any secrets. That was the beauty of our relationship. Total trust, honesty, respect.

I'd always said either we'd get married or move on, and it was time to face the facts. Marriage wasn't in the cards. If you promised someone like Dinah forever, you'd better damn well live up to that promise. Human nature being what it is, I didn't know if I could. Yet the thought that I'd no longer have Dinah as my soulmate seemed so unnatural, so sad, yet a painful reality. In fact, this was the kind of dilemma I'd ordinarily run to her for advice and help with.

"I will love you all my life," I said. "Whatever is good about me, you made it happen. I know it doesn't help any, but I'm taking a lot of you with me. A helluva lot. I'm not kidding when I say that you still excite me every time I look at you. The hardest part about what I'm doing is that I've fallen deeper in love with you than ever. But—"

I lost it. Dinah kept her composure, but I wept as I went out the door and continued in the car. I cried at home. For days I was sullen and withdrawn. My heart ached. A piece of me was lost. I fought the urge to call or run back to Dinah. I missed the closeness we had, the friendship that was so solid, and truthfully I've never stopped missing it every day for almost twenty years.

It seems so childish and selfish now when I write it down. Every time I picked up the phone I wanted to call her. Every time it rang I hoped it was her checking in. Friends fixed me up with some of the most desirable ladies in town, but I ended up taking them back to their homes. They probably thought I was the dullest putz in Hollywood. For the longest time I think I was.

It took several months, but when I finally snapped out of the fog I did so with some flair. Jimmy Hampton and I toured Ohio on the Kenley Circuit, doing summer stock in Toledo, Warren, Dayton, and other cities. After each performance, I signed autographs, a tradition on the Kenley Circuit. It allowed Jimmy to do something I've never seen anyone do better at. With just a glance, he *knew* the party animals, no matter what they had on. I would see a leather micro-mini—he would shake his head "No."

Then we would end up with about five out of a thousand possibilities. Most were housewives, sweet ladies out to tear up the town, but wilder than cats in a jungle. Most had a great attitude and a wonderful sense of humor. We took them back to my hotel suite and had a party. Such escapades open the door to lots of criticism, but the truth is there was more laughter than sex, though there was plenty of crazy sex, too. In the morning, Jimmy would give out the awards: Most Athletic, Most Congenial, Most Talented, and Most Likely to Succeed at Whoever She Took a Turn At. Among the men I have to admit Jimmy always won Most Valuable Player. I won Most Congenial.

# CHAPTER
# 39

I GOT A SHOT AT DIRECTING FOR THE SAME REASON all very bankable actors get a shot. I was hot. The same guys who produced *White Lightning,* the popular moonshine picture we did together three years earlier, wanted to make *Gator,* a low-budget sequel. But the only way I'd agree to play good ol' boy whiskey-runner Gator McKlusky again—and the only way they could afford me—was to also let me get behind the camera.

It was a chance I wanted. As an actor, once you let the bird out of the cage, you can't get it back. But the director says "Action" and "Cut," decides whether to stay back or move in close, and finally puts the picture together in the editing room. The director's voice has the last word, and I've never been at a loss for words.

Clint, who'd already directed a half dozen pictures by this time, advised me to talk to the people I admired. Boorman and Aldrich had already made big impressions on me. But Orson Welles said the first shot in a film is always the most important. I have found that's really true. If you can't tell the story on the first page, it ain't gonna get better on the tenth. Bogdanovich said to cut on movement, something I already knew, but it was kind of him to tell me anyway. And Mel Brooks told me to fire somebody the very first day.

I never had to. Surrounded by great people like Jack Weston, Jerry Reed, Dub Taylor, Burton Gilliam, Alice Ghostley, and Lauren Hutton, my philosophy was that the entire crew made the picture. Although mine was the final word, I was open to ideas; I invited everybody to rushes; I showed my mistakes; and if I made a point about a particular film, they seemed pleased. The rushes were open to anyone who worked on the film. From action to comedy to ethnic humor, I made sure I tried it all in my directorial debut.

Except for one thing. But that happened off screen.

In Savannah, where we spent six weeks shooting, I stuck out like, well, to steal a line from *Gator,* like a bagel in a bucket of grits. The people there just aren't used to seeing actors around town. As I ate dinner one night at the Holiday Inn where we were based, one of the Georgia state troopers helping me out said a fan wanted to come meet me.

Well. I've never short-changed a fan, so a minute later, a guy who would have been played by John Goodman came into my room. He seemed nervous, all jumpy and such, and he barely lifted his eyes from the floor.

"Mr. Raynerds?" he asked.

"Yes."

"Well, you see, I had a bet with my wife, Grace," he said gathering steam. "Ann-Margret or Burt Raynerds. If Ann-Margret came to town first, I'd get to fuck her. If you came to town first, she'd get to fuck you. Wouldn't you know it, you come here first and, well, she's waiting out there in the truck."

"What?" I asked, finding this hard to believe.

"Now, tell you what. You just leave her anywhere you want and I'll pick her up. Just whenever."

"Wait a minute!" I exclaimed, wondering how not to insult the man for his generosity. "Wait. Hold it. I can't do what you're saying."

"Oh, this is going to kill her. It's going to hurt her real bad."

I apologized. "But you see, I pulled my groin muscle. I can hardly move."

"You don't have to move," he said. "Grace'll do all the work."

I finally agreed to go out and say hello to the little woman. The girl looked like June Allyson, I swear. Fresh-scrubbed, adorable, pretty. She started hyperventilating when I approached the truck, which was embarrassing. The three of us chatted for several moments. Before leaving, I leaned forward to kiss her lightly on the cheek, but suddenly there was a grouper stuck to my mouth. We all hugged, and I promised that I'd tell Ann-Margret what a treat she had in store next time she was going near Savannah . . . I did, too!

I liked *Gator.* I think Jerry Reed was extraordinary; it's the best thing Lauren Hutton's done, and when I watch the picture I think that I'd work for that director. Given the budget, it was good. After the film came out, I wasn't deluged with offers to direct, but the movie did well at the box office, a fact that failed to impress the highbrows and Hollywood's filmmakers.

That's an old story, though. I'm convinced it's because I simply had too good of a time making films, and they didn't want to forgive you for that.

I treated life like, Let's chew up every minute. Laughter was the best medicine and I felt, by God, I would prove that you could make a lot of money, do good work, have fun, make a lot of friends, and all that corny stuff while still having a career. That couldn't have been any more evident than when I satirized myself in Mel Brooks's hilarious picture *Silent Movie.*

Mel's idea was to send up all my car movies by sticking me in a wheelchair in a chase scene, but I suggested another idea. The beleaguered director, played by Mel, would drive to my house. On the roof would be a huge sign in blinking lights saying "Burt Reynolds's house." Inside, it would be all mirrors. I'd play an arrogant, obnoxiously vain putz—in a word, to a lot of people, me.

It was a scream. But how could it be otherwise when my big scene required taking a shower with Mel, Marty Feldman, and Dom DeLuise? Since it was a silent picture, we could say anything and no one would hear it in the theater—and Mel did. I remember him saying, "Roll cameras," then looking down at me and saying, "Jesus, look at the size of that swansticker. Are you going to want separate billing for that?"

*Nickelodeon* was opening in New York. After the picture's premiere in mid-1976, there was a postscreening party at "21," the exclusive restaurant on West 52nd Street. The place overflowed with celebrities from movies, TV, and sports. At one point, I looked across the restaurant and happened to make eye contact with tennis star Chris Evert, who was with fellow pro Pam Shriver.

Before leaving, a waiter handed me a note. I opened it up and saw a phone number and a name underneath: Chris Evert. No message, nothing else written. Only her name and number. But I was as intrigued as I was flattered. As soon as I got back to my suite at the Carlyle, I called.

She was one helluva wonderful surprise. From TV and papers, I knew Chris was one of the best women to ever play tennis. Somewhere along the way I also picked up that she was a very cool head on the court, rarely showing emotion. I think she'd been dubbed the Ice Queen. But for the two hours we stayed on the phone, we cracked jokes and discussed movies, and she was anything but cool and reserved.

We had a lot in common. Both of us were from around the same part of Florida. We loved sports. And because of our fairly similar professions, we had trouble connecting with other people. Well, I didn't have to be clubbed over the head. Chrissy was a doll, and as soon as I figured out she was unattached I asked her out.

We had a terrific time. Sparks definitely flew. But Chris, at the height of her career, traveled constantly, hopscotching from Europe to the United States to Australia as if these were short commuter flights.

My schedule was hectic but not like hers. As a result, I flew to a few of her matches and she engineered several visits to L.A., but the awful truth was bad timing. Or just a lack of it. Despite great chemistry, we only went out maybe a dozen times over the span of a year.

I did have the audacity to get on a tennis court with her once when she was at my house. This was back when I could still run. Even so, it was a disaster. Although I wasn't much of a tennis player, I was still fast and hated to lose. I struggled, stretched, and managed to get two points off her the first game we played. I thought, Shit, that's pretty good. Maybe I have a chance at getting a game or two if we play an entire set. Then Chris switched hands.

"What the hell are you doing?" I asked.

"Now I'll use my right hand," she said.

We never played tennis again. But I just admired the hell out of that young lady. Still do.

Chris was a thoroughbred, and about everything any man ever wanted as a brood mare. Certainly as a mother she was going to be extraordinary. As a person, she was all class. And as a friend she was the best, and still is.

# Chapter 40

ALTHOUGH MY OLD FRIEND HAL NEEDHAM LIVED IN
my guesthouse, we rarely saw one another. On those
occasions when both of us were home, we spoke over
the intercom more than we did face-to-face. Like me,
he had a burning desire to direct. I beat him to the
punch, but Hal didn't lose sight of his goal. In fact, it
spurred the competitive son of a bitch to work
harder.

One day he gave me a script he'd written. Titled
*Smokey and the Bandit,* it was scrawled on a yellow legal
pad in his own handwriting. Cheap bastard hadn't
even had it typed. But I sat down and read it anyway.
Now Hal and I had one of the tightest friendships in
show business. He'd directed second unit footage
and coordinated stunts on six of my films. My God,

we'd lived together longer than either of us had lived with any of the women to whom we'd been married.

So it was hard to tell him I thought it was the worst script I'd read in my life.

"However, it's got a couple things going for it," I said. "We've got a clock on the picture. We have to get people from here to there in a certain amount of time. That's always good. And the characters are lovable in a real folksy, blue collar sort of way. No one in America can say we're over their heads."

*Smokey*'s plot was simple. Bandit, a slick con man, hotshot driver, takes a job for $80,000 smuggling Coors beer into Georgia from Texas. Along the way, he picks up a runaway bride who's being chased by the hapless groom she left at the altar and the sheriff father, the Smokey. It was a screwy chase picture, but Hal's fun, outlaw, hell-bent sensibility made it sparkle.

"I'll tell you what," I said. "If you can get a studio to approve it, I'll do it. You direct. I'll star in it."

At my suggestion, Hal got his buddy James Lee Barrett, who'd written *Shenandoah,* to do a rewrite, the first of several eventually done. Then he took the script to Mike Medavoy, my friend and one of the good guys, a studio executive at MGM. Medavoy wanted to make a movie with me—but not *Smokey*. Instead, he handed Hal the script of *Convoy* and said he could direct that one if I starred.

Hal, who'd never directed, considered the bigger-budget offer and said, "No, it's mine or nothing." That's the reason I love Hal. He's a hell of a man.

Universal, his next stop, agreed to make the movie, but under a host of stringent conditions, which caused the first of many fights. They wanted Richard Boone, whom I adored, as an actor, but I was dead set on Jackie Gleason playing the Sheriff. I thought his performance in *The Hustler* was flawless. He was one of those guys, along with Duke and Mitchum, with whom I wanted to work before I died. I haven't worked with Mitchum yet, and the Duke is gone.

I'd met Jackie once in Florida, where he lived, and he'd done an impression of a Southern sheriff that caused me to fall down laughing.

Overly polite to women, Jackie explained, those sheriffs would get the man and say, "Look, you sumbitch, what the fuck you think you're doin'?"

Having Gleason play the sheriff was wild and chancy, but that's what I loved about it. But the studio and I fought and fought. I didn't know the extent of my power and how to use it. I'm sure Kevin Costner says, "The Indians will be played by Indians," and that's that. Nobody argues. But I was ignorant, and instead of laying down ultimatums, tried to reason with the suits. But I eventually got Gleason and then waged another war—this one to get Sally Field.

The studio suggested just about every big-name actress at the time, but I was adamant about Sally. I'd never met her. I just knew her work on "Gidget" and "The Flying Nun." As crazy as most people think that is, I could see the talent way inside.

"But if she can be good in that kind of shit," I argued, "just think how wonderful she'll be in good material."

They countered that Sally wasn't sexy.

"Bullshit," I said. "Talent is sexy."

The suits finally caved in, but then I faced an equally fierce battle with Sally herself. About to star with Joanne Woodward in *Sybil*, the deeply disturbing, Emmy Award–winning TV movie about a young woman with multiple personalities, Sally wanted to escape her sitcom past. She knew *Sybil* was her breakout, a role that was going to put her on the map, maybe win her an Emmy, and at last she'd be considered a serious actress. A goofball adventure like *Smokey* wasn't on her agenda, and she's someone who won't do something unless she loves it.

But I called her anyway.

"This isn't where I'm at," she said, explaining *Sybil*. "I don't want to do something that's silly."

"Thank you for saying that about my career," I replied.

Sally laughed. I interpreted that as a good sign, an opening.

"Look, you and I are very much alike," I said. "People in Hollywood don't understand why I am where I'm at. They don't think I've done anything really good. But, gee, my pictures seem to make money. You, I'm sure, have been kidded enough already about flying around in a nun's habit."

"Yes," she agreed hesitantly.

"This picture might not be *Two for the Road,* but I think a lot of people might like it," I continued. "If you won't do it for yourself, do it for me. Because I really want to work with you. And"—long pause—"being in a hit movie is not a bad thing."

Then I switched tactics. For the next few minutes, we just talked about everything. I kept her laughing.

"If you do this picture, you'll get to see fabulous places like Waycross, Georgia," I said, "birthplace of Pernell Roberts."

"Oh, great."

"Now there is one problem I forgot to mention," I said. "I should've been upfront about it. But—"

"What?" she asked.

"Well, you'll have to work with the No. 1 box-office star guy in the world."

"You?"

"That's what the trophy on the hood of my car says!"

"I heard you could talk birds out of trees," she finally said.

"What does that mean?"

"It means okay, I'll do it."


In the end, I think Sally caught my enthusiasm, and basically trusted me when I promised the picture would be funny. For some reason, we still hadn't met when the crew convened in Atlanta the night before shooting began in fall 1976. I called her hotel room and asked if she wanted to go out for dinner or a drink, so we would at least know each other prior to our first scene.

We went to a nearby restaurant, a lively honky-tonk, where she immediately saw songwriter Paul Williams. He and Pat McCormick were going to play the millionaire father and son duo who hire Bandit to bootleg the beer into the state. I had named them Big Enos and Little Enos. I knew Paul had written some great songs, but I didn't know which ones. Sally, though, got real excited and started mentioning "Old-Fashioned Love Song" and other titles.

"Why are they called Big Enos and Little Enos?" she asked.

"Dammit, because it rhymes with penis."

"That's very mature," she said.

"Thanks, I don't like to be too hip for the room."

Over dinner, we got to know each other. I sensed that she kinda liked my confidence, and I definitely enjoyed making her laugh. In blue jeans and a T-shirt, she looked like a kid just out of high school. But Sally's razor-sharp instincts made her a tough one—smart, funny, adorable but also very damn strong. She knew good from bad. After dessert, we stepped onto the dance floor, pretty brave of me, considering my limitations as a dancer. But I joked my way around the dance floor, too.

"You're very funny," Sally said.

"Thank you, ma'am. We do our best," I said, dipping into my Southern accent.

Although we'd met only hours before, Sally and I seemed to click on many different levels. Movies, ambition, sports, family. As we danced, our conversation flew back and forth like a Tracy-Hepburn movie.

"You're not at all like I thought you'd be," she said. "Which means you're exactly like I thought you'd be."

"What does that mean?" I asked.

"You sneak 'em into the sack, don't you? I mean, you surprise women."

"Are we going into the sack? This is only our first date."

"This is not a date," she retorted.

"It is to me, 'cause I'm paying the check," I said. "Unless you want to."

We sat back down at the table. Then Sally looked at her watch and excused herself. She wanted to call her two boys back home. Another thing I was to grow to admire about her. After she returned, we talked for a while longer, mostly about the work ahead and our philosophies on acting. Work or otherwise, there seemed no limit to how much we had in common.

That discovery was intoxicating. Excited about starting work, filled with enthusiasm over my co-star, I let my guard down in front of this woman. As we walked back to the hotel, I said something terribly corny, something that revealed the Tom Sawyer in me who wanted to impress Becky Thatcher.

"I could flat fall in love with you, lady," I said.

It wasn't a line, and she could tell that.

Taken aback for a moment, she said, "Oh, now that I didn't expect from you."

"Nobody's perfect," I said. "I sure never said it before at this stage of the game."

"That I don't believe."

"Then that was your first mistake."

I wasn't kidding. I'd never said anything like that after just meeting a woman, and I knew I really could fall in love with her. In fact, I knew I already had.

ONCE shooting began, Sally saw me in a whole different light. I, of course, knew what the rest of the country found out when *Sybil* aired, which was that she was one of the finest actresses in the world. But I think she was shocked that I knew what a forty lens was, had an expert bead on all the stuntwork, and that when we rewrote, even Gleason, the Great One, took my suggestions.

Of course, Jackie was brilliant on his own. For instance, it was his idea to have the toilet paper coming out of his pantleg when he left the Bar-B-Q, which put me on the floor. I just began calling Sally's character Frog, making up stuff about her past, like the idea that she'd been a dancer. Audiences enjoy thinking they're watching two people fall in love in a movie—and they were. That was part of the magic.

Hal worked lightning quick, reigning over crew and camera with instincts that made him, in my humble opinion, the best action director in the business. We moved all over Georgia. But one night about a week or so into the picture, which took only about six weeks to complete, Sally rode back to the hotel with me, acting as if she'd just figured out a big secret.

"You're directing this movie, aren't you?" she asked.

"No, I'm suggesting," I said.

"Yes, but we're all taking the suggestions."

"Okay, well, I'm sort of with the actors and Hal takes care of everything else. Why?"

"No reason," she said. "Like everyone in Hollywood, I'm just try-ing to figure out why you are who you are."

By the time we came back to L.A., Sally and I were heavily in lust and falling in love, heading for that solitary place where nothing mat-tered except the tiny insular world both of us occupied when we were together. When postproduction was 99 percent finished, Hal screened *Smokey* for Universal's execs. To a person, they hated it.

But he'd made a horrible error. He hadn't put in any sound effects yet. There was no music. Punches didn't smack. Cars crashed without the sound of metal crunching. The lack of all this was too glaring to anyone from the tower.

"Never show suits an action picture without a track," I said. "In other words, a car chase that doesn't have screaming wheels isn't really a car chase to these guys. They don't know how you make a movie. Every-thing's got to be obvious."

We spent a week preparing a temp track, one that would later be replaced with more precise sound effects. Then we ran the same friggin picture, frame for frame, for the same friggin group of suits, and after-ward they laughed and applauded. The same picture they slammed one week earlier as a piece of shit was now brilliant.

In summer 1977 the studio, in its infinite wisdom, only planned to release *Smokey and the Bandit* in the South, where it immediately caught fire. Encouraged by its success—duh—they took a chance and the pic-ture opened nationwide a few weeks later. *Smokey* proved it wasn't just a moonshine picture whose appeal was limited to good ol' audiences south of the Mason-Dixon line. Though critics panned it, *Smokey* broke box-office records all over the country, over $100 million the first go-round.

Sally and I, vacationing in New York at the time it went wide, showed up at a party Universal threw at "21." Until then, we'd avoided reading reviews or checking the box office in the industry papers. So when Universal chief Lew Wasserman literally ran over to us, I whis-pered to Sally, "We're either a huge bomb or a tremendous hit." Lew told us the good news. They anticipated grossing more than $150 mil-lion. By the end of the year, only *Star Wars* had grossed more than *Smokey*.

Lew shook our hands and congratulated us. But this is one of the traits I loved most about Sally: As soon as he left, she started hugging me, punching me in the arm, and screaming through clenched teeth how unbelievably great this was, never covering her joy. She had a similar reaction once when we took a week-long cruise on a 110-foot yacht, a present from my friends Bernie Little and Auggie Busch, Jr., and the Budweiser people. On boarding, we met the large crew, and Sally behaved decorously. But as soon as we were alone on the deck, she looked at me with a glint of disbelief and excitement in her eyes. Then she scanned the enormous deck and all of a sudden started jumping up and down like a little kid and screaming, "Yes! Yes! Yes!"

She grabbed the moment and laughed with tears of joy. She took nothing for granted. I had always been the same way. I think that's what made our relationship so special. Sally was the love affair of my life. But what you sometimes learn, and indeed I learned, is that the person you love most may not be the one with whom you should spend the rest of your life.

# CHAPTER

## 41

T HE FIRST TIME I WAS OFFERED $1 MILLION FOR A movie, it had the strangest effect on me. Seated at a choice table at Ma Maison—a restaurant so trendy its phone number was unlisted—I listened to the president of Warner Bros., Ted Ashley, tick off the deal for me to star in the story of the stuntman *Hooper*. Never had I imagined making such an incredible sum of money for doing something I loved.

Rather than feed my ego, it scared the breath right out of me. I had a full-fledged anxiety attack. My chest tightened and I began hyperventilating. I asked Ted if he minded if I lay down on the floor. A strange request, but not in Hollywood. I slipped from my chair to the floor. Ted continued talking, ". . . and you're very big in France already, so . . ." tallying those mind-boggling figures, which finally caused me to lay flat on my back. People carried on as if this was normal behavior. Maybe it was.

"Does anyone happen to have a Valium?" I asked.

Instantly, I was showered with pills—blues, yellows, and whites. A few years later, director-writer Jim Brooks incorporated this very scene into *Starting Over*. Hyperventilating became a regular thing with me. I never dreamed help would come from Clint Eastwood. He quietly helped me make sense of this flight of confidence by telling me that he hyperventilated, too. Appreciative of the support, I still couldn't picture Clint gasping for air.

"I can tell you what the matter is," he said. "You think you don't deserve it, so you're punishing yourself. You don't deserve a million a picture, but then who does?"

"So what do I do?"

"Nothing," he said. "Think about it. You've spent over twenty years climbing the ladder. This reward hasn't come overnight. You punched in every day. You've earned it. It probably balances out at fifty bucks an hour. Stop worrying. Get back to work."

It made sense, but other factors complicated as quick a return to the screen as planned. After *Smokey*, I had a three-day break before the scheduled start of *Hooper*. But health problems I'd ignored for more than a year caught up with me. Weak, down twenty pounds, and chronically short of breath, I fainted several times, threw up, and felt my heart beat so rapidly I imagined a time bomb in my chest. I felt sure I was dying.

After a battery of tests in L.A., I flew to West Palm Beach, where a doctor gave me the six-hour low-blood-sugar test and diagnosed the problem: hypoglycemia. A severe case of low blood sugar—he ordered a complete overhaul of my around-the-clock lifestyle. In lieu of drinking and breakfasting on Hostess pies, I was to eat something healthy every thirty minutes and take B-12 shots daily. I had been driving wide open for too long, and now I was running on empty.

It made sense. Forget the shit going on inside me, all I had to do was look in the mirror. If an actor was going to play a major asshole, I'd advise him to look at pictures of me from that period. I was buying clothes the Coasters or the Platters would say were "too glitzy" to wear on stage—only I wasn't performing. I went back to Levi's and boots.

*Hooper* was shelved for a year and I got in good shape for *Semi-Tough,* in which me and Kris Kristofferson played two football stars, quarterback Billy Clyde Puckett and receiver Shake Tiller. Jill Clayburgh gave a wonderfully smart performance as our roommate, the team owner's daughter. Others included Bert Convy and Brian Dennehy in his first good role, and a large ensemble of very large real-life Dallas Cowboys.

Despite director Michael Ritchie, who'd never seen a jock much less worn one, the picture was a wonderful experience. Opening in November 1977, it overcame disappointing reviews and made lots of money. I basically played my friend Don "Dandy" Meredith, the legendary Dallas Cowboy quarterback whose off-the-field exploits were more interesting than anything he did in uniform. Dandy Don quotes Shakespeare, Robert Service, Edgar Allan Poe, or Dan Jenkins. He sings Hank Williams, and is funny enough to be a standup comedian.

After warning Sally that I'd probably go a little crazy while making *Semi-Tough*—in the name of research, of course—I introduced myself to the Dallas Cowboys Cheerleaders on the first day. In real life, the Cowboys prohibit players from dating the girls. But I made one point perfectly clear.

"I do not play for the Dallas Cowboys," I said.

Over the course of the movie, I became very close friends with a cheerleader, one of the nicest gals you'd ever want to know. I never knew if word got back to Sally, but I had the best gal in the world back home. Someday I knew I was going to have to be a grownup. I didn't seem to know how to get my act together.

Nor could Kristofferson. He had played varsity football at California Polytechnic. One morning we were in the trainer's room together, getting taped before shooting a game scene. I looked like a display for Johnson & Johnson, having had surgery on both knees and my shoulder, not to mention lots of other injuries. Kris flashed me a devilish grin and said, "Hey, I believe you and I are probably in the best shape of any forty-year-old actors in the world."

"Better than Jim Brown?" I asked.

"Well, he's not really an actor," Kris said.

"Yes, he is," I said. "What's your point?"

"Burt, I believe we can run on these guys."

"We're playing against the Dallas Cowboys starting defense," I said. "Are you out of your friggin mind? We couldn't play checkers against them."

"Really?"

"I know you won a Rhodes Scholarship and I never graduated from college, but take a word of advice," I said. "Don't say anything about ever playing college ball. Remember now: If they ask you if you played any ball in high school or college—and they will—tell them no. Say you were in the drama department. And you might want to say it with a little lisp."

I'd already spent some time hanging out with the players. I'd told Meredith stories and joked around with them. Most of them liked my movies. They were my audience. But my experiences with *The Longest Yard* had taught me that they were going to get bored real quick while we made this picture. Making movies is a lot of hurry up and wait. And once they got bored, they'd try to find someone to destroy.

When we took the field the Cowboys came over and shook hands and complimented us on some of the pictures we'd made. A few asked me about playing for Florida State.

"No. That's all PR—I was a drama major," I said with a wink. "You know Hollywood publicists."

But Kris told them all about playing for Cal Poly.

"I went both ways in those days," he said. "Started at end, and I thought about playing pro ball but I got a Rhodes Scholarship."

I got a queasy feeling that something real bad was going to happen. It was like anticipating a car wreck.

The first play called in the huddle was a sweep to the right with me carrying the ball. As I prepared to take the handoff, I looked over the line of scrimmage and saw eleven wide-eyed happy killers from the Super Bowl championship team staring at Kris and chanting, "Cal Poly! Cal Poly! Cal Poly!"

With some trepidation, the quarterback called the signal and handed me the ball. I started my sweep right. Then eleven guys hit Kris. I mean they were programmed to deliver pain, and they carried out their mission. Kris was carried off the field with a broken wrist and three broken ribs. He turned out to be a hell of a good guy, and has never seemed to back off his beliefs.

But as they carried him by me, I couldn't resist saying, "You know, for a Rhodes scholar you are really dumb."

# CHAPTER
## 4 2

ALTHOUGH SALLY WOULD LATER BLAME ME FOR not letting her attend the Emmy Awards when she was nominated for *Sybil* in early 1977, that's not what I recall. First, we went to the People's Choice Awards, where she was also nominated. But Jane Alexander's memorable portrayal of Eleanor Roosevelt in *Eleanor and Franklin* captured the award.

It's an honor to be nominated, but only one person goes home with a statue—and Sally wasn't that person. Now, she's not a real good loser. In fact, she's the worst loser I know. On the way home that night, she was a witch dressed up like Cinderella. Really pissed.

"I played seventeen friggin people," Sally said. "She played one."

"You're right," I said.

We once saw Meryl Streep in a play off-Broadway when Meryl was the new hot actress. Indeed, she proved untouchable as a talent. But about halfway through the play, Sally leaned over to me and whispered, "I could act her right off the fucking stage."

"I'm sure you could," I said. "But aren't we going to enjoy this?"

"No, we aren't," she said, and a few minutes later we left.

When the Emmys rolled around, we were holed up at the plush San Yisidro Ranch in Montecito, about eighty miles outside of L.A., rewriting the script for *Hooper*, an action-packed tribute to aging stuntmen and the young turks replacing them. Sally brought some expertise to the subject. Her stepfather was Jack O'Mahoney, arguably the greatest stuntman ever. In fact, when guys list the top five, it's always the same—Yakima Canutt, Mahoney, Davey Sharp, Hal Needham, and Dar Robinson. But not necessarily in that order.

"Well, are we going to the Emmys?" I asked.

"I can't stand it," Sally said. "God, I'm such a poor loser, but what if I win?"

"I guess that means yes," I said.

"Oh, God, I hate this," she said.

"I guess that means no," I said.

I would've gone if Sally had really wanted to. Believe me, this is a strong lady—if she had wanted to go, we would have gone. Either way, I didn't care. But I didn't say we couldn't or wouldn't attend. Our relationship wasn't that one-sided. In fact, we were in a rustic bungalow at one of the most luxurious hideaways in southern California, writing and laughing as we worked on the script. We loved being by ourselves. It was one of our greatest times, writing together, creating characters.

Even though we didn't go, we still watched the Emmys on TV. With Sally nominated, how could we not? Both of us held our breath from the time her category came up to the moment she won. As soon as her name was announced, we sprang off the floor and hugged, kissed, and screamed. Then we got on the bed and jumped up and down for a half hour, giggling till we fell down, made love, and then fell asleep.

I'd never been that much in love before or since. Everybody was a blur except for Sally. Just as I'd been in her corner throughout *Smokey*, she became my biggest supporter when I took a risk on co-producing, directing, and starring in *The End,* a twisted black comedy about death. The script by Jerry Belson had been around for seven years. Everyone was afraid to make it. Upon discovering he's dying of an incurable disease, "what Ali McGraw had in *Love Story,* "a real estate salesman decides to help matters along by committing suicide. Yet no matter what he tries, he can't seem to do the job right. It was black, but it was funny. There were laughs that were longer than any I can remember in a theater.

Screenwriter Belson introduced me to his script. I took it to a friend, producer Lawrence Gordon. At the time, Larry's assistant was Joel Silver, who would go on to produce the *Die Hard* movies. He was a bright, ambitious schlepper, who ran errands, picked up lunches, whatever needed to be done. I called him Irving, after Columbia's legendary genius Irving Thalberg, because he was clearly brilliant. So much so that I once told Larry, "Someday you're going to be working for that guy. And you know what? You ain't gonna like it."

It would be me who needed the snakebite kit, but that wouldn't be for a number of years.

In the meantime, Warner Bros. agreed to finance *The End,* but only if I would make two decidedly more commercial pictures for them, including *Hooper.* They got what they wanted, and I received what every filmmaker dreams of yet few ever get: total creative control.

At the risk of sounding like a pompous ass, I knew that no one else could direct *The End* but me, because no one I'd encountered had my sort of completely bent, dark, tortured sense of humor. Maybe Blake Edwards could, but I didn't know him then. From the first time I read the script, I saw the film as a chance to say something about my philosophy of living. My goal was to experience everything and go out swinging. I'd seen few movies where before someone dies they scream, "Screw you!"

I'd been in the tunnel myself, seen the white light and fought kicking and screaming, "I want to live!" I wanted that in this film. I also wanted to talk about the inhumanity of being in a hospital, the cold, businesslike manner in which doctors and nurses treat patients. But it all had to be funny. There's a reason everyone hates to go to a hospital, even to visit, so to get people to go to a movie about dying . . . well, it was a very brave project.

I don't think there's any question that the brilliant ensemble cast, which included Joanne Woodward, Sally, Dom DeLuise, Carl Reiner, David Steinberg, Myrna Loy, Pat O'Brien, and Robby Benson, turned a disturbing subject into the kind of offbeat tickler that I hoped for. Contrary to predictions, it wound up grossing nearly $40 million, a wild success given its $3.7 million budget. I'm even prouder that it still plays in art houses, often with *Where's Poppa.*

I'd steered a bleak idea around a dangerous curve, come in under budget, and made an enormous profit—not to mention getting outstanding performances from my actors and incredible reviews. However, once again the serious filmmakers in New York didn't care. I might as well have been a kid again, trying to win favor from my father.

Liza Minnelli told me that Martin Scorsese once remarked to her that I was the only real movie star left in the world. But when she asked why he didn't work with me, he simply said, "Because I don't want to." But that was his prerogative. I would love to work with him. Francis Ford Coppola was simply devious. In 1978, he had me up to his San Francisco home to discuss starring in a film he wanted to make on the maverick car builder Preston Tucker. Coppola showed me at least a half dozen different endings to *Apocalypse Now,* and also screened home movies of Tucker, commenting on how much he looked like me. I left thinking it was a cinch. In fact, he told me as much.

A few days later I heard from Paramount. Francis wanted to make *Tucker,* all right, but also six other pictures Coppola had tied to the deal. In other words, he was trading—I got a movie, he got six. Hurt, I called him to ask if he didn't believe in me enough to put the other projects aside and go ahead with this picture he'd personally told me was so dear to his heart. He gave me some kind of bullshit answer. But the truth was that the movie didn't get made for ten years (and it wasn't very big, either). By then, he wouldn't give me the time of day.

I knew what I was up against. I came from the same New York acting schools as Pacino and DeNiro. I knew I couldn't outdo their brilliance, but given the same material I would have surprised people. I was a rich, single, highly approachable actor who loved people and felt no need to conceal the fact that I was having a tremendously good time.

My mistake was accessibility. I thought I could win respect by working harder. But it ended up costing me everything.

# CHAPTER
# 43

ON THE END TABLE IN THE PANELED LIVING ROOM of the ranch house where my parents lived, there was a small black-and-white photograph of me and Sally. It was in a pretty needlepointed frame that also carried a message: "To Fern, Love Sally."

My parents were as far removed from Hollywood as one can get on this planet. They watched the interviews, glanced at the tabloids, and heard all the "crap," as they called it, about their boy. Tight-lipped by nature, my mom and dad described me to reporters simply as a "good man" or "our son, Buddy." They refused to believe a word of whatever was being bandied about from barrooms to hair salons until it came directly from my lips, and no matter where in the world I was, I called them every Sunday.

After Dinah, they learned not to get their hopes up about marriage, yet neither Mom nor Dad hid the fact they were smitten by Sally, a spitfire of personality, warmth, and determination. She was their kind of woman, and after awhile they began dropping subtle hints about whether we were or weren't going to get hitched.

My answer never varied. I definitely planned to, but beyond that vague scratch of a commitment loomed a question mark of mythic proportions, one so large I never seemed able to get around it. The problem boiled down to lifestyle. One weekend I was happy to stay around Sally's home and repaint a room, but the next I wanted to go on the road with Willie Nelson.

There were endless opportunities for distractions. Money poured in. From *Smokey* alone I received more than $5 million, a portion of which I used to buy a Mediterranean-style home on 3.8 acres on Carolwood Drive in ultra-exclusive Holmby Hills. With the rest, I started construction on my fantasy, a dinner theater in Jupiter, Florida. I also acquired a helicopter and jet, the BR fleet. I paid two crackerjack pilots $100,000 apiece to sit around all year in case I had the urge to go someplace.

Sally and I let our whims direct our destinations, though we never had to stray far from home. The more money I made, the more homes I acquired: two in California, three in Florida, plus a mansion in Georgia that looked exactly like Tara in *Gone With the Wind*, which was why I had to have it. I also had land in Tennessee, where Dolly Parton would build her amusement park, Dollywood.

So why settle down? I asked myself that all the time.

Sally made it look so easy, though. She was a model mom to her two boys, Peter and Eli—aged seven and three when I first entered the scene—from her first marriage to writer Steve Craig. They lived in a comfy house in Studio City, where she was always doing something— fixing the gate, waiting to meet a plumber, dealing with pets. Wearing what seemed like her uniform—cutoffs and T-shirts—she drove carpools and waited in line at the grocery store like everyone else.

Now I marvel at her, but it drove me nuts that she could leave the house without a dab of makeup on. I said things like, "You can't go out like that. You're Sally Field." I still can't figure out how she managed to shop, prepare three meals a day, help her boys with homework, discuss my scripts and projects, and still pay attention to her own acting career.

If we'd combined households, I might've been forced to work on issues I otherwise avoided, but at forty-two I was set in my bachelor ways. Eli, the baby, was little enough so that I could get away with hugging him, but Peter was older, more complex, and real smart. He resented me. Not only did I make demands on his mother's time, I didn't show him enough respect. He was right.

God, that boy was bright. And I didn't make the effort I was capable of. For instance, I promised to take the boys fishing, something I wished my dad had done with me. I whetted their appetite with stories from my childhood. I told of hunting sharks and riding on the back of manta rays. But when the big day arrived, I said I was too tired, and hired a fishing guide to take them while I stayed home.

Sally buried me for that, and rightly so. I should have won asshole of the year for that alone. No matter how tired I was, I should've put in the time. I should've taken Peter to museums and ball games. I should've been the fun-loving guy who entertained their mother so effortlessly. Because of her, I became a much better father when my time came. Like Dinah, who gave me confidence, Sally taught me humanity. But she didn't get back what she gave. Not even half.

She never knew the best of me. If she had, maybe we actually would have gotten married. I proposed three or four times; she did the same to me. But each time one of us would back out, saying we wanted that deeper level of commitment at different times. After one argument— not the best time to propose—I said, "Well, let's just get married." Much to my chagrin, Sally said no, which was a nice lesson in humility.

But I also remember her, on another occasion, saying, "I would like to get married."

"Good," I answered, "I hope you find the right guy."


ONE thing I never took for granted was Sally's talent. Like me, the work was incredibly important to her. But we had different approaches to the business. While she'd rather starve than do a project she didn't love, my philosophy was to look at all the zeros and say, "Well, after I finish this piece of shit, I'll do something I love." But we respected each other's judgment equally.

After Sally read the script for *Norma Rae*, she gave it right to me. I finished it one night when we were in bed.

"What do you think?" she asked.

I looked at Sally for a long time with both loving jealousy and admiration for the performance I knew she was going to give. I envisioned the whole movie in my head, and I knew it was the launching pad that would put her into orbit. *Norma Rae* was about a true heroine, and nobody's more heroic than Sally.

What did I think? I set the script in her lap and said, "The envelope, please." I also made grumbling noises about being jealous, but off she went with Martin Ritt.

Sally's movie opened to critical raves in winter 1978. I had similar expectations when I went off to make *Starting Over*, a psychocomedy in which I get dumped by my wife, Candice Bergen, and tutored on the single life by Jill Clayburgh. Director-producer Alan Pakula wanted one of those serious New York actors in the role, but I desperately wanted it for myself. My agent Sue Mengers thought I was nuts.

"You can't play a guy who can't get a date," she said.

"The hell I can't," I said. "I wouldn't even know how to start to get a date in a singles bar today."

Together, Sue and I pushed like two halfbacks struggling for a first down inside the ten until I finally got a meeting with Pakula. I'd read and reread Dan Wakefield's book and Jim Brooks's screenplay. We talked about the character, Phil Potter, an unsuccessful, overly sensitive writer. Pakula knew I'd done my homework and sensed my eagerness, but he was being polite and not about to make any offers. So I simply asked for a shot.

"Well, I don't think you're the image," he said.

"Image?" I said, acting surprised. "You're too smart a man and too good a director to worry about image. You could direct Roy Rogers in this picture. But let me tell you something absolutely true. I've never been able to pick up a woman in my life. Not in a bar. Not anyplace.

"I'm terribly uncomfortable and shy," I continued, "and like anybody else I don't want to be shot down. The jokes and wisecracks are nothing but protection against a lot of pain that's hidden inside me." The speech was true. I knew it; did he?

"I've played a lot of parts," I said. "But I've never played me. And this is me."

My impassioned speech had an effect—a small one. I wasn't handed the job, but Pakula offered me the chance to test. It was a nod. I'm sure he expected me to say, "Fuck you," and storm off. After all, the Theater Owners of America had named me the Number One box-office star in the world. People who are Number One don't test. But I said, "Absolutely. When?"

I'm sure I surprised the hell out of him, and also myself. I hadn't tested for a part since *Rosemary's Baby* in 1967. But while I have my problems, fighting for something I believe in isn't one of them. The director witnessed this himself by having me test four separate times. When shooting began over Christmas in New York City and Boston, the role was mine.

Without my trademark mustache, I played my part closer to the real me than I'd ever done before. During rehearsal of a scene in which I kissed Jill's neck while she moaned with pleasure, I broke from the script and ad-libbed, "Hey, wait a minute! I'm not that good." It was something I'd say in real life, but Brooks knew it was just like my character and added it to the script. James Brooks is the finest writer I've ever worked for; the kindest and most unselfish.

But if restraint and vulnerability were a departure for me, the picture's biggest surprise was Candice Bergen doing comedy. Until then, she was regarded as this glacier-cool blond who took pictures, acted occasionally, and lived an adventurous life. Early in the picture, though, she had to sing, something she can't do well enough even to fake. From that hideous Bogdanovich adventure, I knew exactly how she felt—embarrassed and inhibited. One day I flat out told her she had one choice—to go for it.

"Look, we're real bored with you saying 'I haven't made up my mind whether I'm going to be an actress or a photographer,' " I said. "You can't get away with that after a certain age."

"I don't know if I agree," she said. "What's your point?"

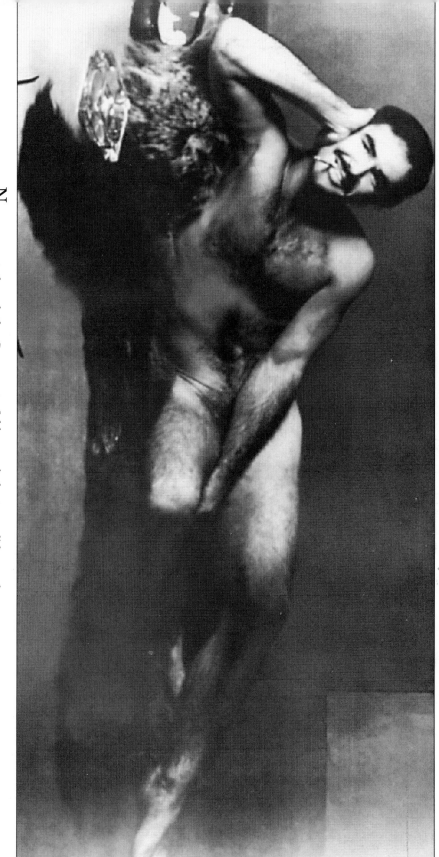

No comment, though the *Cosmo* centerfold caused plenty, as did my spleenectomy scar.

PHOTOGRAPHED BY FRANCESCO SCAVULLO

With first wife Judy Carne, outside the house we lived in after getting married.
BURT REYNOLDS COLLECTION

On the set of *Smokey II*, I admired this great lady and brilliant actress—too good for me at the time. COPYRIGHT © BY UNIVERSAL CITY STUDIOS, INC. COURTESY OF MCA PUBLISHING RIGHTS, A DIVISION OF MCA INC.

It was impossible to look at Catherine Deneuve in *Hustle* and not admire this fantastic woman.

Farrah had great teeth, great hair, and would go on to become a great actress after *Cannonball Run*.

My favorite picture of us, it shows how much I respected this lady who changed my life.

Cowboy great Roy Rogers with one of his biggest fans.

The finest and most talented cast ever assembled —that of *Evening Shade*, of whom I'm very proud. TONY ESPARZA, CBS

My sister, Nancy, Dolly Parton, Pop, me, and Mom. BURT REYNOLDS COLLECTION

The lovely Pam Seals, laughing, looking beautiful and oh, so buffed. BURT REYNOLDS COLLECTION

"The Countess" and me, before I dropped anchor. MARIO CASILLI/PHOTOGRAPHY © 1994

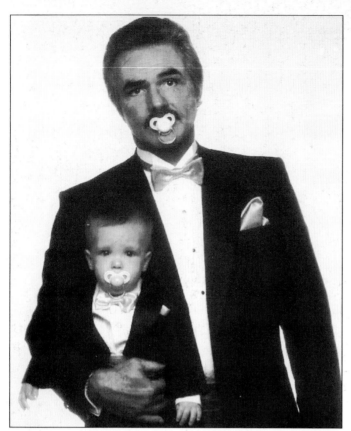

Quinton asked for a
pacifier, and I did, too.
MARIO CASILLI/PHOTOGRAPHY
© 1994

Quinton with his future
coach, Florida State legend
Bobby Bowden.
BURT REYNOLDS COLLECTION

"My point is that this is a part you can get nominated for. But there's only one way. You have to sing. Go full out. You've got to be brave."

"What do you mean?" she asked.

"You and I know you can't sing, but you have to act like you think you sing great. If you don't make a fool of yourself, then you're not doing it right and you won't get a laugh, and if you don't get laughs, you don't get nothing." Candice was brave as she could be—and, boy, did she sing out.

As I predicted, Candice would get an Oscar nomination, but the more immediate reward was confidence. As an actor, you only get that by venturing into the most dangerous places. Off-screen, she and I took a rather perilous sojourn of our own. At the start, I had thought she was untouchable and she had thought I was this asshole from the car movies—misperceptions based on stories we'd read or heard. We discovered how wrong we were simply by being ourselves.

The first real intellectual woman with whom I became close, Candice was accomplished in so many fields, including horseback riding. One day we took a couple of horses through Central Park. I think my horsemanship impressed her, but I was fascinated to discover that one of the love affairs of her life had been with Mahan, my gypsy horseman from Spain who owned Destaphanado.

From then on our friendship got closer and closer, kind of like two planets colliding. She took me to Mike Nichols's place for dinner and was surprised when I cracked a joke that made him laugh. In turn, I introduced her to Willie Nelson, who she thought was a bit rumpled. But I warned her that before the day was over she'd love him. Indeed, before he left the set, Willie had laid some of that magical voice on her, prompting Candice to come up to me and say, "He's very sexy, don't you think?"

Allies on the set, friends off, I didn't kiss Candice until the picture was practically over. We'd hung out together in Manhattan, making all the gossip columns, but nothing happened between us. Both of us were involved with other people, so we fought the urge for as long as possible. Then one day as we rehearsed a scene where I answered the door, she said, "We're going to end up doing it, aren't we?"

I had no comeback. Giving little thought to what a major prick I was being to Sally, I said, "Dear God, I hope so."

"Well," she said, "let's get it over with."

We remained platonic friends, but nobody had ever said that to me before. Candice is extraordinary. Back then, she was only beginning to discover the depth and range of her talent—both as an actress and a woman. I knew her future would be as bright as she was. On my way home, I knew mine was somewhat questionable.

# CHAPTER
# 44

OUTSIDE THE DRESSING ROOM DOOR WAS AN ENOR-
mous gold star that read, "Superstars Burt Reynolds
and Sally Field." It was a joke, but everything else
about the Burt Reynolds Theater, which opened at
the end of January 1979 in Jupiter, Florida, was more
serious than almost any regional theater in the country. I'd put $2 million of my own money into the pro-
ject, which gave me a chance to give something back
to my hometown.

Except for the Palm Beach crowd, most people
from that area had never seen an actor live on stage
before, but I brought in the theater and Hollywood's
best. The sold-out opening of *Vanities* starred Sally,
Tyne Daly, and Gail Strickland. One month later I arrived to direct and co-star with Sally in *The Rainmaker*.
Over the next fifteen years, until I sold the playhouse,

such actors as Martin Sheen and Carol Burnett would come down and for very little pay take the sort of chances they didn't get on film or TV. I would just ask the actors, "What's your favorite play?" or "What's your biggest challenge?" Singers want to act. Actors want to sing.

Martin Sheen was in five plays at the theater. One was *Mister Roberts,* directed by Josh Logan. Charlie Sheen and Emilio Estevez played some of the smaller roles. Here are other actors who appeared there:

Kirstie Alley and Parker Stevenson—Three one-act plays called *Answers*

Charles Durning—*Mass Appeal* (won the Florida Drama award—did over five plays at the theater)

Julie Harris—*Death of a Salesman* (won the Florida Drama award)

Farrah Fawcett—*Butterflies Are Free* (her stage debut)

Ossie Davis—*I'm Not Rappaport*

Robert Urich—*The Hasty Heart* (We took this production to Washington, D.C. I attended with Nancy and President Reagan.)

John Goodman—Unknown character actor then. We thought, "He was good!"

For Sally and me, it was an opportunity to forget the pressures of Hollywood and work on our relationship. Despite outward appearances, we had problems. Sally felt I didn't try to balance my work schedule as much as she did hers. She wasn't thrilled about Candice, and she also blamed me for "pushing her into" a movie as shitty as *Beyond the Poseidon Adventure.*

I don't believe I or anyone else could talk Sally Field into doing a film, no matter what was offered. If she did the film, it was because she needed money—and, exactly as I told her, no one even knows she did the damn thing. But once you reach sainthood as she has done, she is allowed to do a clinker now and then.

Yes, I pointed out that the money being offered her for that movie was phenomenal. The film script sucked, but Michael Caine would be great to work with. And bad films die a quick death. She listened to her business manager and did the film. She also worked with Caine again twice after that, so they both respected and liked each other. Talk about dying: *Operation C.I.A.* plays on TV more than that film. She did the smart thing—she took the money and ran.

I left do to my next picture in July. *Rough Cut,* a movie about a retired jewel thief who returns for one last diamond caper, filmed in England, Holland, and Hawaii, teamed me with Lesley-Anne Down, who, along with Catherine Deneuve, was one of the two most beautiful women I'd ever seen at that time.

Intended as a slick, Cary Grant–type film, the picture turned into a contentious test of wills when producer David Merrick meddled with Larry Gelbart's excellent script and fired a handful of directors—including Blake Edwards. He finally settled on Dom Siegel, one of Clint's mentors. But Don had aged since *Dirty Harry.* Not that that's bad, but a movie takes on the director's energy, and he could barely stay awake between shots. Maybe it was my acting.

Lesley-Anne and I had another problem between shots, though that stopped as soon as Sally flew over for a visit. Until then, I worked too closely with my co-star. Her personal life was a bad dream. She was so good inside and very sweet, but surrounded by real bad people. But she was a superb athlete who amazed me one day by catching a football over her shoulder at a full run. Sally also caught on immediately.

"You're screwing her," Sally said. "Who do you think you're kidding?"

Sally was like that. She was able to walk on a set and say, "You're screwing the craft services girl," and be very close to right every time. On *Rough Cut,* she watched only one scene between me and Lesley-Anne. She just gave her one of those Norma Rae looks—"I'll kick your ass!" To me, she said the same thing—only with a little more edge. And real loud.

We had a lot of stresses tugging at us, but London put Sally over the top and we broke up. It didn't last long, though. Somehow I talked my way into another chance, which certainly wasn't typical of Sally. If someone screwed up, she had the ability to erase them off the face of the earth. But after four years together, we knew each other too well and had too much in common to give up so easily. Neither of us was a quitter.

In the fall, Sally and I became Frog and Bandit again in *Smokey and the Bandit II,* the stunt-packed sequel that would open to record-breaking business in August 1980. Contrary to rumor, she had no problem doing the picture. Never. Not only was she paid an enormous amount of money, but I think she wanted to play the string out to the end.

Would I see the light? Or was I destined to remain Peck's bad boy?

This wasn't a secret. Before Hal shot the film's most dramatic scene, in which Frog tells Bandit it's all over between them because he's never going to take life seriously—a problem that struck close to home—I suggested Sally write it. She thought that was a swell idea and went off and rewrote what amounted to a two-page monologue by herself. Until then we'd always enjoyed rewriting together, as we'd done on *Hooper,* but clearly this time I knew she had things to say on her own.

No problem. I made sure Hall, who liked to roll-'em, show-'em, cut, print, and move on, gave her whatever time she needed. She'd earned the respect, that's for damn sure.

"Let's really shoot this beautifully," I said.

It was a night shot. We found a beautiful location beside the water. A full moon hung overhead like a solitary lightbulb. The water was like silver rolling in toward the beach. Sally was as primed as I'd ever seen her. If I hadn't known her so well, I would have been intimidated by the intensity I saw in those brown eyes. Right after Hal said, "Roll 'em," she looked up at me and said, "You'd better stay with me."

"I've never had a problem before," I said.

My job was to counterpunch, not compete. But no matter what I did, Sally intended to blow me off the screen if she could. I held my own. I've never phoned anything in in my life. But Sally was remarkable, crying real tears, pausing for emphasis, using her body perfectly. Clearly, the lines she'd written were about us, our relationship, everything she'd wanted to say for a long time and some things she'd already said in private. Afterward, Hall called me over.

"I'll shoot it again," he said when I huddled with him. "But can she do it any better?"

"Probably," I said.

"I could use some coverage," he mused, trying to convince himself.

"If I was directing that's what I'd do," I said. "But why don't you ask if she wants to do it again."

Sally looked at him as if he was nuts.

"What the hell for?" she asked.

To be sure, she'd done it the way she'd wanted. She'd said it all. The whole shoot, from Georgia to Las Vegas, was like that. Through it all, Sally and I had perhaps the most heated affair of our relationship. The sex was angry—well, wonderful and mean—but we couldn't keep from doing it. By the time the picture finished, she seemed to be working as hard as possible to hate my guts.

Before returning to L.A., Sally simply said, "It's over, pal." And that was it . . . just about.

OVER the next few months, we had occasion to speak several times. When Oscar nominations were announced, I congratulated her on receiving a Best Actress nod for *Norma Rae,* and she bristled with anger that the Academy had overlooked me for *Starting Over.* It was very obvious. Candice nominated, Jill nominated, the director nominated, the writer nominated, the cinematographer nominated, yet even the reviewers had called me "the core" of the movie.

"How can they not also give it to you?" Sally asked.

"I don't know," I said. They forgive you for being rich, reclusive, or in rehab, but God forbid you have too much fun and make the work look easy. Maybe that's my cross to bear. Sally, of course, had enough other reasons for not forgiving me anything, yet I persuaded her to have dinner with me. One last attempt at reconciling, we made plans to have dinner with football-star-turned-actor and artist Bernie Casey and his wife at Cafe Four Oaks in Beverly Glen.

It started out nice—until I picked Sally up. On the way, we got into a horrible argument. Truthfully, I don't even remember why. As soon as I pulled up to the restaurant she sprang out of the car like a jackrabbit and started running. I froze, watching Sally disappear into the darkness, looking at the valet, who wanted to give me a parking ticket, and wondering what I should do about Bernie and his wife, whom we were already thirty minutes late in meeting.

I darted into the restaurant and found our guests.

"The good news is I'm here," I said. "But the bad news is Sally isn't and I've got to go chase her. I probably won't be back. I hope you understand."

Bernie, as always, was so understanding. He said, "Go, man!" So I then ran outside and started down the street, hunting for her in people's hedges and driveways, shouting, "Sally! Sally!" It took awhile, but I found her walking through the dark canyon and persuaded her to let me drive her home, a momentous achievement given the situation. She remained perfectly silent while I apologized the entire way. But after I dropped her off, that was it.

The next time I saw Sally was on television the night of the Academy Awards. I'd retreated to Florida, as if I could snub Hollywood's grandest night by leaving the state. I also didn't watch the rest of the ceremony. After Sally won, which I was certain she'd do, I realized that this was a journey that I had also taken with her, and because I was an asshole I wouldn't and shouldn't be there when she crossed the finish line.

Long after the telecast finished, about one A.M., I finally turned the TV back on. At that hour, I thought all the shows dealing with Academy Award results would be over. Alas, there would be no escape from Sally. God put her directly into my bedroom via the airwaves as celebrity journalist and onetime friend Rona Barrett questioned her about the big evening.

Asked by Rona what she thought while running down the aisle to collect her award, Sally had no difficulty answering. She said, "I was thinking, Fuck you, Burt Reynolds. Fuck you, Burt Reynolds. Fuck you, Burt Reynolds."

I turned off the TV. Message received, Captain. No reply necessary. I didn't cry, but I felt as if I'd been run over by a truck. They had bleeped the F word, but I heard it. I walked out onto the porch, where Sally and I used to sit and gaze up at the stars, talking about our dreams, and I said the serenity prayer. Later, I remembered something Dinah had told me about relationships, which helped me realize that Sally couldn't hate me with such fervor if part of her didn't still love me. A little anyway.

I have no doubt why the breakup was so bitter and painful because we both were so passionate and both so deeply in love. We tried to be friends again when I visited her on the set of *Back Roads,* the second picture she made with Martin Ritt. Again, one night Sally asked me to read a script, this one an early draft of Robert Benton's *Places in the Heart.* As before, I told her, "The envelope, please."

But a failed romance is like a death in the family. You don't survive it and not change. We'd survived three breakups, and the past had consumed us. I knew the very best of Sally; my biggest regret is that she never saw the best of me. She saw only the boy. She is a remarkable woman, the best mother, the greatest companion when you're down. She has the courage of a lion. Her talent I always saw—the rest only now I see, much, much too late.

Shortly before she married producer Alan Griseman, who she has since divorced, Sally called to tell me the news herself. It was a courtesy, so I'd know before I read it in the paper. Her announcement left me speechless. I tried congratulating her, but couldn't seem to get all the syllables out of my mouth.

"I want you to know something," she said. "No man will ever see the Sally Field that you saw. Goodbye."

Click.

That was it. She was gone.

And I thought, Isn't that a pity on so many accounts.

# CHAPTER
# 45

ALTHOUGH CRITICIZED FOR NOT TACKLING heavier material, I had the notion that more often than not people liked going to the movies to forget their problems rather than be reminded of life's big issues. The public picked John Wayne over Montgomery Clift almost any day. My pictures had the same appeal. Which explains why in 1981 it was me rather than Marlon or Pacino who was voted the Number One box-office star for the fifth straight year, something no one had ever done before. It also explains why I received $5 million—at that time the highest salary ever paid an actor—for five weeks of work on *Cannonball Run*.

I always said my success was the result of simply working hard at making it look easy. But the fun I had also came through. How else do you explain the appeal of a dopey picture like *Cannonball Run?* Filmed in Georgia, the car-race comedy, which included a cast ranging from Roger Moore to Bianca Jagger, was a nonstop party. Dean Martin alone guaranteed a good time. He told me about an incident when, as he was about to go on stage while holding a glass of booze, a stagehand stopped him and said, "You can't go out there with that drink, Mr. Martin."

Without missing a beat, Dean said, "Well! I ain't going out dere alone!"

He was so quick, much funnier than Jerry with a comeback. In our first scene together, Dean played a priest and wore a strand of beads around his neck. I was supposed to say, "I'm going to stuff those beads up your nose." Instead I messed up and said, "I'm going to stuff those bleeds up your nose." Dean fired right back and said, "If you do, I'll bead all over you."

But once we got Dean for the movie, I also added Sammy Davis, Jr., as a second priest. Sarah Miles had introduced me to Sammy originally, but Sally and I occasionally went to parties at Sammy's house in Beverly Hills. Talk about eclectic groups. We saw everyone from Sinatra and Sugar Ray Robinson to porn star Marilyn Chambers and her pals. Leaving one night, in the car, I asked, "What do you think goes on after we leave?" We just started giggling.

On the *Cannonball* set, Dean and Sammy were always among the holdouts late at night. Usually we were in my room or one of the actors'—Roger Moore, Dom, Jamie Farr, Doug McClure, Susan Anton, Adrienne Barbeau, etc.—everyone pretty well lubricated, trading stories until about three A.M. That's when Sammy really got going, as if he was about to do the first of two shows that night, which prompted Dean to say, "Oh, da little guy's going to sing again. Oh, shit. I'm going to bed now."

"Aren't you going to sing, too?" I asked.

"I don't sing, Bertie," Dean said. "I ain't finished a song in twenty years. Da little guy'll sing. I sleep now."

While down there, Farrah Fawcett and I stirred up a storm of gossip in the tabloids, though nothing happened until after those stories appeared. Farrah, beautiful beyond belief and a fine athlete, was the kind of wild down-home Texas girl I dreamed of marrying for about two seconds. We were two of a kind. We heard the rumors that I'd turned into the kind of bad boy character who'd caused Sally so much heartache and said, "If we're gonna get blamed for this, what the hell."

Nothing like that lasts on a movie set, even when it's someone as wonderful as Farrah. But we clicked for far longer as confidantes. When Farrah explained how desperately she wanted to escape her *Charlie's Angels* past and be considered a serious actress, no one identified with her as much as I did. I did monologues on the subject, entire one-man shows. When I suggested she do a play, she asked why I didn't do one, too.

"I have," I said. "They don't care. But with you it's a lot different. You're younger. You'll surprise people. Shock the industry. It'll be a major event."

After the picture, Farrah came down to my theater and made her stage debut in a production of *Butterflies Are Free*. A success, Farrah used the poise and polish she gained there as a springboard for landing the lead in the off-Broadway production of *Extremities*, which changed her career forever. The industry felt she had taken a risk. So look . . . she's an actress now.

I had to do the same. Following *Paternity*, which was one of those movies I thought would be a big hit, I felt I had to sharpen my chops. The comedies were nice and profitable, but they were getting a little too light. I suddenly felt like Faulkner's dog. If he doesn't go up against a bear every once in a while, he can't call himself a dog anymore.

Author Sidney Sheldon first mentioned William Diehl's novel *Sharky's Machine* to me at a party, and soon afterward Clint sent me a copy of the same best-selling book with a note saying, "This is *Dirty Harry* in Atlanta." He was returning a favor; years earlier I'd sent him a copy of *The Outlaw Josey Wales*. After reading *Sharky's* overnight, and discovering it combined elements of two of my favorite movies, *Laura* and *Rear Window*, I persuaded newly formed partners Orion Pictures and Warner Bros. to acquire the screen rights for me.

It's the story of a detective who investigates the attempted murder of a high-priced call girl and finds himself wading through the dangerous play-for-keeps world of the two men with whom she's involved, a politician and an underworld figure. The kind of film Aldrich would've been great at, I knew from the get-go that I had to direct. It was my baby.

Granted complete creative control, for me only the third time this had happened, I assembled my dream cast. After interviewing countless actresses, Rachel Ward entered the room. As soon as I saw her, I told myself, "If this girl can talk, she's got the part." Because in the film I spend hours on stakeout watching her and recording her voice, I wanted it to sound very sexy. It turned out she didn't have the voice I wanted. However, I remembered that Howard Hawks had sent eighteen-year-old model Lauren Bacall to the beach and instructed her to scream her head off all night long. By morning, she had gotten a node on her throat and returned to Hawks's office with that famous Bacall voice.

I told Rachel to do the same thing. To this day, she has a sexy rasp in her voice. I'm not saying it's a good idea for everyone, but it certainly worked for two beautiful ladies.

Shooting began in March 1981. On the first day I walked onto the set and faced this extraordinary cast—Brian Keith, Bernie Casey, Vittorio Gassman, Earl Holliman, Darryl Hickman, Henry Silva, and Charlie Durning. Let me just say this about Charles Durning. He may be America's finest actor working today. And as a friend, my God, I'd take a bullet for him any time. He's honest to a fault, loving to the point of being embarrassing. Tough? He can put down near any man on the floor in seconds. Brave? How about two bronze and two silver stars.

The film also had one of the best crews I had ever worked with. I thought, If you've ever been right, you better make sure you're right every time with this bunch of people. Have your shit together.

And I did. Right down to the soundtrack, for which I gathered the greatest jazz musicians of the day. A jazz fiend, I went through my record collection and called my own list of All-Stars—Sarah Vaughan, Peggy Lee, Julie London. I also had Joe Williams, Shelly Manne on drums, Bobby Troup on piano, Tony Tescadero on guitar, Abe Brown on bass, Eddie Harris on sax. I even slipped trumpeter Chet Baker into the country and made him sing. The sessions were extraordinary. Nobody took a break. They just jammed.

The picture opened at the end of the year to critical reviews that were beyond my expectations. I knew my third outing as a director had been right on. The best I could do. But when even the *New York Times*'s

Vincent Canby also got it, I was bowled over. The reviews made me hot as a director:

*Burt Reynolds is as valuable behind the camera as he is in front of it.*
                              —*Janet Maslin, the* New York Times

*Reynolds has a feel for the director's craft that could, someday, permit him to break the genre bonds.*
                              —*Richard Schickel,* Time *magazine*

For a sparkling moment, I was like Rob Reiner after *Stand By Me* or Ron Howard following *Splash*. I had respect from a group of people who ordinarily didn't look in my direction. The time was right to move in the direction that would have made me even now the hottest director in the biz. Sound arrogant? All I know is what too many great actors have said—I was born to direct movies!

Everybody had a script they wanted me to direct. They flooded my office. It was one of those moments where I needed a strong agent or manager to sit me down and ask, "What do you really want to do when you're fifty-five or sixty? Act? Direct? Both?" There's an immutable reality in Hollywood: No matter who you are, you're only as good as your last picture.

Over the past twenty-five years, I'd had two great scripts and a couple of very commercial ones handed to me, but my turn had finally arrived. I was an absolute movie freak, an obsessive, passionate, knowledgeable freak of the highest order. I loved movies. I loved the process of making movies. Although I loathed to admit it, I also discovered I loved being in control. You get that only by directing.

But the people around me said, "Shit, you're getting millions of dollars to act. Grab the brass ring now while you're hot. You know you can always direct."

But the years roll by, and people now only want the flavor of the week. You have control of your life once or twice in a lifetime, if you're lucky. I dropped the ball both times. I found out it's not true that "You can always direct."

# CHAPTER
## 46

I'D KNOWN DOLLY PARTON SINCE SHE WAS A BEAUTI-
ful chubby-cheeked singer working with Porter
Wagoner. I knew, like many others, that she was
bound for stardom. But after the first preproduction
meeting for *The Best Little Whorehouse in Texas,* she revealed a side of her personality that few people ever
saw. We were in her suite at the Bel Air Hotel, listening to director Tommy Tune, his co-director (I had
never been directed by two people; it sounded very
dangerous), and producer Stevie Phillips discuss this
much-anticipated movie version of the smash Broadway musical.

None of them seemed to make any sense whatsoever. We were adapting this story of a sheriff who's
pressured to shut down a popular brothel run by his
girlfriend. But Tommy Tune, a gentle soul who

seemed to be floating on some kind of energy field that I had never been on—and never ever wanted to be on—just talked about the cosmos, spinning bones on rugs, lights, astrological shit, and more. His friend nodded and embellished Tommy's ideas. My eyes bounced from one to the other. I wondered if they gave any thought to the camera. I envisioned these Moonies huddling after each take to decide our fate.

There was no doubt Tommy Tune was a genius director on the stage. But I doubted if he was meant to direct movies, at least on Earth.

Stevie was another case. Tougher than nails, she had her own ideas about the movie and didn't hesitate to mention them. At that meeting, however, she was hung up on getting Johnny Carson for the part of the evangelist, eventually played by Dom DeLuise. Johnny's people had already nixed the offer, but Stevie boasted that she'd get him, because she *always* got what she wanted.

"Johnny won't do a movie," I said. "Never."

"Just a fucking minute," she snapped.

"Okay. But only 'cause you asked nice," I said calmly.

Until then, the atmosphere had been very weird, needless to say. Now it was also tense. Throughout everything, Dolly silently sat in her chair, looking as sweet as ever. Whatever her thoughts, she kept them cloaked behind a bright red lipsticked smile that looked as if it came straight from a candy store. But I knew this woman. Back when she sang with Porter you didn't have to be a rocket scientist to know she was real bright and street smart. Likewise, I knew she was holding back, looking real sweet (something I have never learned to do) and thinking, "What the hell are they talking about?" They left, feeling real good about Dolly and okay about me.

The door hadn't closed on the three of them for more than two seconds before she said, "Get Lew Wasserman on the phone."

"You know, he's more than just a figurehead over at Universal," I said. "Maybe we should start with Sid Sheinberg, the president?"

"Get Lew!" she snapped.

"All righty." I called the studio and asked for the big man himself. His secretary answered.

"It's Dolly Parton and Burt Reynolds calling," I said.

Lew took the call and was gracious as always. Then Dolly grabbed the receiver.

"Listen, get your ass over to the Bel Air Hotel," she said. "And bring Sid whatshisname."

Then she hung up. My jaw dropped. I ordered room service, lots of vodka and tonics. About a half hour later Lew and Sid showed up. Then she calmly explained that the two of us weren't "doing this movie with these crazy people."

"You've got a contract," Sid said.

"I don't give a damn," she said. "We're not doing it with them. They're nuts. I'll buy my way out before they turn this picture into a piece of shit."

They calmed Dolly. I was essentially a bystander. A fascinated one, but a bystander. After some discussion, they asked who she wanted to direct. She named Colin Higgins. Of course, Colin was the only director she knew; he'd directed her only movie until then, *Nine to Five*. I hadn't worked with him, though I was crazy about *Harold and Maude*, which he'd written, and I enjoyed *Nine to Five* a lot. I had no objections. Neither did they.

But you know, of course, back in New York, who was blamed for the firing. Not a woman who'd made only one picture. It had to be the guy who was Number One and was exercising his enormous clout. To this day, I'm sure Tommy Tune and Stevie Phillips love Dolly, but they think I'm a piece of shit.

Prior to shooting, I saw Dolly perform at one of the hotels in Las Vegas. After the show, she told me to wait for her up in her suite. It was much later than I thought, but she rolled into the room wide awake, gabbing and laughing with a couple of friends—her makeup woman, who'd been a friend since childhood, and a rollicking little old wardrobe lady from Tennessee. One time, our cameraman William Fraker (a great friend whom I did five films with) asked her, "How ya doin', darling?"

She said, "Okay. I was out last night and a guy said to me, 'I'd like a little pussy.' And you know what I said?"

"What?" Fraker asked.

"I said, 'So would I, you son of a bitch. Mine's the size of a god-damn Chevrolet.' "

In any event, Dolly's friends stayed a short time. They were fun, and we laughed a lot. Then they went to their rooms, leaving me and Dolly alone. Ever since she and Porter Wagoner had parked their tour bus where I was filming *Gator* in 1975 and spent the day visiting, Dolly and I had always had a flirtatious relationship. Fun, lighthearted kidding. And I was truly smitten by her. But then I'm sure lots of men feel that way about Dolly. She is truly one of a kind. Yet nothing had ever happened.

But up in her suite Dolly got a funny look in her eye.

"All right," she said, "let's just get this humping business over with."

I paused for a minute, repeated the words to myself, just to make sure I understood what she'd said, and I asked, "What?!" But Dolly was as serious as a heart attack.

"Let's just hump and get it over with, because when the movie starts we've got to work."

Whether we did or didn't, I'm not going to say. But once the picture started, there wasn't any fooling around. None. In fact, one day after shooting returned to Hollywood from location, I noticed this guy leaning against a post. Incredibly handsome, he wore a sheepskin jacket and cowboy hat, and watched everything. I figured he was an actor making a western somewhere on the lot, because ours was a closed set and nobody ever came by.

"Check out that good-looking guy over there," I said to Dolly. "Who do you think he is?"

"That's Carl," she said. "My husband."

"No shit!" I said. "Nobody's ever seen him. Why don't we take a picture together?"

"He's pretty, all right, but you do that, darlin'," she purred, "and I'll kill ya."


COLIN Higgins had in mind Mickey Rooney for the role of Governor. Well, let me say right here and now that every year I vote for Mickey Rooney to get honored in Washington for his career achievements and contributions to the movie industry. However, I had another actor in mind. So I got Colin's ear one day. "You know, Colin, when the industry sees Mickey sing and dance up a storm, what's the surprise? He's been doing just that since he was five! But now you take a fellow like Charles Durning, no one in the industry really knows what a great song and dance man he is. You know he taught dancing for years. And who do you think will get all the credit for that brilliant, offbeat casting? You!" Charles got the part and was nominated for an Academy Award.

With Dolly, Charlie Durning, Dom, and Jim Nabors around every day, filming the damn movie was so much fun I hated to go home. My only difficulty was with two of the producers, Edward Milkis and Tom Miller. I called them Mucous and Midler. Every few takes, they had some stupid suggestion, and I'd say, "Don't talk to me, talk to Colin. This is a director's medium."

Colin, one of the dearest and most talented people around, didn't want to fight. I loved to fight. Somehow I found it easier to put up with their putzy suggestions than to argue, but when I asked for new brakes to be put on the police car I drove, nobody seemed to hear me. Day in, day out. Having done just a few "action" films, I knew the importance of good brakes. In the opening of the film, I had to drive that vehicle very fast and pull to a screeching stop that would send up a spray of dirt in a 360-degree circle. That was impossible without brakes.

This picture had a tremendous budget, more than $20 million. But just like most films, they will step on hundred-dollar bills to grab at change. None of the police cars had good brakes.

Well, even if I'm not respected as an actor, I'm the Picasso of car pictures. I've done more car movies than anyone in the business. And I know how to make it right. So one day I asked Colin and the production manager to take a ride in my car. After making sure they were belted in, I put the pedal to the metal, headed down a straightaway, picking up speed until the needle on the speedometer was around seventy.

"You want me to come in pretty hot, Colin?" I asked.

"Eh, eh, yeah," he said.

"About this hot?" I asked.

"Maybe not this hot."

Then I turned to the production manager.

253
MY LIFE

"I've asked you to get some brakes for the past week, haven't I?" I asked.

"Yes. Yes, you have," he said nervously.

Then I stepped on the brake pedal, which hit the floor without even slowing the car down a drop. Even so, I turned the wheel, sending the police car sharply to the right and straight into a ditch upside-down, where we finally rolled over and stopped. Nobody was hurt, but Colin had peed in his pants and the production manager was whiter than a ghost. Although upside-down, I turned around and smiled.

"Now will you please get me some brakes?"

Aside from that, everything went smoothly until the picture's premiere in Austin, Texas. The governor, the mayor, and the University of Texas band were all there. It was some big opening night. During the credits, the screenwriter, Larry King, sat behind me and Dolly hissing, "You cunt! You cunt! You ruined my movie." In my best Sheriff Ed Earl style, I threw him into the aisle and yelled, "I'm gonna hit you so hard both your parents are going to die." But before I could get to him, a couple of state troopers hauled him away. It was a great start to the film; the crowd loved the opening act, and the entire movie was a smash. We made the headlines the next day with the "I'm gonna hit you so hard your parents are going to die" quote.

Following the Austin event, another star-studded premier was scheduled for the next evening in Miami. Generous, good-natured soul that I am, I offered Dolly and an associate of hers a ride on my Hawker jet; they both accepted. Here's the thing, though. When you're on a private jet, it's not a good idea to call the person who owns the plane an asshole, something her associate did at about 25,000 feet.

For some reason, we were discussing Joan Rivers, and this person and I got into an argument about whether or not she was funny. I didn't always think so, because her humor came at the expense of individuals who had no forum in which to answer her back. Unlike Don Rickles, her attacks were very personal, and I thought she had too much talent to do that.

"Well, you're an asshole," her associate said. "You don't understand what she does."

"I'm an asshole? Is that what you just said?"

I saw Dolly suddenly getting real uncomfortable. I walked into the cockpit and told the pilots to land the plane. Baffled by this sudden change in flight plan, they told me we weren't near any airports.

"I don't care," I said. "Land the damn plane right now!"

I don't know where they put down, but somehow they found this little airstrip in the middle of nowhere. There wasn't even a building in sight. A few houses and farms, otherwise it was empty and still. The door opened and I glared at Dolly's associate.

"Get out," I said.

"What?" This person didn't think I was serious.

"You should never call someone an asshole on their airplane."

With obvious, understandable apprehension, the associate walked down the aisle, turned around, and said, "Well, come on, Dolly."

"I didn't call him an asshole," she said. At which point I happily closed the door.

Although the associate never made it to Miami, I paid the price. For the next four years, Joan Rivers didn't step on a stage without cracking a Burt Reynolds joke. Personal, unforgiveable jokes. The movie made Universal lots of money, but I entered a period when what happened off the screen overshadowed everything that happened on it.

# CHAPTER
# 47

FOR THIRTEEN YEARS I WAS RANKED AMONG THE top-ten box-office stars in the world (something no one else had ever done before), but starting in 1977 I began a five-year stretch at number one that was extraordinary. It was a wonderful feeling, an honor that was beyond anything I ever thought could happen. But it also rendered stirring insight about success, particularly success in Hollywood.

At the beginning of your career, you start climbing a mountain that is actually a giant dung heap. You're trying to reach a beautiful rose garden at the top. Nobody warns you the air up there is extremely thin, so once you finally reach the summit you can't smell the flowers. Nonetheless, standing on top is something of an achievement in itself.

Still, there's a price to pay. Whether you walk

down the dung heap with some dignity or tumble down, by the time you reach the bottom you've lost your sense of smell.

By 1982, I'd picked a nice bouquet. But before starting down the mountain I made *Best Friends,* a romantic comedy about two writers who get married. My co-star was Goldie Hawn. Our first time working together, she defined the term *professional.* Soon after the shooting began, she was devastated by her father's passing, but whenever director Norman Jewison needed her she wiped her tears and nailed her lines with impeccable timing.

Few people know how bright and incredibly wise Goldie is in real life, in addition to being funny. We became terrific friends. I would have to say working with her was the best experience I've ever had with an actress. But that picture allowed me to meet another bright, sexy actress, the legendary Jessica Tandy. Thrilled to meet her, I searched her out the first day we were on the set and said, "I've always heard how sexy you are."

"Yeah?" she said, smiling. "Thank you."

I meant it.

I didn't hesitate in taking advantage of Jessica's background and experience by peppering her with questions, specifically about playing Blanche opposite Marlon Brando in *A Streetcar Named Desire* on Broadway. My curiosity about such things was insatiable. She told me that Marlon was always brilliant, never less, and added, "But there were nights when he soared to the sky and took us all with him."

That blew me away. To have one of the greatest actresses of our time say that he took her with him . . . how impressive. And Blanche is a role that's pretty hard to take anywhere. Jessica's comment made me wish I could've been on stage with them to experience that, or just to have been in the audience one of those magic nights.

Interestingly, she also told me that Jack Palance understudied *Streetcar* and was partly responsible for Marlon's famous nose. They used to box in the theater basement during lunch, and one day Jack popped Marlon good and broke his nose. Marlon came upstairs bloodied but not complaining, and because Stanley wouldn't have had his nosed fixed, he didn't either. The movie did well; not great, but very well. The song "How Do You Keep the Music Playing" was nominated and should have won, according to Mr. S. It's one of the most beautiful songs ever written for a movie.

Following that picture, I made a decision for which somebody should've punched me in the nose. No, much worse. Writer Jim Brooks asked me to be in *Terms of Endearment,* a picture he started writing back when we made *Starting Over.* Jim was making his debut as a director on *Terms,* and from the beginning he wanted me for the part that earned Jack Nicholson an Oscar. During *Starting Over,* he studied me, observed all my hair jokes, the pseudo-macho jokes I did on myself, and my laugh-at-the-world attitude toward life.

But when Jim asked if I would do it, I declined. To this day, when I tell people that story, they stare at me as if my IQ just dropped a hundred points right in front of them. Then, when I explain the reason I turned down an Oscar-winning part—in a movie that captured five Academy Awards and received five additional nominations—was because I'd promised my old friend Hal Needham I'd star in *Stroker Ace,* I see them wondering if I had a hundred IQ points to lose.

Clearly I didn't. My agent and manager should've locked me in a jail cell until I came to my senses. I didn't know how to exercise my power. But I felt I owed Hal more than I did Jim. Needham could've waited; the world wasn't clamoring to see another race-car picture.

Now I know that's the point at which I lost my sense of smell. The keen sensibility that had guided me from my Hyde Park apprenticeship to the top of Hollywood deserted me without a clue as to what I'd done until it was too late.

But the ever-shifting currents of life are like that. They're as deceptive as the Chattooga River on which we made *Deliverance.* As I had learned, there's no reason to fear the roaring white water and jagged rocks. With rapids, you can see the danger. It's right in front of your eyes. If you've done your homework, you know what's happening and what needs to be done in order to survive.

It's the smooth water that'll kill you. You relax, and when it gets calm, you have to be the most alert.

• • •

I first met Loni Anderson when both of us guested on the "Merv Griffin Show" in 1978. There was no sense at the time that anything would happen between us at some future date. I was heavily involved with Sally, and Loni was married to actor Ross Bickell, her second husband. In fact, the most memorable conversation I had that night wasn't with Loni but with her husband.

"It's rough, I know," I said. "Your wife's working and you're not. But hang in there."

Three years later, I was honored as Entertainer of the Year. The program was one of those big televised tributes that drew everyone from President Ronald Reagan and Clint Eastwood to my parents. Before dinner, Jimmy Stewart erased any doubts my father might've had about my career by saying to my dad, "Burt, I . . . I . . . I just want you to know your son's doing very well."

Loni also attended, doing promos for the network during commercial breaks. Still popular from playing the sexy blond secretary on the sitcom "WKRP in Cincinnati," she knew it was a coup to be among the A-list movie crowd. Loni mingled with the stars, but before the night ended she snuggled up beside me and in a breathy voice whispered in my ear, "I want to have your baby."

Hmmm, I thought, looking at this voluptuous woman who was poured into a skin-tight gown, that's an interesting way to say hello. Guess I still had it.

Through the grapevine, I learned that Loni had been separated from her second husband for a year and a half. During that time, she'd lived for quite a while with her "WKRP" co-star Gary Sandy, a nice guy, though after I asked Loni out, he warned her, "He has had a reputation for eating women alive."

"I'm sure he meant that as a compliment," I said with a slight laugh as Loni and I talked on the phone. "That's the image some people have, I guess."

For our first date, I invited Loni to spend New Year's with me in Florida. She arrived in Miami, where I picked her up in my helicopter. It was already dark, and through the the night sky we flew along the inland waterway back to Valhalla, my Mediterranean-style retreat. Between the

Christmas lights reflecting off the water and the boats all lit up, it was extraordinarily beautiful.

The ensuing four days alternated between the singing violins and crashing cymbals of a frenzied sexual marathon. During the nonstop animal passion, both of us, I fear, lived up to every sort of preconceived notion. And it was great. Better still, Loni seemed as if she'd wear me out before I got old.

At some point during the weekend, she asked, "What is the longest period you've ever gone without having sex?" I said something like three or four months.

"What about you?" I asked.

"I think a day or two. That's all I could stand," she said.

Then she told me that one time, back when she was working in the theater in Minneapolis, she'd been so sexually frustrated she picked a cute guy out of the crew and took him to bed. "And he almost left his wife," she said. "Can you believe it?"

And I thought I was fast.

Raised in St. Paul, she said she learned to fend for herself very early. At eighteen, in her senior year, she married for the first time. Divorced three months later she said, she discovered she was pregnant. After the birth of her daughter Deidra, whom Loni's parents raised to be quite a young lady, Loni put herself through college, taught school, and began working in Minneapolis theater. She made the move to Hollywood rather late. Married to an actor, the two of them came West. She decided to become a blond; it was a good move. About the time "WKRP" made her a star, her second marriage collapsed. She blamed career pressures for driving them apart, but also mentioned having dated a married actor, years earlier.

"I didn't know you went out with him," I said.

"Nobody did," she replied. I thought, sure, because he was married.

The affair had occurred back in Minneapolis, where he starred in a play in which she also appeared. In a nice way, I tried asking why, if she knew he was married, she went out with him. True, I joked, this actor was incredibly handsome, but he wasn't known for his great sense of humor, you know?

"He took me places," she explained, as if, Doesn't that explain it all?

The woman defied explanation. She was unlike any other with whom I'd ever been. Exhausted from four days of lust and laughs, I thought I'd hit the jackpot. I couldn't believe what a great time we'd had together. As Loni left for L.A., where she was about to finish the last season of "WKRP," I promised to see her as soon as I returned.

# CHAPTER 48

SOME GUYS HIT THEIR FORTIES AND HAVE A MID-
life crisis. I, on the other hand, fell in love. Loni and I
dated for about two months before the news leaked
to the public. In February, we were sighted vacationing at my friend Jim Nabors's beachfront home in
Hawaii. Several months later, a photographer am-
bushed us on my Carolwood property, but I managed
to bump him hard enough to ruin the film. I was
lucky that's all I ruined.

Finally, the *National Enquirer* got photos of us together, but it was only after I brokered a deal. Hearing the *Enquirer* was offering $25,000 for a shot, I
called a photographer I knew, had him take photos,
and then he sold them to the tabloid. After I gave
him some money, I donated the rest to charity.

Our relationship was a tough secret to keep.

Loni and I spent weekends together at my place in Malibu. During the week, I parked my Rolls-Royce, a car I'd always felt ridiculous driving, in front of her home in Sherman Oaks—a pretty little place with average-sized rooms and closets. She didn't need anything bigger . . . yet.

Beyond the backyard pool, Loni had a rather large guesthouse. One day I asked if she'd had it built. Not only did she answer yes, Loni described how during construction she would sunbathe in a skimpy bikini—hers were small enough that I could hide them in my ear—then laughed as she said, "It drove the workers crazy."

On another occasion, Loni took my sister shopping. As they drove down Ventura Boulevard, Loni pointed out Casa Vega, a dark, windowless, Mexican restaurant, and mentioned that at a cast party held there for one of the TV movies, she'd engaged in a furtive passion session with the leading man on a back table. Later, Loni reiterated the same story to me as if it were cute.

"How was the salsa?" I asked.

"Hot," she said. "Very hot."

I couldn't figure her out. But what was to figure out? Loni's hint of promiscuity excited me, I suppose, in exactly the same way Judy's amorality had twenty years earlier.

She was also independent. Shit, she'd raised a kid (well I'm sure she helped her folks raise her), taught school, and become a successful actress. In terms of survival skills, she was a Green Beret with battle stripes. I would come to realize I didn't have half her knowledge in that area.

And above all else were her looks. With her platinum blond hair, impossible curves, perfect skin, and blinding smile, Loni seemed to combine the best of all the great Hollywood blonds, Marilyn Monroe, Jean Harlow, and Judy Holliday. To an old high school football player like me, she was a grown-up homecoming queen whose attitude said yes, yes, yes.

She always looked impeccable. Of course, I would later realize she spent five hours in front of the mirror getting to that point even to run out to the store. It was an image she believed in more strongly than the person beneath the coloring and make-up, which was okay up to a point. For instance, I didn't think she needed to refer to herself as a "star"—to me, to our friends, or to anybody.

"Let other people call you a star," I said. "Just say you're a working actress. When you look like you do, you're going to get a million compliments anyway."

"Well, I think you have to believe in yourself," she answered.

"I'm not talking about that."

"But I don't want to run into people who think I'm a star and disappoint them," she said.

"The guy at the drugstore? I don't think he'll complain if you look clean, have on a nice dress, and say please and thank you. People generally like that."

Loni wanted to be Marilyn or Harlow, that unattainable blonde after whom she'd modeled herself—a movie star. After "WKRP" was cancelled, she wanted me to help her make the jump into film by playing one of *Cannonball II*'s two female racers. But those parts went to Susan Anton and Catherine Bach, and when I explained to Loni that I didn't want to waste the fascination we'd generate as a couple in a part that barely crossed paths with mine, she understood. As soon as casting began on *Stroker Ace,* Loni got the female lead, the Dixie girlfriend of my Southern-fried racer.

*Stroker* had some funny lines, but nothing that compared to those uttered off-screen by Kirstie Alley. Nobody knew who she was, except that she hung out with Parker Stevenson, who played one of the film's drivers, but everyone checked out Kirstie's smoldering good looks and sexy voice.

"Hi, what are you doing here?" I asked one day.

"I'm just here to fuck Parker," she said.

I became an instant fan of Kirstie's. Her ribald sense of humor kept things lively. The first night Loni and I had dinner with her and Parker, the future "Cheers" star turned to Loni and asked, "Do you ever go by a construction crew and want to take them all home and fuck them?"

Loni stalled, but was stumped in an instant. Now, I have a pretty good idea about why she was uncharacteristically tongue-tied. So was I. But maybe if I'd been more like Parker, who smiled and puffed his cigar as if to say, "What a girl," I'd be much wealthier today.

We had a great time working in Charlotte, North Carolina, but

*Stroker* suffered the same defect that plagues every racing movie—predictability. The cars went in circles, and the hero won.

AFTER *Stroker,* Loni brought over bags and her stuff each time she spent the night, until gradually everything she owned was transferred from her Sherman Oaks house into my three-million-dollar Beverly Hills fixer-upper. Barbara Streisand lived two houses away. Rod Stewart was next door to her. Gregory Peck was adjacent to the British rocker. I gave Loni a Rolls-Royce to complete the royal picture and even affectionately called her the "Countess."

I bought into the perfect-looking image Loni and I put out as a couple, but I also needed it more than anybody else. After *The Man Who Loved Women* became my second box-office disappointment in a row, the critics came gunning for me. Writing that I was on my way out—after thirteen years in the top ten—they made me out, at forty-seven, to be an old gunfighter hearing the footsteps of younger, faster triggermen named Cruise, Stallone, and Schwarzenegger.

But with Loni beside me, it didn't matter. We formed a double-bill everybody wanted to catch. *People* magazine described us as the quintessential blend of beefcake and cheesecake. Trailed by paparazzi and reporters, the Countess was convinced that she'd finally arrived. The nonstop publicity also enabled me to make believe nothing had changed in my career.

# CHAPTER
# 49

OVER THE YEARS, CLINT AND I HAD TALKED ABOUT working together, but for one reason or other—usually having to do with scripts or scheduling—we never got around to it. Finally, at the end of 1983, Blake Edwards, with whom I'd recently worked on *The Man Who Loved Women,* approached us with *Kansas City Jazz,* a Prohibition comedy he'd written especially for us. Retitled *City Heat,* both Clint and I wanted to make it.

Unfortunately, the first meeting between Clint and Blake fared only slightly better than that of Custer and Geronimo. Both are close friends of mine, but as soon as Blake brought out lunch—caviar and champagne—I knew my beer and pretzels buddy was going to fly south on this one. Imagine Stanley Donan asking Gary Cooper to tap dance. They didn't have like minds on this one, which happens. On the way back to the studio in Clint's truck, I figured we'd find another project.

"This ain't gonna work," he said.

"I got a feeling," I said, and after pausing added, "All right, we'll do something else together."

"Well, we might be able to work this out," he said.

I thought he might have reconsidered something Blake had said, found a common idea, and wanted to set up another meeting, but instead, the next day I was notified that Clint wanted to get rid of Blake and wanted my opinion of Richard Benjamin to direct. I didn't know him, other than that I'd loved *My Favorite Year*, his first outing as a director two years earlier. Blake never got over it. Thinking back on it, he had a perfect right to be very angry.

It didn't take long to figure out why Benjamin got the job. Not only was he talented, Benjamin was also petrified of Clint. Their exchanges were almost comical, many times better than the picture itself, particularly when imagining Benjamin's monotone voice and Clint's ability to say volumes without uttering a word.

Benjamin would say, "We've got to get coverage on—"

Then, in the middle of his sentence, he'd see Clint shake his head.

"No, we've got the two-shot of Burt and Clint," he corrected. "That's gonna be good. We'll move on."

Nevertheless, judging from the fight scene we shot the first night of filming, I had no doubt the picture was headed in the direction I'd hoped. Clint agreed. Set in a diner, the scene was perfect—taut, exciting, visually sharp—a great beginning, except for one major setback: I got hurt.

The injury not only affected the rest of the picture but in many, many ways altered my life forever. It was an accident. It occurred when one of the two enormous guys I had to fight, neither of whom were great stuntmen, clobbered me on the side of the head with a heavy metal chair. He was supposed to use a special breakaway chair made of balsa wood, which was how we'd done it in rehearsal.

But the guy was so strong he didn't realize he'd picked up the wrong chair. It's understandable. When a director yells, "Action," people react differently. The adrenaline really flows; they get caught up in the action; they perform on instinct. That's why a professional boxer-turned-stuntman is usually the worst person to fight. I know from experience that if he sees an opening, he's going to hit me. He knows he shouldn't make contact, but he has trained to do that his whole life.

Well, the guy who hit me couldn't have picked a worse weapon. Swinging the chair as if it were a baseball bat, he caught me directly on my right jawbone. It offered about as much resistance as an eggshell. It just shattered. Stunned, I still fell as rehearsed, but instead of getting up, I remained on the ground. With pain shooting through my head, I knew I was hurt. How badly I was hurt remained to be seen.

Staggering to my feet, I made it to a chair and told everyone I was fine, or that I'd be okay with a minute's rest. Like any crusty old football player, I figured I'd had the wind knocked out of me, but that I'd bounce back once I caught my breath. Helped back to my trailer, I lay on the bed while my brother Jim applied acupressure to ease the pain.

That didn't work. Still, despite a blinding headache, blurred vision in my right eye, and something going on with my jaw—intensely severe pain, though I could still open it—I finished out the night and left caught up in everyone's excitement. I knew if the whole picture had this much action and humor, we had a big hit. That night I took a load of Excedrin PMs and got a few hours of sleep.

When I awoke the next morning I knew, without any hesitation, that I was in deep, deep shit. My head, particularly my face and my eyes, hurt merely upon getting out of bed. In front of the mirror, I studied my face. There were no telltale marks. But I could not open my mouth without a severe stabbing pain. I couldn't chew without that pain getting unbelievably worse. Moving about, I grew incredibly nauseous, like permanent seasickness.

Excited about working with Clint, I was determined to finish the picture. I called my doctor and got Compazine pills for the nausea. I'd deal with the pain later. I knew something was royally messed up, that I'd probably need some major fucking surgery, and simply decided to drink milkshakes and pace myself—anything rather than walking away. I'd never done that before and I wasn't about to start, especially after waiting so long to work with the big guy. But it might not have been the best time to play Mr. Macho.

COMPARED to me, Clio Goldsmith, the actress slated to play my girl-friend, was worse. About a week after the accident, I arrived at the studio for a 6:30 A.M. call and saw a body lying motionless on the pavement in front of the gate. I thought some poor schmuck had tried to crash the gate or been run over. Something horrendous. Then I saw Clint stand-ing near the body and he looked pissed. I changed my mind and thought, Christ, he's gone and done it. He's finally killed someone.

Along with Gene Hackman and myself, Clint's got one of the more volatile tempers in the business. He just picks his moments better than me.

Some years earlier I'd witnessed one of those moments. He was making the second *Dirty Harry* movie when I visited him on his San Fran-cisco set. During a break, we had a beer at a nearby diner, formerly a railroad car. People left us alone, except for one woman who clearly was drunk. She pestered Clint for an autograph, waving a wet napkin in his face, until she pushed him too far.

"Please, let me finish my beer," he asked. "Then I'll sign."

"You fucking movie star," she said in a raised voice.

Having stunned the room and turned heads, she then pirouetted as only a drunk can do, picked a full beer mug off a table, and dumped it over Clint's head. I have never in my life seen anything like what hap-pened. One minute I was sitting with Clint, and the next he was Dirty Harry. Springing out of his chair and fighting to maintain control, Clint went to every person in the railroad car, grabbed the glasses out of their hands, and doused this woman. No one complained. As she began to scream, he picked her up, walked her outside, and threw her in the back of a taxi. After slamming the rear door, he kicked the side in for good measure. Then he handed the stunned driver a $100 bill.

"Drive her as far as this takes you," he said. "Then kick her out."

On reentering the diner, Clint yelled, "Who brought this broad?" Everyone turned their heads. Not a soul "brought the broad." Finally, Clint sat back down with me, and then, in typical Eastwood fashion, said, "I guess that was a little over the top, wasn't it?"

In any event, I drove around both Clint and the body lying on the

269
MY LIFE

ground, parked, and walked back to see who the hell he was staring at. I recognized the woman on the ground as Clio Goldsmith, whom Warners had brought over from Europe because of a movie called *The Gift*. She had on a mink coat and was unconscious. I thought of a song that went, "We've got a dead skunk in the middle of the road."

"What's a matter, partner?" I asked.

"She's imitating a fucking speed bump," he said.

I looked at her for a moment, then poked her with my foot to see if she was really out. Someone from Security eventually carried her away and got her medical attention.

"I have two words for you," I said to Clint.

"Yeah?"

"Madeline Kahn."


MADELINE showed up the next day. A hostage to my failing health, I loved her being there. My condition slowly started to frighten everyone, including the man of steel himself. On about the third week, Clint saw me arrive for a night shoot. My timing was off already, and I wasn't laughing and kidding around with the crew; I was just sitting till it was time to shoot. Pale and tanked on Percodan that night, I barely made it from my car to the trailer. I'd already cost the production one day, the first time in my career I'd ever missed a day, and though I felt as if I could easily follow Clio onto the pavement, I vowed not to repeat that ignoble feat. Then Clint said, "Come on, let's take a walk."

We turned a corner that put us on a street resembling a scene out of the thirties. Lit up and heavily trafficked by costumed extras, all part of one of our costly night shoots, I half-expected Clint and I to duck into a speakeasy and have him give me hell. But the storefronts were as phoney as my assertion of feeling okay.

"When you're feeling poorly, old friend, it's really the shits, isn't it?" Clint said.

I let him see the crack in my game face. But that was his intent all along—to check me out.

After circling the block, he asked somebody to get Benjamin. He always called him Benjamin, as if that was his first name. Moments later, the director came running, looking at my ashen pallor and then at Clint as if to ask, "What's wrong?"

"Benjamin," Clint said, "I'm sick."

"What?" Benjamin asked.

"I'm sick. Tell everyone it's a wrap."

Benjamin wrapped for the night and I went home and rested. His gesture, which cost thousands of dollars, was considerate beyond thanks, but Clint couldn't get sick every night, and I exhibited the strain of trying to work despite the overwhelming, often debilitating pain. My weight dropped from 200 pounds at the start of production to about 150. My face was thin, haggard, and pasty, my cheeks sunken, and my lack of energy probably made me a few enemies among the cast and Warner Bros.

With a stellar cast that included my old roommate Rip Torn, the wonderful Jane Alexander, Irene Cara, and Richard Roundtree, everyone began the picture convinced it was a surefire hit. In retrospect, somebody like Richard Brooks would've done a better job directing, if only because Benjamin is so goddamn nice. If we had stopped trying to incorporate every subplot and instead stayed with the Tracy-Gable relationship in *Boomtown,* I believe our core audience would have loved the picture. They didn't give a shit about the kissing crap as much as they wanted to watch Clint and I go at it—and then get together and beat the shit out of everyone in sight.

Ultimately, I blame myself for the picture's disappointing performance in 1984. For Clint and I to come off effectively on screen as a sort of macho odd couple, we would have had to work with equal force. His natural rhythm required me to counterpunch with a certain energy, a perceptible vigor, like Jack Lemmon going against Walter Matthau. I had to dance while he stood still, like I did the first night of shooting.

But I didn't have it, and that'll always be one of my biggest regrets, because I know what Clint and I were capable of delivering. We still could be Tracy and Gable, but no one wants that to happen these days. But just trying to stand upright and not vomit consumed all my concentration then. I wasn't interested in contributing creatively, discussing stunts, dialogue, comedic gags. Nothing. Very unlike me. I just wanted to finish the film, so I could spend whatever conscious moments I had at home battling the constant pain, nausea, and ringing in my ears.

And if that didn't work, I figured I'd just check out.

# CHAPTER
# 50

Somewhere in the dim recesses of my mind I remembered what it was like to be so young and strong that injuries didn't matter. When my knee shattered, I practically willed myself through surgery and back onto the field. I practiced a technique called Mind Tricks Body, Determination Conquers Fear. Over the years, I'd grown older, sure, but my competitiveness was as fierce as ever. My mission, as I saw it, was still to squeeze every last drop of fun out of life. I wanted to live it for everybody.

At forty-eight, few men in the world were as poised as I was to rattle the cobwebs of middle age. In any emergency I was always at my best. I had all the toys. A fleet of cars sat in the garage, a jet and helicopter waited at the airport, a yacht was docked in

Florida, and homes all across the country were poised for blowouts.

However, by early 1984, my life was quite different than I'd planned. Like a torture victim, I spent almost every day curled up in a fetal position. Soon the room had to be completely darkened or I would scream. I prayed for an end to the suffering. I thought, I can only take this for a little while. I had no idea that for two more years I would be in my own private hell. The slightest sound killed my head. If a light was on my eyes felt as if needles were plunged into them. I couldn't eat, and my inner ears were so screwed up I couldn't move without being overwhelmed by dizziness.

In May, I struggled out of bed and probably further damaged my ears by flying to Fort Lauderdale for the opening of Burt and Jack's, a restaurant I opened with a dear friend, Jack Jackson, who's kept it a success to this day. Nauseous and weak on arriving, I skipped the festivities and had to go to bed. The hotel doctor, summoned late at night, gave me a shot of morphine, which relieved the pain immediately, and then told me I needed to sleep.

"You don't know how badly," I said.

"Take one of these," he suggested, putting a small bottle on the nightstand. "It's something new. Halcion."

I popped three Halcion. Miraculously, as the Halcion started to relax me, my jaw quit hurting for the first time in months. I fell in love with something that would prove to be the only drug in my life that would rule me.

Over time I'd come to rely on those tiny blue pills, but till then I looked to Loni for strength. I told myself that each day she stayed with me was a sign that she really did love me and that I wasn't about to check out. If a woman of her beauty was still there, I had to hope for the best.

The only times I left my bed was to see a new doctor.

Examined and X-rayed by umpteen specialists, until I felt as if I'd seen every medical school graduate in L.A., I also flew to New York, Philadelphia, Boston, and Miami. Every diagnosis pointed to the same problem: a fractured tempora-mandibular joint, resulting in severe inner ear damage. But knowing what was wrong led me to discover two disheartening facts: tens of thousands of people also suffered from TMJ, and there was no real known cure. Some people actually killed themselves after years of nausea and pain.

However, every expert offered some sort of treatment, therapy, or, in some cases, solution, but for big bucks. They ranged from one guy—well meaning, I'm sure—declaring that my jaw would heal itself, to another doctor who listened to my jaw pop open and shut and then proposed an experimental operation in which he'd implant a metal hinge. Through wads of cotton and his stubby fingers, which were jammed into my mouth, I said, "Screw you."

One thing I learned about injuries from playing sports is that you want to be fixed just enough so you can play. You don't want to be sewn together so tightly you can't move. What's the use of knee surgery if you can't move your knee? I could take pain, I always could play football with pain, but the seasick feeling put me down.

After reading literature on TMJ, I discovered the operation was risky, less than a fifty-fifty chance at improvement. Furthermore, once the hinge was in, you couldn't remove it if it didn't work.

Then came the unbelievable search for a dentist who could do something to fix my bite, which was so far off it actually crushed my eustachian tube. I could no longer fly. I took trains and cars across the country to see one highly touted dentist in Philadelphia. Another time I traveled by rail to Texas. In one periodontist's office, I met a woman whose mouth was stuffed with tissue because, like me, she couldn't find her bite.

"It just isn't worth it," she said, tears streaming down her face.

"Has anyone helped?" I asked.

"No," she said.

"How about this guy?"

"No, no one," she sighed. "It's been going on for two years now. It isn't worth it."

Two days later, she took her own life. Such desperation, I found, isn't uncommon among TMJ sufferers.

Gradually, I realized that I'd joined this tortured legion of people who crisscross the country in search of relief from uncompromising pain and nausea. Motivated by hope, even the faintest glimmer, the reality is usually disillusioning. One horror story followed another. Indeed, I saw a dentist in Beverly Hills who promised results and then proceeded to shave off every one of my bottom teeth, which, by the way, were perfect.

As soon as I realized it, I went friggin berserk.

"Listen, this isn't a goddamn hedge!" I yelled. "These teeth won't grow back! Look at me! What am I going to play—Walter Brennan parts?"

"Calm down. We're going to cap them," he said. "They'll meet and you'll be fine."

He capped my teeth all right. Although they formed a straight line when my mouth was shut, they were so perfectly smooth that I couldn't chew. I couldn't even bite my way through a piece of watermelon. As a result, my mouth was transformed into an unmitigated disaster; though as events played out, I'm not sure if it was the worst in a series of catastrophes.

I believe that many a man's profanity has saved him from a nervous breakdown.

When it got to where blinding headaches, ringing in my ears, and dizziness prevented me from seeing, reading, and thinking straight, I signed over power of attorney to a new business manager. Recently hired, he was impressed with an investment my old, good friend Buddy Killian in Nashville had suggested: a new chain of restaurants called Poor Folks.

Serving Southern food like hush puppies, catfish, and iced tea, Poor Folks originated around Nashville. I jumped on board, and we expanded with great success into Florida. At the manager's urging, the chain pushed into Arkansas and Texas. Bedridden, I listened to people say, "We're expanding," and thought, This is great. If I never work again, at least I'll have something.

As the business manager poured my money into the endeavor, he also convinced Buddy the home office should be in Florida, saying that's what Burt wants. I knew nothing of this and, needless to say, wasn't in shape to be checking everything out. My deteriorating health somehow gave rise to rumors that I was dying of AIDS. I'm sure it started as a joke in some hairdresser's salon, but I did look like death with my weight loss; I'd dropped to about 138 pounds, almost seventy less than normal, and looked as if I suffered from . . . AIDS! This was not a good time to be seen. Reports circulated that I'd checked into a hospital in San Francisco, then another in Phoenix, and so on. I'd put out one fire and another would start. These hospital check-ins were done with B.R. doubles, saying I had tested HIV positive. The whole thing was very well financed.

One day Loni came home devastated. Her hairdresser had heard I was being treated for AIDS and refused to do her hair. Her manicurist also told her to take her nails elsewhere. I would have beat the shit out of him, but he could have knocked me over with his blow dryer.

Also, my friends were bailing out faster than passengers on the *Titanic*. I tried making light of it. I joked about saving money on Christmas cards. But the loss of people who I thought cared caused me a tremendous amount of emotional pain beyond the physical pain that was already killing me. If I didn't have a good enough reason to take pills, I did then. And boy was I hitting those babies big time.

Those who called regularly were Johnny Carson, Dom, Ossie Davis, Charlie Durning, Charles Nelson Reilly, Elizabeth Ashley, Alice Ghostley, Vic Prinzi, FSU Coach Bobby Bowden, Renée Valente, Jim Brown, and, of course, Dinah.

As false reports of my hospitalization continued, I knew someone had it in for me. Things were too organized. It was a fire I couldn't put out alone. At each hospital, nurses confirmed having actually seen me check in, even getting autographs from whoever was posing as me. I was beginning to believe this was a well-orchestrated plot, someone not only wanting to end my career but to make a much larger point.

But what do I do about it? Who can turn that around?

I thought, Shit, I'll call Nancy Reagan. From my bed, I dialed the White House, asked for Nancy, and got her assistant. About an hour later, Nancy called back and I explained my theory. Perhaps I was paranoid, but perhaps I was onto something. Not generally perceived as a warm, compassionate person, Nancy had always been a true, caring friend. Several hours later, she phoned again with news that made me seem not so crazy.

"We believe it could be a right-wing radical," she said, naming a political zealot.

"What?" I asked. "Why?"

"Because he's trying to float a bill that would isolate all gays with AIDS," she explained. "His organization would love a well-known heterosexual who can say he got AIDS from a doctor, someone else, saliva, kissing, mosquito bites, and so on, and thus fan the hysteria. They would love a Charles Bronson, a Clint Eastwood, or you."

Given my condition, I was the perfect target. Eventually, I tried to dispell lingering AIDS rumors by accepting a standing invitation to go on the "Tonight Show." If I had had AIDS, I would have admitted it— hopefully with the same bravery and dignity exhibited by Magic Johnson. Like him, I would've also worked like hell to educate the public and prevent discrimination. But goddammit, I didn't have it.

In my feeble state I had only once choice: to defy rumors by getting better. But then Sally Field fanned the flames in an interview in *Playboy* magazine in which she didn't deny the rumors. "There's always been something going on around Burt," she said. What the hell did that mean? What was going on around me? What was she implying? I was destroyed beyond words.

I knew of rumors that I was a homosexual. But I'm not gay. I have many gay friends just as I have black, brown, yellow, and Native American friends. But that doesn't make me anything other than who I am. And, somehow, issuing denials sounds like a putdown of those who are gay. You can't help what you are.

Then God's mighty wrecking ball found more of me to hit. The Poor Folks restaurant chain, after blazing an unprofitable trail across the South—every state but Florida—went belly-up. Almost every dollar I'd earned was gone. Had I been well and alert none of this would have happened. In fact, as badly as this was managed, the concept of Poor Folks was a good one, and with good management it would have made Buddy Killian and me more money than my whole film career would have done in over thirty-four years. Through my lawyer, I fired my business manager and hired another guy who was totally incompetent instead of dishonest and made the situation worse.

Did I need any more reason to finagle more and more Halcion prescriptions from doctors? Popping fifteen to twenty pills a day, I resided in a pain-reduced cloud, where I spent a lot of time talking to God. It was as if I was practicing a soliloquy from a play that existed only in my mind. I talked nonstop—mumbling jibberish that made sense only to me and the man upstairs. One day I just blurted, "Goddammit!"

Pause.

"Sorry, let me rephrase that. Dammit, God! Why are you doing this to me?"

Pause. No answer.

"I'm choosing to get well. I don't care how sick I am or how much time, guts, courage, and dignity I have to dig up from somewhere, I'm going to get well! Do you hear me?"

No answer.

Though these lines were delivered brilliantly, in my mind, there was no applause.

# CHAPTER
# 5 1

Something that was always unspoken when I saw other TMJ patients in dentists' waiting rooms was how far our own personal hell had gone. Following a lead from another patient, I went to the House of Hearing, a highly regarded ear clinic in L.A. operated by two brothers named House. They were the first people who truly helped me. They inserted little plastic tubes in my ears, the same kind pediatricians put in children who suffer ear infections. Instantly, my nausea and dizziness vanished.

Talk about miracles. After two years of seeing one specialist after another, I wanted to know what they really did. It seemed too simple. Wonderful, sensible people, they were also the first doctors I'd seen who weren't bothered by the AIDS rumors. They treated me like any other patient, without checking my blood, putting their hands in my mouth, and cheering when the tubes worked.

With that problem solved, I only had to get my bite back to normal. I say only. How many dentists had I seen?

God must've been watching like always, though. As I walked out of the House of Hearing, a guy stopped me in the parking lot. He apologized for bothering me, but said he'd read about my problems in various magazines and knew someone he thought who could help. Since my ordeal with TMJ was first publicized, I had received thousands of notes offering remedies and advice. I looked at each one.

"There's a guy in San Diego," he said. "His name's Gus Schwab."

"Gus Schwab," I said. "Okay."

"Don't be put off by the fact that he's got a chair that looks like it's from the 1930s. And a little tiny office. No secretary either."

"Well, I don't care about that Beverly Hills crap. What does he have?" I asked.

"Determination," the guy said. "He won't stop until you're well. And he's cured people. That's the reason they go. Everybody else gives up. But not Gus."

With nothing to lose, I made an appointment to see Gus Schwab and drove to San Diego. Initially, I was struck by the doctor's incredible honesty and his upfront manner, which was unlike virtually ever other specialist I'd seen. He showed me one picture after another of mouths he'd treated that truly looked beyond hope—before and after photos of jaws that had been broken in five places and now were as good as new. Maybe better. He was a funny, tough little guy with tremendous energy and a never-say-die attitude that was so uncommon.

Over the years, I'd been given at least twenty-five different bites and none worked. I'd worn mouthpieces, plastic molds, headgears. Doctors screamed at me not to move for twenty-four hours. I gazed at those "after" photos with envy, like Zsa Zsa Gabor window shopping at Tiffany's. A few years earlier I'd dreamed of winning respect as an actor; now my wish list was topped by a set of teeth that met where they were supposed to.

Gus practiced orthognathy, the alignment of the upper and lower jaws, something for which few dentists had either the patience or pocketbook. Because it required spending days, weeks, and, in my case, months with the same patient, it wasn't the easiest way to make money. In fact, it was almost impossible to make money. There was no revolving door, no other waiting rooms. But his work inspired confidence.

"Burt, I can help you," he said. "I can fix this. But you're gonna have to stay with me."

Thus began a five-and-a-half month odyssey of traveling to San Diego. Sometimes I stayed for a few days, other times Gus scheduled me for several weeks. Every day, for up to six hours at a stretch, I sat in his ancient chair, staring up at his I'm sure near seventy-something-year-old face. With my mouth propped open, he capped every single tooth in my head and redid them one by one.

By the time he finished, Gus had made an entirely new mouth. Even better, it worked. I'd closed my new choppers down on thousands of those tinselly sheets of silver paper until Gus was satisfied my teeth were straight and my jaws aligned. Every few months I returned, because my brand-new mouth changed ever so slightly as it settled in. I had to relearn how to bite and chew—how to, as they say, find home base.

With the pain and nausea all but gone—whatever remained was imperceptible compared to what it had been—I got completely disgusted with myself. I had finally licked problems I thought would kill me, and was close at one time to checking out! Unbeknown to everyone except Loni and perhaps a few intimates, I was hooked on drugs. To numb the pain, I received occasional shots of morphine, but more worrisome, I gobbled up to fifty Halcion a day. Yes, fifty. I know that could kill you. Well, it should have; maybe fifty-one would have.

It sounds impossible. But I had doctors scattered all around the country, from Florida to California and various cities in between. Since they couldn't send medication through the mail, I pulled the old Elvis stunt, showing up for an examination one place, then hitting another office the next day. As any junkie knows, it takes a lot of effort, money, quickness, and so-called friends to support a habit.

When it appeared Gus was going to return me to the living, my lawyer came to the house for an important meeting. Looking like a cousin to the Angel of Death, he deposited a thick, brown accordian folder on my office table and explained he'd been keeping its contents a secret until I was well enough to handle the news. But healthy or not, he couldn't postpone it any longer.

"What?" I asked.

"The restaurant chain—"

"Poor Folks," I said. "I know, it's in trouble."

"No, it's gone," he intoned.

"How bad?" I asked. "Do I have anything left? Am I broke?"

"It's worse than that."

Not only was I broke, the Poor Folks debacle left me millions of dollars in the hole. Buddy and I owed over $15 million to creditors. Basically, it was my entire worth. Nobody had wanted to tell me this news when I was flat on my back. They knew I was taking an enormous amount of pills and figured, maybe rightly so, that I'd take an extra fifty and check out. How could I handle it all?

Well, I prayed a lot, sought refuge with strong friends, and started to gain some weight back. Rather than crash and burn, I kicked myself in the ass for being hooked on the goddamn drugs. My advisers called for me to declare bankruptcy, an action I flat out refused to take. I knew the people to whom I owed money had worked hard and deserved to be paid whatever I could muster—fifty or seventy-five cents on the dollar. To do that, I had to generate income. But I couldn't do anything while I was on drugs.

In early 1986, Loni and I planned a trip to the house in Jupiter, our first in months. I decided to leave three days ahead of her and, unbeknownst to her, go cold turkey off my fifty-pills-a-day Halcion habit. I'd overcome dependencies on Valium and Percodan in the past by locking myself in the house. After one or two horrible days and nights of the shakes, sweating, and nausea, I had fought my way back. I didn't think this would be any different. Rougher, sure, but I was determined and ashamed of the way I looked.

After arranging to meet Loni in three days, I snuck into the Jupiter house undetected. Nobody knew I was home except my assistant. I grabbed a jug of water from the fridge, went upstairs, and laid on the bed. The afternoon was rough but manageable. However, by night I was rocking back and forth on the bed, howling like a wolf from the pain. Shaking, screaming, out of my mind, I started hallucinating.

Terrified, I remembered someone told me years before that my house was built on an Indian burial ground. I then became convinced that the dead Indians were slowly sucking me into a huge grave. I moved farther and farther away from the center of the bed, the spot where I imagined they were pulling. But I kept slipping into the center, then fighting to crawl away again.

During a brief moment of clarity, I decided to get the hell out and go downstairs. But there was no safe haven. In the kitchen, I began shaking like a friggin leaf. Sweat poured off me. Before I could get a drink, I was struck by a gust of hurricane-force wind and blown onto the floor. The windows were closed, the doors locked. But as soon as I got up, I was knocked down by another blast. I might as well have been in the ring with George Foreman.

I hated my fear, my helplessness. I screamed at myself at the top of my lungs.

"You sick jerk!"

I hollered at my hallucinations, at the gremlins who wanted me to stop the madness by taking another pill.

"Get the hell away from me!"

Somehow I made it through the night, but the next day, instead of getting better, I got worse. From experience, I knew that the symptoms, including the shakes and sweats and even the desire to gobble a handful of pills, should have diminished. But I was clearly getting sicker and sicker throughout the day.

And scared. Really scared. I thought about calling for help—something I thought I could never do, but I couldn't make it alone. I started to crawl toward the phone, but before I could, I passed out and lapsed into a coma.

For roughly nine hours I was stuck in a strange, hallucinatory movie, like a reel that looped continuously. It began at a delicatessen, where I sat at a table with a group of comedians, including Milton Berle, Jack Carter, and Jan Murray. We cracked jokes and ate breakfast. After awhile, a blond woman who resembled a young actress I'd known in my salad days in New York entered the scene in a sexy outfit and began dancing.

Later, a psychiatrist I saw a few times explained these as the two different sides of my personality. Wouldn't you know? The mystery behind the Burt Reynolds mystique, the yin and yang, if you will, of my appeal, which people had tried to explain for years, turned out to be a gang of Jewish comedians and a Vegas showgirl. . . . Okay.

The worst part of the hallucination required no analysis. I saw my parents being tortured inside a building. Somebody was trying to get information from them. Knowing my mother and father, they wouldn't talk. As horrible things were done to them, I attempted to rescue them. But no matter what I tried, I couldn't help, and resigned myself to their screaming in desperation.

Then, just as I reached my breaking point, the reel switched back to the comedians. It was surreal, and it went around and around until the bedroom door crashed open and my assistant and several police officers found me.

Unconscious, I was spread like a beaten rug on the floor with my eyes rolled back into my head. But I heard everything. The officers called an ambulance. When the paramedics arrived, they traded information about my jaw problem, took my vital signs, shined a flashlight in my eyes, and even discussed giving me an injection of morphine, which would've killed me. I shouted, "No! No, don't give me a shot!" But nothing came out.

Rushed to a hospital, I sank deeper into the gray netherworld that divides life and death. By the time Loni arrived, my heart had sputtered to a near standstill several times and had slowed to where the doctors suggested it might be time for her to say goodbye. Kneeling beside the bed, she whispered how much she loved me and other lovely, caring things.

At that point, I had the second out-of-body experience of my life. Hovering above the room, I observed everything that happened. Later, my doctor scoffed at such things, but then I reiterated all the conversations that went on around me, including two attendants discussing a new apartment.

"How do you remember all that?" he asked, shocked.

"I'm an actor," I said. "It's my job to remember dialogue."

At any rate, Loni got up from my bed and told the doctor about my addiction to Halcion. It was almost an afterthought. The doctor, however, jumped on it as if she'd just found the missing link.

"He took pills?" the doctor asked. "What kind? How many?"

A shot of liquid Valium jump-started my heart. After a little more, I mounted a comeback. By the next day, I was out of the coma, chatting with a wonderful nurse named Nancy. Several days later, I sneaked out of the hospital. In order to avoid vulturelike tabloid reporters, I checked out at two A.M. Later that day, I was sparring with my new psychiatrist.

"You wanted to kill yourself," he said.

"No," I argued, "I was trying to get well."

Although he didn't buy that, his primary concern was starting me on a detox program. Drastic but safe, he prescribed phenobarbital in a decreasing amount. I began by taking twenty-one pills and reduced the amount by one each day. In other words, twenty-one pills the first day, twenty the second, and down you go. He also got me a male nurse, this huge, apelike sweetheart who, he said, would be essential in getting through the tough days to come.

On the first day, I downed twenty-one phenobarbitals, felt swell, and went to sleep. I continued to feel great for the next week, until I got down to about fifteen pills. Then it started getting a little bumpy. By the time my allotment dropped to four and three pills a day, that coma looked as if it might be coming back. I didn't think I'd make it.

But my nurse handled me perfectly. He yelled at me. He called me a chickenshit when I wouldn't get out of bed. He laughed when I tried choking him and knocked me back like a fly on the wall. He forced me to walk around the tennis court. He dropped me in the pool and coerced me into swimming—one lap at first, five the next day, and finally I was pushing myself to swim thirty or more.

For the first time in years, my appetite returned. I started on spaghetti and graduated to fish, chicken, and then a big, incredibly delicious hamburger. About a month later, I'd regained thirty-some pounds. With my weight around 170 pounds and my old strength returning, I had to convince people in Hollywood that my next performance wasn't going to be the Wax Museum.

This could be an entire book about my bout and final victory over Halcion. Since that time it has become a very, very controversial sleeping pill. I understand they don't even make the tens anymore—just fives. The years, yes years, I took so many, I'm sure millions of brain cells were blown away. Thank God we have a few billion back there, I'm told. Otherwise this would be one of those books other people write about your life after you're dead.

Thank God for friends like Johnny Carson. Accepting his long-standing invitation, I made a dramatic, highly emotional, first public appearance on the "Tonight Show." I'd thought about dispelling persistent AIDS rumors by joking that I'd had only a mild case. Instead I held up a little black notebook, which, I told Johnny, contained the names of all the people who'd supported me through the long illness.

Then I opened it. The pages were empty.

"It's always nice to know who your friends are," I said, and though I may not have looked 100 percent, I heard the audience cheer and felt like I was on my way back. I felt like saying to the audience—America— as someone said in shock, "Dear God, you like me, you really like me!"

# CHAPTER 52

IN TERMS OF STAGING A COMEBACK, THE BEST AD-
vice I received might have come from Joel Silver, one
of the most influential producers in Hollywood as a
result of blockbusters such as *Die Hard*. At my lowest,
I couldn't get him to return a call, even though we'd
known each other since making *Hooper*, when he ran
errands for producer Lawrence Gordon. But as I
started to get around a bit, he called. No matter what
happened, by God he called.

Not only was I thrilled he remembered my number, I got excited when he began telling me about the
problems he was having on the Whoopi Goldberg
picture *Jumpin' Jack Flash*. In typical Joel style, he described it as a little catastrophe.

"I just fired the goddamn director," he said,
"and each day is costing me a fucking fortune."

Thinking I had a shot at the job, I met with Joel in a trailer on the *Jumpin' Jack Flash* set. Mind you, it's difficult in this business to look at someone you remember as a bright kid, a flunky, and listen to them tell you what to do as if they really know what they're talking about. But Joel's brilliant. He's positive.

"I want to give you some advice about how to get this AIDS thing behind you," he said.

"What do *you* think?" I asked.

"You've got to do an action picture where you just fucking kill guys everywhere," he said. "All over the screen."

"Very good, Joel," I said, believing the script was about to come over the table.

We continued talking about action pictures and then returned to *Jumpin' Jack Flash*. Our thoughts couldn't have been more compatible. What a guy. He knows I can direct, so I get *Jack Flash* and then we do *Kindergarten Kid*. If we were in a choir, we would've been standing next to each other. But then Joel lit my short fuse, a fuse that was shorter now than ever before, and started up an anger that was capable of killing easily. He mentioned a rumor that was going around, and it made me furious. I didn't even try to restrain my anger, since I knew for a fact it wasn't true. I grabbed Joel and out he went—through the trailer door. I stepped right over him.

"It's assholes talking that kind of bullshit who almost killed my career," I screamed.

Running toward my car, I said "hi" to Whoopi.

"I guess you won't be directing," she said.

"It's a damn good bet," I replied.

Joel hired Penny Marshall, while I stood on principle, which didn't pay as well. She was off and running. Me? Well, I got a job with two of the most talented people in the business, Robert Altman and William Goldman. God was starting to smile, and I thought I'd hit paydirt again.

It turned out I would hit something else.

WHEN I was hired to star in *Heat*, the trades handled it like any other casting notice, but for me it was a godsend. *Heat* was adapted from William Goldman's novel about a gambler who gets in trouble with the Vegas underworld. Until producer Eliot Kastner called in mid-1986, nobody in Hollywood had wanted to offer me a job. I was damaged goods, yesterday's headlines, and though the town loves comebacks and gives awards to survivors, it loathes fire sales.

I didn't realize how much anger I'd repressed over the past two years until I had to get a physical. Normally for a movie physical, a doctor drives by, yells "Cough," and stamps okay. But I took eleven blood tests. Yes, eleven blood tests! Somebody cute was saying, "I don't believe it," ten straight times. By the ninth test, I'd turned into Dirty Harry and dared them to "come and get it."

By the time *Heat* came along, I was a powder keg of anger. Perfect, if I can use it. Unless you have a constructive outlet for such fury, though, it'll come out in some horrible, uncontrollable manner. A heart attack, a fight, somewhere—it has to.

Well, the picture's main ingredients—director, writer, and star— formed a pretty volatile stew. Altman and I had been dying to work together for more than twenty years. He'd offered me *M*A*S*H* in 1969, but I'd been in the hospital, recuperating from parasites I picked up in Asia. When we met in Vegas I realized we might have to wait another twenty.

"I don't trust him," Altman said, referring to Goldman. "He smokes a pipe." Jesus, I love Altman, loved him then and still love him now. But William Goldman smokes a pipe! Who cares?

"Listen, Bob, you and I have known each other for a long time," I said. "What the fuck has that got to do with the fact he's a great screenwriter?"

"I can tell," he said. "He's one of those guys with the pipe and the sweater who won't change a goddamn word."

"Well, what do you want to change?"

"I like to improvise."

"I know," I said. "So do I. But only when it's shit. This is good."

The crux of our discussion concerned a clash of styles, not anything personal, but unfortunately this difference surfaced pretty late in the game. On Friday night in my suite at the Sands Hotel, two days before shooting was scheduled to begin, Altman continued airing his concerns in a now-infamous meeting with Kastner. It ended with Bob hitting the producer with a beer bottle. If I'd done that, it would've cost me $9 million. Bob said, "Sorry, Burt, but I can't work with this asshole."

This left the picture without a director, and Eliot vowing to stay on schedule.

"We've got the crew on Monday," he said.

"We aren't going to get anybody," I countered. "What self-respecting director's going to step in without any preparation, take another director's locations, cast, script changes, and so on? Unless he's desperate for a picture. Desperate!"

But Kastner had already lined up Dick Richards. I hadn't heard of him. With evident sarcasm, I asked if he was a TV director.

"No," Eliot said. "He did some really great movies."

"Which ones?" I asked.

*The Culpepper Cattle Company,"* he said.

It was among my favorite westerns. But I also knew that Hal Needham had directed 75 percent of the picture. I'd also heard that one of the guys on the film had a terrible fistfight with the director.

"He also did the remake of *Farewell My Lovely,"* Kastner said of the film he also produced.

"Great," I said. "Mitchum hit him. Not only hit him, but he dragged him onto Pacific Coast Highway and said, 'Let's see if you can direct traffic.' "

"Well, he also did a film with Hackman and Catherine Deneuve," Kastner said.

"Say no more," I said. "Hackman hit him, right?"

"Yes," he admitted. "And so did Deneuve."

"Catherine hit him, too?"

I repeated this fine résumé. Three pictures, four punchouts. Sounded lovely to me. Eliot then pointed out that Richards hadn't been hit on his last movie. I asked who starred.

"Martin Sheen," he said.

"Martin Sheen?" I asked incredulously. "He thinks Hitler is a good house painter. Martin's like Jesus. He wouldn't hit anyone. Listen, I'll make it easy. I don't want to work with someone who's been hit by almost every actor in the business."

Needless to say, budget considerations won out and Richards showed up on Monday full of enthusiasm and ideas. He couldn't refrain from talking—talking to everyone. But everyone heard a different Dick Richards. Sweet to the producer, he criticized extras, verbally abused crew members, and took advantage of others in all kinds of bully ways. He made the wardrobe lady his private clothes cleaner. I hated his type, and told him so.

I watched him slowly undo the cast, including Peter MacNichol and Howard Hesseman. Then one night he started in on me. It was during a scene in which the boy in the movie gets killed and dies in my arms. I wanted to play it exactly as Goldman had written, going for the most impact. However, Kastner and Richards began the trouble by debating whether or not it would be good for the box office if the kid died. Then Richards wanted to shoot the scene in a convoluted manner that veered entirely from Goldman's intent.

Unable to make up his mind what he wanted, Richards decided to shoot it two different ways. That was total bullshit. It was easy to know which ending Richards was going for. I took offense. Was he going to print both? Was I going to have at least an opinion?

"Let's not play games here," I said. "We disagree, but let's work it out to where we're both happy."

To make a long argument short, he got in my face and jabbed me with his finger on my chest. I counted four times. Others said it was only twice. Regardless, I didn't realize how much anger I had stored in me. The punch traveled only about eight inches—from my chest to his chin. He was about four inches taller than me. But it was like a bazooka, loaded with all the frustration and rage of the past two years.

I didn't even see him fall. Assuming we'd take five, I just turned and walked back to my trailer. A few minutes later, the makeup guy and assistant director came and asked what I wanted to do. Irritated, I sighed "Oh shit, he was wrong but you can't hit people anymore," and walked back to apologize. Richards, though, was still out. In fact, not only was he splayed on the pavement, the crew had outlined him in chalk like a body at a crime scene.

I thought he was dead. At which point, Vegas being Vegas, the two off-duty police officers who guarded the set approached me.

"When he threw that punch at you," one of them said, "you had no choice but to—"

"It's okay guys," I said. "I appreciate it. But I nailed the asshole."

Later that night I went to Richards's hotel room to make another apology. He was having dinner with his only two allies on the picture, Kastner and the art director. Kastner did not look good. I didn't waste time saying I was sorry.

"I lost it," I said. "No matter what you said, I shouldn't have hit you."

"What are you going to do about it?" Richards asked so smugly I sensed he'd rehearsed this moment.

"What do you want me to do about it?"

"I want a car," he said.

"A car." Well, I thought, just keep your head, old cock. "Okay. What kind of car?"

"A Jaguar," he said.

"Okay." Now just keep your head, old cock—so what if it's a forty-five-thousand-dollar car?

"A yellow one."

"Okay, a yellow one." Keep your head, old cock.

"And I want a ribbon around it. And I want you to give it to me in front of the crew."

Once again, they had to separate me from Richards. I wanted to hit him so hard he'd have to roll down his socks to take a shit. I was trying, I explained, trying very hard to be nice, but he was such an asshole it was almost impossible. However, the next day I ordered his Jag, a yellow one, and apologized in front of the crew. As soon as I finished, he disappeared. Later, two Teamsters reported having seen him take a swan dive off a prop truck. After being helped up, he complained of headaches. He also couldn't see.

Why didn't he have eye trouble after Mitchum or Hackman hit him?

I said, "Oh, shit, here it comes."

Richards went back to L.A. Production shut down until Kastner got a director to finish up a lackluster movie that nobody—neither those in it nor those who went to see it—gave two shits about. It was all there—

Bob Altman and a William Goldman script. And all of Hollywood waiting to say, "We're sorry we said you were dying."

In the meantime, I received a call from noted L.A. attorney Howard Weitzman, who now represented Richards. As soon as I heard Weitzman's voice, I knew Mr. Richards was going for the major bucks.

"I'm a big fan," Weitzman said. "But you're on the other side and we have to work this out."

My lawyers were O'Melveny & Meyers, a wonderful, staid firm. They had been handling my stuff for twenty years. The problem was, Mr. Weitzman proceeded to kick their ass. My punch ended up costing me and my insurance company $500,000. It was the costliest one-punch fight in my history. Hell, for $500,000, Tyson can have two on me! If nothing else, though, my performance both on and off the screen quashed any doubts about my physical health. That's the good news. The bad news is, I was suddenly perceived as a crazy, moody mental case. Gee, it felt good to be back in the movie business.

# CHAPTER
# 53

Y OU'RE ONLY AS GOOD AS YOUR LAST PICTURE. BUT
not your last party, and it certainly didn't take into
account picture charades, the fast-paced, wildly animated game I hosted at my house on Saturday nights.
On those evenings, my parties were downright sensational. Carol Burnett and Alan Alda are very competitive. They are both loaded with cleverness and ability.
But can you imagine them going up against the brilliant Orson Welles?

Talk about wild. For years my house was a mag-
net for weekend fun among a closeknit group that
included Mel Brooks and Anne Bancroft, Carol and
Dom DeLuise, Ricardo and Georgina Montalban,
Robert Preston, Esther Williams, Bette Davis, Betty
White, Charles Durning, his wife Maryann, and others. After dinner, we divided up into teams, the men

versus the women, and played a highly competitive game of charades.

We began drawing because of Fred Astaire. Too shy to get up in front of everyone, he preferred to watch. But one night as he was about to pass the bowl of titles, I pulled out a blackboard and said, "Draw it."

"What?" he asked.

"Draw it. Draw the title," I said. "If you're too shy to act—draw!"

Fred selection was *The Fleet's In*, the 1942 Dorothy Lamour musical. Always the perfectionist, even at play, he drew one tiny sailor after another. They were so minuscule that people got up from their chairs and crowded around the blackboard. The guesses flew. Unfazed, Fred took his time making sure his sailors were lined up as straight as a chorus line. Then Carol Burnett screamed, *"The Fleet's In!"*

From then on, we drew our charades. No one was as fiercely competitive as Bette Davis, who hated playing games—or so she claimed. She'd try to stay out of the screaming fracas, pretending not to be interested, but somehow Bette always found herself in the middle of the fray. In fact, you knew the night reached a crescendo when her famous voice rose above the din of guesses and shrieked, "Goddammit, Orson, you fat bastard! Keep drawing! Keep drawing!"

I never knew why Bette liked me, but in the last few years of her life I frequently took her places. I adored her stories, but the one I remember the most was the night she asked me to meet her at a party at Bob Aldrich's house. That afternoon the news was out that Joan Crawford had passed away. I was talking to a movie critic from *Playboy* magazine when I noticed a slight commotion in the room. Then, suddenly, people parted, as they did when she came into the room, and, as always, this tiny woman made a beeline for me.

"Well, the cunt died today," Bette said.

"Ah, Bette, I don't think you know this gentleman," I said, worrying about her frankness in front of a journalist. "He writes for *Playboy* magazine, Sex in the Cinema."

Bette immediately said, "But she was *always* on time."

I had heard that Merv Griffin sold the rights to the game show his wife thought up, "Wheel of Fortune," for a staggering amount of money.

"Oh, yeah," I said. "How much?"

"Something like $175 million."

"Really," I said.

Then I sprinted to the nearest phone and told my lawyer I had invented a game show. Calling my Saturday night parlor activity "Win, Lose or Draw," I called my old friend Bert Convy and together we pitched it to various companies. Merv indicated why he's so rich by offering to produce the show in exchange for 80 percent ownership. That kind of business advice I'd already gotten. Game-show production giant King World passed, but the King Brothers, who I like a lot, asked if I'd host a talk show instead. I passed. (Oprah didn't.)

Finally, with Bert as co-producer, "Win, Lose or Draw" sold to Disney, who turned it into a day- and nighttime favorite that ran for three years. It made a nice sum of cash for everyone involved. Millions of dollars—but not enough to help me.

Money woes stayed with me. This is another book, but I got rid of some properties, and I grabbed whatever pictures were offered. Admittedly films like *Malone, Rent-a-Cop,* and *Switching Channels,* all made between the end of 1986 and the middle of 1987, boosted my bank account. But they were making me part of an endangered species: an old actor. However, there are times when you can be artistic, and times when you have to be realistic.

This was one of the latter, but I never would've predicted the effect it had on me. Like a goal-line stand, I found out what I was made of. At age fifty, I realized life wasn't all about money and toys. They sure were fun, but they didn't guarantee happiness.

I had the past to prove it. I found myself pondering and yearning for the stability, companionship, and richness that comes from marriage and a family. Things you can't buy.

ALTHOUGH raised a Baptist, I was never formally religious. I just always believed in God. I enjoyed talking with God. As one-sided as the conversations were, I still enjoyed replenishing my soul by praying to a higher, mightier authority, a spiritual Father who knew the answers to questions we couldn't explain.

Beyond the house and barn at my ranch, beyond the screening

room, plane hangars, and recording studio, I envisioned an old-fashioned chapel. It was the perfect spot, toward the lake and under a grove of enormous shade trees whose branches hung and turned in the breeze like a corps of ballet dancers. I noticed deer took sanctuary from the heat there, and it seemed a place where I might, too.

In 1985, I began construction of the chapel—a place where I'd either die or get married, depending on my health. A year later, it appeared likely Loni and I would recite our vows there. Both of us thought we had a promising future together. Her timetable was a little different from mine, but that was okay with me.

I had a great excuse for waiting. I didn't want to have the ceremony any other place than the chapel. But my financial state slowed work on it to a snail's pace. Whenever Loni raised the subject, which was often, I gestured toward the unfinished chapel and said, "When it's done."

On the other hand, I couldn't wait to become a parent. In my fifties, I felt that time was running out. If I had a boy, I wanted to be able to throw a football, hit baseballs, and participate in the mayhem of having a little Tom Sawyer. If I had a girl, I wanted to be in good enough shape to send a warning to all the boys in the county by at least looking as if I was capable of beating the shit out of the first one to ask her out.

Loni supported my dream. During my illness, I don't remember if we slept together, and if we did I wouldn't have known it. But Lord knows, by the end of 1986, with the return of my strength, we tried. And tried. And tried. Until I felt I was back in spring practice going through two-a-day sessions.

Nothing happened. Since she'd had a child, albeit twenty-one years earlier, Loni used that as proof she had no problem conceiving and convinced me that I must have had some mechanical problem. If that was a possibility, I wanted to know—that's how serious I was about becoming a parent. I saw a fertility specialist, where a nurse handed me a *Playboy* magazine and pointed me toward the bathroom.

"We need a specimen," he said.

"You've gotta be kidding. Isn't there another way?" I asked.

"You can do it at home," he said. "You can have sex with your wife in the morning and run the semen over here immediately."

All the guys sitting in the waiting room applauded as I said, "I'll use my own material, thank you!"

For the next week and a half, Loni and I had sex every morning and then I ran my little sample into Beverly Hills as the office opened. The doctor found my sperm was not only normal, but strong enough to do the job. However, Loni, who turned forty in 1987, still never got pregnant. Not even a false start.

Shortly after Christmas, 1987, our luck changed. We got news of a pregnancy, not Loni's. A local politician, someone who is still one of my dear friends and who remembered I'd talked about adopting a child, called and said she'd been contacted by a teenager who was about a month pregnant and definitely wanted to give the baby up. This could possibly be the best present I had ever received.

"It's too early to tell if it's a boy or a girl," my friend said.

"I don't care," I said. "It doesn't matter."

"Burt, the reason I called is this young lady has never been on drugs, has a great relationship with her parents, and expects to have the child by natural childbirth."

"That's great," I said. Then kidding, "Too bad the dad isn't a pro football player."

There was a long pause. Then she burst out laughing. "Burt, he's called B.R. by his teammates because he looks so much like you, and he is a very well known professional athlete. This was a one-night stand to him. So he's already out of the picture. He may look like you, but the last thing this young man wants is to be accused of being the father of this young lady's child. She wants to give the child a life—and then move on to her own."

I was standing there with tears running down my face.

Over the next few weeks I found out skeletal details of the mother's background. Young and healthy, she was both drug and trouble free. She lived with her father. A while later, I even saw a picture of her. Knowing Loni as I did, I returned the photo before she saw it. I feared she'd walk away if she didn't approve of the girl's looks.

The opportunity and excitement accelerated our race toward the altar. Two actors living together didn't give the most stable impression in the world, and the birth mother could change her mind about giving up the baby until right after its birth. But if marriage bettered our chances, and everyone said there was no doubt it would, then we'd get married. Loni and I were headed in that direction anyway.

Loni also deserved it, considering what she put up with while I was sick. She stuck around when most smart women would have left. If she stayed because she became rich by staying, who knew? From what I saw, Loni displayed grit and stick-to-itiveness, an important ingredient in any marriage. She seemed truly devoted in a long-lasting, loyal, for better-or-worse sense.

Some people tried opening my eyes in very public ways. Goldie Hawn, for instance, came right out and said that Loni wasn't right for me. She described a lunch she'd had with Warren Beatty at the NBC studio commissary when Loni came over to their table. Without taking her eyes off Warren, she'd said, "Hi, Goldie, remember me?" and then proceeded to tell Warren that she'd had a *Bonnie and Clyde*–type suit when she was in school.

"Too obvious for you, B.R.," Goldie said.

I thanked her and then, of course, married Loni.

After six years of what appeared to be the most publicly and privately devoted courtships on record, our engagement just seemed to happen on its own. We talked about it, laughed, backed out, cried, consulted our agents, and got out our calendars. But I don't remember proposing. I once asked my buddy Joe Namath if he actually remembered proposing to his wife (a beautiful lady, by the way), and he couldn't remember having done it either.

Joe Willie and I decided women have this magic power. It's extraordinary.

The real clue that three decades of bachelorhood were about up came when our business managers began negotiating a prenuptial agreement. I had only two real priorities: I was adamant she couldn't touch Valhalla or the ranch. It would've killed my father to lose any part of the ranch. I didn't care about anything else. Little did I suspect this lady would try to do a little rewriting on the Magna Carta.

In the event of a split, Loni's and my assets—my treasured western art collection, for instance—would remain separate, including any money we earned during the marriage. Since Loni was a millionaire on her own, we also agreed there'd be no alimony.

There was one loophole. Paragraph 23. If we had a child, it read, Loni could void the entire agreement. I didn't think it included adoption, and after I learned it did, we were too close to getting the baby for me to dare jeopardize our getting that kid. I'd leave it to the Big Guy upstairs. If we started squabbling and the mother found out and took the baby back, I would've died.

I truly believed Loni was going to be a devoted, caring mother. I thought her daughter Deidra had turned out wonderfully. She was a straight-A student, a graduate of UCLA, and a teacher. How could anyone argue with that?

In the early spring, after three years of procrastination, the chapel was completed. Suddenly, my old excuse was no good. A wedding date was set for mid-June. Since Loni was busy shooting *Whisper Kills,* one of three consecutive TV movies she made, I planned the event, including the design of her wedding ring—a seven-karat, canary-yellow diamond encircled by smaller diamonds. Once a director, I guess, always a director.

Somehow we managed to send out invitations—to such friends as Ann-Margret and Roger Smith, Dom and Carol DeLuise, Robby Benson and his wife Karla DeVito, Jim Nabors, Bert Convy, and my neighbor Perry Como, as well as two dozen apprentices from the Institute for Theater Training—and keep details of the pending nuptials a secret. Still, word leaked. One Palm Beach cafe offered a Loni Burger "stacked" and a Burt Sandwich—"ham with a lot of lettuce and adorable buns."

WITH an armada of helicopters buzzing overhead, Jess Moody, a Baptist minister, commenced the early afternoon ceremony, the same time my parents had wed. I'd known Jess since he was my preacher in Florida, and now he was in L.A., so I brought him and his wife, Doris, down. Vic Prinzi reprised his role from thirty-five years earlier as my best man. Loni's daughter and sister Andrea served as her attendants. As Jim Nabors sang the "Lord's Prayer" and "Our Love Is Here to Stay," I heard Perry Como, who followed with a song, say, "Boy, he's loud."

Dr. Moody, like any great preacher, went on a little long, especially for my mother's taste. Mom, God love her, had broken her hip for the third time. In poor health, she never left her bed, but for this occasion she was wheeled to the front pew. Finally, as Jess arrived at the actual vows, my mother, in a voice louder than Jim Nabors's, said, "Good, let's get on with it!"

I broke up and dropped the ring. I don't know why, but Mom's comment struck my funny bone and I got the giggles. Loni glared.

As the crowd flowed out of the chapel, the helicopters, which had been hovering above, zoomed in, the photographers and their tele-photo lenses hanging out the side like the gunners in *Apocalypse Now*. They were so loud and disturbing I had to talk my father out of shooting them down.

"Gimme five minutes," he said. "I'll get rid of 'em."

"Not a good idea, Dad," I advised. Actually, it was.

We then joined everyone for the reception in the helicopter hangar, which was decorated with a forest of plants, flowers, and a home-style buffet overflowing with caviar, beef Wellington, shrimp, crab, salmon, ham, biscuits, and chocolate fondue. Those who had room could dive into a three-tiered, heart-shaped wedding cake, topped by a couple who looked just like us.

"I'm a very lucky man," I said, raising a glass of champagne. "I married my best friend today."

"I feel like Cinderella," Loni replied, daubing her wet eyes. "I married Prince Charming."

Later, she relayed a similar thought to my assistant, although off in a corner, away from eavesdroppers, she added, "I'm the first woman who could win his kingdom."

By the time of our planned getaway at dusk I couldn't help but anticipate the start of our honeymoon. To divert the paparazzi, Ann-Margret and Roger climbed into my black-and-white helicopter, branded on the side with a bright red BR, and sped off. In Miami, they were met by about fifty photographers, who let out a mix of groans and laughter when the two decoys stepped off the aircraft.

Meanwhile, Loni and I climbed aboard my friend Bernie Little's jet copter and dashed to Key West, where we transferred to his opulent 125-

foot yacht, the *Golden Eagle,* and set out on a leisurely, romantic cruise around the Bahamas. Any notions I had of amour were erased by rough seas, which caused Loni to get horrifically sick. Even though we turned back and had a decent time sailing the calmer waters in the Keys, it was a bad omen.

# CHAPTER
# 54

I WAS A BASKET CASE ALL THROUGH AUGUST, THE
month our baby was due. Worse than any husband of
a pregnant wife. The actual date was August 31. I
couldn't wait. There weren't hallways long enough
for me to pace at night. Used to calling the shots, I
drove myself crazy, worrying about things I couldn't
control, like whether the birth mother would have
the child and not want to give him up.

My nervousness was compounded by the fact
that I was in Portland, Oregon, playing a sixty-five-
year-old character for the first time in my career.
*Breaking In*, a John Sayles–penned comedy that was
later honored at the New York Film Festival, was
being directed by the internationally respected Scot-
tish director Bill Forsyth. On the phone constantly, I
talked to everyone I knew in Florida and L.A., think-

ing they might hear something before me. I had a baby store deliver about $2,000 worth of stuff—in both blue and pink.

Finally, I was paged at the hotel late on the twenty-eighth. The woman who arranged everything was on the phone.

"Burt?" she said.

"Come on, Mary, tell me what it is?" I said anxiously.

"You've got a little linebacker!"

For the first time in my adult life I was speechless. I put the phone down and cried. When I talked with Loni a few moments later, I cried all over again. And I repeated the drill when I called my folks and told them about Quinton—named after the famous journalist Quentin Reynolds, who reported war news on the radio when I was a boy, and after one of my favorite times as an actor playing Quint on "Gunsmoke."

With my prayers finally answered, I flew back to L.A. to meet my son, who arrived three days old.

Prior to that, I thought all babies looked like little generic sacks of oatmeal. Big ears and bald heads. Yet their parents would always gush, "Isn't he the most beautiful baby you've ever seen?" Well, frankly, no, I'd think. They all look alike. I had no understanding how parents loved so blindly.

Then Mary handed me Quinton. Without even thinking about the words as they came out of my mouth, I cradled him in my arms, tucked in the corners of his swaddling blanket, patted his gorgeous head of black hair, looked up, and said to Loni and Mary, "Now that's a beautiful baby." They laughed as I added, "With that head of hair, he looks a quarter Cherokee. Like his pop."

"He even has your sideburns," Loni chimed.

We're so much alike, friends have sworn I must've secretly had someone carry a baby with my sperm. Maybe someday I'll use that story. In fact, I started worrying what I'd tell Quinton about his real parents even before we got him. I once asked David Steinberg, the father of two adopted girls, what he told his kids about their birth parents.

He said in a tone so straight both of us broke up, "They drowned."

I didn't know I could love anyone as much or as deeply as I did Quinton. The first afternoon he was with us I sat in a rocker and gave him a bottle. That night I tucked him in bed beside me and fed him throughout the night. Loni, reminded of past hardships, I think, wasn't crazy about the thought of changing dirty diapers. But not me. I didn't know how domestic I was until my friend Victor showed me how to diaper, bathe, and feed.

"Don't be scared to lift him," Vic instructed.

"Well, I don't want to drop him," I said.

"What does he weigh? Seven pounds? Pretend he's a football."

Something I understood. I quickly got to where I held Quinton like a ball and swung him around with confidence. My dad was worse. As soon as Quinton was old enough, he bounced him on his cowboy boot. Once Quinton learned how to kiss, they went at it like they'd discovered something new.

"What's wrong with this picture?" I said. "Dad, what happened when I was a kid? Was something wrong? Did I smell?"

"Possibly," he said. My dad looked at me in a way I'd never seen before but nonetheless understood. It was his smile, the sparkle in his eye, his obvious, overwhelming love for his grandson, and his pride in both of us. In that look, I heard all the words he'd never been able to say to me over the years, everything I'd wanted to hear. After fifty-two years, we finally began to have the kind of close, father-son relationship I'd dreamed about since I was a boy, and the catalyst was my son Quinton.

Quinton had us all mesmerized. He received a standing ovation when he took his first steps at ten months. Two weeks later, he uttered his first word—"Da-da." The biggest thrill of my life occurred when Quinton walked into a room full of people and picked me out.

"Dada," he said. "I love you."

I might not have been a matinee idol any longer, but I was Number One in this young man's eyes. Such unconditional love had an instant effect. Just picking my son up made all my problems disappear. He forced me to mature, something others had tried to get me to do but failed. He didn't care what I did for a living, that I was famous or lived in a big house. He loved me just because I was his dad.

An interesting thing happened as I tried living up to such a lofty responsibility. As my comfort grew with Quinton, I also became more comfortable with myself. My life took on greater clarity and focus. I quit searching for father figures and finally grew up. I faced myself and became a man.

Loni, it appeared to me, had a somewhat more difficult time adjusting to motherhood again. We ran through a whole corps of nannies, all of whom complained to me in private that Loni, who didn't rise from bed till eleven, refused to help. Only when I came home, they said, would she take Quinton, hold him in her lap, and present a quaint little picture of domesticity.

I got the sense she didn't know what to do with a little boy. Like every toddler, he constantly fell and bumped into things, collecting his share of scrapes and bruises. I found myself, as if a sage old father, explaining to Loni that this was part of raising a boy. Boys were physical. He was going to get bloody noses.

"You can't fall apart," I said. "You have to realize that Quinton's like every other boy. You're going to tell him not to climb a tree, and he's going to promise he won't climb it. But as soon as you walk away, he's going to shimmy up as high as he can, and then he's going to fall."

"Then he won't climb a tree," she said. "Yes, he will," I said.

"And what about when he plays football?" I asked.

"He won't play football either."

Stating that Quinton wasn't going to be allowed to play football was sacreligious. As soon as he was born, he received a full four-year scholarship to Florida State. I'd already informed the school's legendary football coach Bobby Bowden to pencil in the name Quinton Reynolds at halfback for the 2006 season.

"We've got awhile to go before we get to that place, Loni. And I might be in a walker by then. But I guarantee you, that boy's going to play whatever the hell he wants to play." The argument was premature.

At the end of the year, I signed with ABC to star in the private-eye series "B.L. Stryker"—six two-hour Movies-of-the-Week, most of which I directed. They were also sold overseas as features, and rotated on the wheel in the U.S. with *Kojak, Columbo,* and one other two-hour movie. The network agreed to shoot them in Florida, which enabled me to sell Carolwood and move to Jupiter full-time.

Not only was the business arrangement ideal, so was the change in lifestyle. I painted clouds on Quinton's bedroom ceiling. He and I began our days together at the breakfast table. He waved goodbye as a helicopter picked me up at the dock and shuttled me to work. Nights were reserved for bedtime stories. For Quinton's first birthday, celebrated at the ranch, I gave him a hand-crafted rocking horse with his name carved on both sides.

An exquisite piece of craftsmanship, it was, I know, an embarrassing splurge at $10,000, but I figured Quinton would pass it down to other generations of Reynolds's. The day it was delivered I didn't have my checkbook and asked Loni to write one. Five days later my business manager received a call from her business manager, who went berserk, screaming that Loni's account hadn't been repaid and that she was always bailing me out. The rudeness with which it was handled and the letters that were Fed-Exed were unbelievable.

"What the hell's going on?" I asked her. "We're married. Don't married people do stuff like that? Or is my money yours and your money yours?"

"Don't worry," she assured me. "You're right."

I wired her business manager $10,000 and told him maybe he should look at some "loans" that were never "repaid," nor asked to be, from my side.

Loni and I spent lots of time together. While I worked, she made an impression at the boutiques along stylish Worth Avenue in Palm Beach. At night, we ate at my Back Stage restaurant or at Camanella's in Palm Beach. In 1990, I sold the dinner theater, but I still taught midnight classes at my Institute for Theater Training, where Loni also lent encouragement to the apprentices.

Without the big expense of a home on the most exclusive street in Beverly Hills and other cutbacks stemming from the move, my financial burdens lifted so that I started to breathe. If "Stryker" had gone five years, I would've had it made. But after the second season, the network cut the number of episodes from six to four, which wasn't cost-effective for me. In other words, they forced me to pull the plug. I was an actor out of work again—living in Florida. Not an ideal situation.

# CHAPTER
# 55

Wнат do you do after you've killed thou-sands of people in the movies and hunted down every conceivable bad guy a private eye could ever chase on TV? I'd never done a four-camera show, but every-body who knew my sense of humor always told me, "Boy, are you made for a live audience." You're al-ways hot in Hollywood at what you've never done.

Apparently the industry agreed. Flooded with of-fers from top producers wanting to schedule meet-ings, I finally tested the landscape with two writer-producers, one from "Designing Women," a show whose Southern sensibility and crisp writing I enjoyed. The other was Hugh Wilson, who I liked very much and whose writing I loved. Hugh envi-sioned me and Alex Rocco as partners in a restaurant situated on the wrong side of an island in the Bahamas.

"I don't think I want to be chasing bikinis down the beach," I said. "I love you guys, but there's got to be a time when I don't do that. I've got to play my age. I doubt I could catch them anyway."

I had lunch in a tiny Italian restaurant with the husband and wife producing team of "Designing Women," Harry Thomason and Linda Bloodworth-Thomason. She had created the show, and together they formed one of the more influential, dynamic partnerships in the business. In other words, they got things done.

"Let me say what I'd like to see you do," Linda started.

She spoke and Harry listened. It was part of their act. Her bad cop to his good cop. I'd get to know it well.

"What's that?" I asked.

"A Jimmy Stewart kind of thing," she said.

She caught me off-guard right away. I'd imagined the same thing, but it's not something you come out and say.

"That's interesting," I said.

"Do you like the name Wood Newton?" she asked.

"I guess so," I said.

As she laid out the scenario, I detected a familiar ring. My character ran a small-town newspaper in the South. Kind of Andy Griffith but with his own printing press. I'd done my homework, though. She'd written a similar script for Hal Holbrook, which had been pitched to CBS. But the network had wanted Hal to do a pilot and he didn't feel with his stature that he needed to audition. So she had a script laying around.

"Look, I don't play lawyers or journalists," I said. "Number one, I don't like them. And number two, that's not who I am. My audience is Middle America. I play blue-collar guys."

"So what do you see?" she asked.

"If I wasn't an actor, I'd probably be a football coach."

Linda thought for a moment. She looked at Harry, who was a smiling blank wall.

"I don't know," she said.

"Wait a minute," I said. "The guy sitting next to you coached football for fifteen years in Arkansas." Then I started in on Harry. "What if

I play a coach in Arkansas? It's the South, where football is a religion. But I never win a game.''

For the next ten minutes I riffed on about the character, detailing how Newton had been a local football hero who'd returned to the scene of past glories after playing pro ball. I also fleshed out the small town. I suggested a Charlie Durning–type character. Then all three of us talked about how every small Southern town had a black-owned barbecue place, where you got great barbeque and very good philosophy on life.

"Wouldn't Ossie Davis be great in that part?" I said.

"Yeah, we love that," Linda said.

By the time dinner finished, we'd fleshed out the entire town, characters, and named a dream cast of actors that included Elizabeth Ashley, Hal Holbrook, and Marilu Henner. No question we had a show the network would buy, which they did in a blink. The next hurdle was casting the various roles. The money for that kind of cast was a dream, but we began in earnest about a week later when I was watching the Tony Awards. As Michael Jeter, who won for *Grand Hotel*, gave his acceptance speech, I called Linda and Harry and told them to turn on the TV.

"There's our Barney Fife," I said.

Ironically, Durning also won a Tony that night for *Cat on a Hot Tin Roof.*

"Maybe we should think about him for the Durning part," Linda said. "But we'll never get him."

I said, "You'll never know unless you ask." Durning, who works whenever he wants, asked what time we wanted him and where. Ossie, dear old friend Ossie, one of the most respected talents in the business, came on board, too. Ann Wedgeworth (my suggestion for Durning's wife), a friend since she was eighteen years old, pregnant, and married to my New York roommate Rip Torn, said yes. Hal, Marilu, and Jeter signed on. Wonderful, wise, and crazy Elizabeth agreed, too.

"Hollywood is a sea of assholes," she told Linda. "But Burt Reynolds is an island. I'll do it!"

•  •  •

I'M also someone who enjoys surprises. After deciding to do the series, I leased a fifteen-thousand-square-foot mansion on Mulholland Drive without mentioning a word to Loni. It had the feel of a castle, with breathtaking views, marble floors, Hearstian fireplaces, and high ceilings. In the backyard, a pool and spa gave way to a tennis court, and beyond them, steps led to a waterfall and gazebo designed for afternoon tea. I felt certain the Countess would be as pleased as I was.

She reacted coolly at first because she didn't help pick the house. Then she saw the bedroom—two separate TVs, one on one side of the bed and one on the other, and enough closet space for Lana, Doris Duke, and Imelda Marcos together.

"It's fifteen thousand square feet," I explained.

"I love it," she said.

The house was completely furnished when she arrived, something else I'd taken care of. But before we moved in, there was still work to do. It took three days just to unpack and arrange Loni's clothes and shoes. Her closet, the size of a small home, also included a marble bathtub so big Quinton could've taken swimming lessons in it. I unpacked everything myself, hung all Loni's clothes and put away all her shoes before she ever saw the place.

By the end of the week, we were pretty settled in, enough so that I invited Harry and Linda over for dinner. It immediately threw Loni into a tizzy of insecurity. Knowing only that the Thomasons were wealthy, she figured they lived even better than us, not realizing no one lived better than us. As a matter of fact, Harry and Linda lived very simply. About an hour and a half before they were to arrive, Loni surveyed the dining room table and freaked out. I was in the shower.

"We don't have any plates!" she screamed, panicky.

"What?" I said. "What are you talking about? I saw the table Clarence set. They're plates—little salad plates, dinner plates. We have lots of plates."

"No, no, no, not formal plates," she said.

"Well, it's not a formal dinner," I said. "Harry and Linda are coming over to discuss the show, and I thought it would be nice if they met you and Quinton, too."

"You don't understand," she said. "I'm not going to have a dinner at my house with those plates. I hate them."

Wrapping myself in a towel, we inspected the dining room table together. What looked fine to me was an embarrassment to Loni. Even though it was dark outside and stores were closed, Loni wanted to rush out and buy a complete set of formal china. I asked where, but she had no idea. She just wanted to get new china.

It was easier to agree than fight. I called a guy I knew who owned a pricey china store on Ventura Boulevard. Although he'd just gotten home, he turned around and met Loni at his store. It was a smart business move on his part. She returned to our house thirty minutes later having spent $5,000 on a new set of formal ware for six.

"Aren't they beautiful?" she said as Clarence placed them on the table.

"Yes," I said. "But for that amount of money, we shouldn't eat on them. We should hang them on the wall!"

Such extravagances became routine after the move. From the time "Evening Shade" began, I was consumed by the perpetual, eighteen-hour-a-day struggle to make the series everything I believed it could be, which wasn't necessarily, and usually wasn't, the way Linda saw it.

We began butting heads on the pilot. According to what I had read and heard, Linda was involved in a major fight with Delta Burke, who had left "Designing Women" over creative differences, and it set her on edge, affecting her mood and how she dealt with people. After the first scene, an exchange between me and Durning in the doctor's office, she ran over to me and started to complain that Charlie was too over the top.

I put my arms around Linda, hoping the packed audience would think we were congratulating each other about the printed scene rather than fighting. It threw her off stride. She asked what the hell I was doing.

"It's one thing to fight Delta Burke and her husband," I said. "But I'm rather well liked out here. It would be bad and would make Delta look very good if we had a public fight. But more to the point, I heard you say Durning is over-the-top. Which he may be—he's just come from the Broadway stage (for which he won a Tony). And he's getting monstrous laughs.

"If you had produced the 'Andy Griffith Show,' Don Knotts would have been fired and Barney Fife would've been played by Robert Stack because he's never over-the-top. Now what is it you wanted to tell me?"

"You're grammar is bad," she said. I was dumbfounded. "What? Very few football coaches, and all the great coaches I know personally, including Bear Bryant, speak with perfect grammar," I said. I ripped Linda for delivering her criticisms of the actors in front of an audience on taping night. The proper place would've been dress rehearsal, but she rarely attended them. Always running late, she had no compunction about changing scenes and writing new dialogue at the last minute.

I directed the second show, which should've caused her to keep her distance. Like me, though, Linda can't help herself. I felt she always needed to be in control. She probably felt the same about me. After a scene in which Michael Jeter, one of the greatest physical comedians since Chaplin, did something that wasn't in the script, she came roaring down to the floor, fuming about Jeter.

"Tell me exactly what it is," I said.

"He's just over-the-top," Linda exclaimed.

"It was Durning last week," I said. "Jeter is over-the-top tonight. It'll be Elizabeth next week. But you know something? Before this show is over, they'll all be nominated for Emmys."

My prediction turned out to be true. Linda's exceptional talent wasn't being questioned. But I knew she took offense every time someone strayed from the words as she'd written them. People like Jim Brooks worked with his actors; he enjoyed a good suggestion. Linda went apeshit when someone got a laugh she didn't write. That's why she hated it when I got laughs by just reacting. Look, no dialogue!

"But I'm directing this episode," I said. "And I like what he's doing."

"We'll see when we get in the editing room," she snarled and then stalked off.

Our fights were legendary. Eventually they led us straight to the network president, Jeff Sagansky, who regarded Linda as television's reigning genius. But even with the odds stacked against me, I fared okay. No one wants to be a 500-pound gorilla. The suits make you into one, but it was a role I could play as well as anyone. By that time, I was engaged in another pitched battle for control, except the stakes were higher.

# CHAPTER
## 56

IN THE FALL OF 1990, I HAD NO REASON TO SUSPECT any serious discord in our two-year-old marriage. There were a few minor sour notes. I'd turned down the part Kevin Kline played in *Soapdish,* a funny soap opera spoof that was written in my rhythm and would have for the first time in years paid my old salary. It also starred Sally Field, which wasn't a problem for me. But Loni was absolutely positive it would ruin our marriage and everyone in Hollywood would be laughing at her.

"It would kill me if you worked with her," she said.

The public would've loved seeing Sally and me together again. I'm positive that the movie, which became a hit with both critics and moviegoers, would've also rekindled my film career. But in deference to Loni, I turned it down.

What the hell was I thinking about? Where was my agent? I couldn't afford to be so nice.

Loni wasn't as considerate when I complained about her spending habits. Shopping might have been a way of life among Hollywood wives, but Loni turned it into an art form. One morning I gave her a brand-new platinum American Express card. At lunchtime, I borrowed it so I could pick up some toys for Quinton at a sporting goods store. Much to my embarrassment, the kid at the register told me the card was maxed out. In only a few hours, she'd spent an astounding $45,000.

On another occasion our houseman drove her to Neiman Marcus, where, I've been told, the saleswoman thought it was Christmas every time she walked in. She had Clarence wait in the car, explaining she'd be only a few minutes. According to him, she zipped out in no time, but mentioned somehow having spent $25,000 and still not gotten everything she wanted.

That was the problem. She purchased everyday clothes in triplicate and the fancy dresses she wore whenever we went out or she had to make an appearance were custom made at Courtney's by her favorite designer, Robert Turturice. Such creations cost between $4,000 and $10,000 a shot. But she wore each dress only once if she wore them to an event. I went into shock when I found that out and heard her explain why.

"It's been photographed," she said, her tone implying that she didn't believe I didn't already know that.

"What does that mean?" I asked. "It's got Kryptonite on it or something?"

"I never wear a dress once it's been photographed."

"Where's that written?" Here I was, busting my ass to get out of debt. "Who made that rule? Jackie Onassis? I mean you never said that before when you paid for them."

"Men can do it with tuxedos, but women can't. They can't."

"Yes, they can," I argued. "You just push it back six events, get a flower sewn on, and who'll care?" I was flabbergasted. "Where do these dresses go when you're done with them?"

"I give them to poor people," she said in all seriousness.

What a nice thought. I could just see some lady in the inner city walking around the block with her new Turturice gown on.

"You give a ten-thousand-dollar designer dress to a poor person? Where are they going to wear it? The Poor Person of the Year Awards? Why not give them to your daughter? Or to my sister? I know Nancy ain't getting them."

"They don't have the figure for them."

No matter how ludicrous her point or how loud I yelled, we were going to remained deadlocked on the issue. Loni's jaw tightened. She rolled her eyes. All signs pointed to her stalking out of the room at any moment.

"I have to dress in the style that everyone loves," she said. "I have to dress like a star."


Even by a star's standards, Loni rang up astronomical bills. The $1,000 cash allowance I gave her every week barely made a dent. Her clothing bills alone hit $10,000 a month. She spent $600 on keeping her dark hair blond and another $500 on manicures, pedicures, and cosmetics. Her personal trainer, Magic Mike, charged $100 a fifteen-minute session. If we went out, she had someone come to the house and do her hair at $100 a pop.

Also, Loni got better and younger looking every couple of months. She treated cellulite as if the Surgeon General had issued a warning against it. Veins, sags, blemishes were all anathema to her. While she constantly improved, I grew older without a fight. Do you know what sort of self-confidence that requires from a man? If we'd stayed together, I would've needed a walker about the time she began cheerleader tryouts.

After I started "Evening Shade," our life together underwent a drastic change. Prior to L.A. and the series, we spent practically every day together. We doted on Quinton, shared romantic dinners, walked the beaches, and took spur-of-the-moment vacations. But the show occupied me from dawn until the wee hours of the night, eliminating that much freedom.

I still made time for Quinton. We ate dinner together almost every night. Afterward, I climbed into his Corvette-shaped bed and, resting beside him, read our favorite bedtime story, then went back to the studio and edited trailers. I was aware of the sacrifices my schedule caused, but saw them as temporary. In three to five years the series would be sold into syndication, and I planned on stepping back into the slow lane with between $25 and $100 million in my pocket, my back porch money.

Whatever our disagreements, I never thought of Loni as anything but supportive, and I never thought that she might be unfaithful. I really believed that we were the couple atop the wedding cake. I never thought we'd topple from the upper tier.

Was it ego? Of course. That, and assuming she wouldn't risk losing this lifestyle.

Maybe it was also naiveté. I believed that when you promised, in front of your family and loved ones, to love, honor, and cherish till death rather than divorce did you part, you tried to keep that promise.

Then I got hit with a lethal dose of reality. From the time we moved to Florida, Loni and I always shared a portion of our lives—be it teaching, lending support, or simply finding jobs—with young, good-looking guys and girls from my Institute of Theater Training. Terry Warren, a former FSU linebacker, ingratiated himself more than other apprentices by displaying the linebacker's work ethic. After gaining my trust, he joined us in L.A., working as an assistant and Loni's occasional escort for dinner or theater when I wasn't able to go.

As far as I could tell, I had no reason to suspect any funny business. Then one day in October I finished rehearsal much earlier than usual and came home, where I walked in quietly and found my wife and Terry beside the pool. Wearing the briefest of swimsuits, neither could see me peering through the glass window, but from my vantage there was no mistaking lust for like. The situation made me suspicious about them, as I'd been many times before.

Finally, I stepped outside. Wide-eyed and mouths agape, they tore apart reflexively and probably entered the same suspended world of incredulity that I'd left. They probably also thought I was going kill them with my bare hands. Seething with a boiling rage but somehow managing to remain absolutely silent, I turned and stormed into the bedroom.

A few moments later Loni opened the door. I noticed Terry peeping in from the background and shot him a look that in unmistakable language said, "Get the hell out of here!" Loni shut the door.

"Get your clothes and get out," I said very quietly.

What a silly statement that was. Loni's wardrobe filled two closets the size of small rooms, and the overflow was scattered throughout the house. There was more in storage across town at Elizabeth Courtney, a costume supply house.

"It's going to be very interesting to see how you do with him financially," I continued. "He doesn't have a job or even a car. In fact, he drives one of mine. And at his age he's not going to be able to do much for you except walk around with a permanent erection."

"It's not what you think," she said. "It'll never happen again. It just felt . . . he was young and I was flattered . . ."

It's scary to see your life turn into a TV movie. Suddenly, Loni dropped to her knees and started weeping. Not one of the greatest actresses, she nonetheless gave a brilliant performance. I'd rank it with Susan Hayward in *I Want to Live* or Vivien Leigh in *Streetcar*. In fact, it was a lot like *Streetcar*. Loni crawled, pulled at me, clawed, and wept. Finally she just cried, "I can't live without you!"

Again, I was unbelievably stupid. I could have grabbed Quinton and walked out, given her everything in the house but him. I would have been so much richer now. And I'd have my son. But after Terry got the hell out of Dodge, he left without a word, and I gave Loni another chance. But the reconciliation was in name only. I couldn't look at Loni without wondering what else happened that I didn't know about. Every thought I had was colored by suspicion.

Loni let some time pass. Perhaps a week later, she rolled over in bed and tried getting amorous with me. I pushed her off.

"No," I said. "No way."

She sat up and turned on the light.

"How long is this going to last?" she asked. "How long are you going to punish me like this?"

"I don't know," I said. I really didn't. "I don't know if I will ever be able to make love to you again."

And I never did.

# CHAPTER
# 57

OURS BECAME A MARRIAGE OF INTENSELY DIS-
jointed moments only a Swedish director could love.
Holding hands and smiling at paparazzi at a glamor-
ous opening. Arguing inside the car on the way
home. Cozied up in a booth at a favorite restaurant.
Snapping at one another in bed.

"I think you should get some help," Loni said
one night.

"For what?"

"You know, being impotent."

One lie piled on top of the next, transforming
our homelife into a prison of discontent. It was impossible to believe that we had once appeared so
close and happy that Steve Martin asked who the hell
*we* fantasized about. My Emmy nomination for "Evening Shade," which should've been cause for joy, cre-

ated a small ripple of pleasure. If Bergman had filmed us, it would've been hailed as his masterpiece.

Only Vic Prinzi knew the truth. I also confessed my pain to Pam Seals, a petite blonde who managed the cocktail lounge at Malio's, a popular sports hangout in Tampa where I went whenever I visited Vic. I'd known Pam since 1988, but nothing happened between us and after my marriage collapsed, it seemed unlikely we'd ever get together.

Malio Iavarone, the restaurant's owner, offered to fix me up with any girl in the place, but when I said I would like to meet Pam, he laughed. She was serious, hard-working, and as a rule never went out with any admirers from the bar, and there were plenty.

"No chance," he said.

"Good, then that's the kind of lady I need to talk to," I replied.

I managed to strike up a phone friendship with her that was extremely lopsided. I talked about my problems, and she listened, occasionally offering bit of sound advice about coping in this incredibly difficult time. At a time when I needed a good female friend, she was there. Because whatever could go wrong did go wrong.

It was like Murphy's Law. How bad did it get? In September I won the Emmy for Best Actor, a triumphant moment that was extraordinary. Against almost insurmountable odds, I'd fought back and won. Yet the next day it was just a statue. I was still miserable. I should've been full of joy, but instead I felt lousy and depressed. This wasn't me.

Burt Reynolds was a fun guy who played hard, drove fast, and made people laugh. How'd I get caught up in some Eugene O'Neill nightmare?

AGE is a funny thing. Although you gain wisdom by living a long time, you lose just about everything else. My mother, who suffered from a weak heart and bad hips throughout the last five years of her life, once told me, "After seventy-five, things just start breaking down and they don't get fixed. You don't die, you just wear out."

That reminded me of a scene in *The End* that failed to make it to the final cut. After learning I had a fatal illness, I walked into the Intensive Care Unit at the hospital and found a patient who had tubes sticking out of every part of his body. I sat down beside his bed and stared at him, trying to feel what he was feeling as he breathed his final breaths. Finally, I asked what it was like to die. The part was played by Sam Jaffe, the wonderful actor who had played Dr. Zorba on "Ben Casey."

"It's not a good thing," he said.

My mother tried doing it on her own terms. Early in 1992 I was relaxing in Florida during a break from "Evening Shade" when my houseman greeted me at the door late one night with news that Mom's nurse called and asked me to get to the hospital. It was three A.M., but my brother drove me there.

I'd given up trying to impress my parents long ago, but I don't think I ever stopped trying to earn their affection. I anticipated the worst and expected to see my mother hooked up to tubes and machines. On her best days, she breathed oxygen from a tank. But when I walked into her hospital room, she was, despite the hour, sitting up in bed without her oxygen mask. Her hair had been done and she'd put on some lipstick.

"Hi, Mom," I said, curious. "How're ya doin'? What's going on?"

"Sit down," she said in a soft but firm voice.

"Yes, ma'am," I replied, pulling a chair close to her bed so I could hear easily.

"I'm going to tell you something and I don't want you to answer me," she explained. "And then I want you to get out."

"Yes, ma'am."

After a long silence in which she stared at me intently, she said, "You were the greatest thing that ever happened to me in my life, and I love you."

"I love—"

"Now get out," she said, cutting me off.

Maybe I'd seen too many movies. After leaving her room in a daze, I sat in the car and cried. My brother cried too. He went up to her room and she was asleep. We thought for sure she was going to pass away. In fact, several days before that, the doctors had warned us she could go at any moment. Afterward, Dad and I had stood in the hospital corridor and balled our eyes out. But Mom was so strong. She went home looking great, and I went back to L.A.

Six months later she finally succumbed. She'd made her peace and let all her worn-out body parts slow down. It was the summer of 1992. Fortunately, I was back in Florida, shooting *Cop and a Half,* but I had to be called back from location in Tampa. She went in the middle of the night with my dad holding her in his arms. We'd made a pact—her, Dad, and I—that we'd all be buried on the ranch, behind the chapel.

At the end, Mom was fond of telling us and anyone else within earshot that she'd had a wonderful life. Indeed, there was no reason to doubt her. She had a wonderful marriage, three children who would do anything for her, and a grandson who was single-handedly responsible for adding four years to her life. She lived past her ninety-second birthday. But as we said goodbye, I thought about the fact that all of us get one shot here, one ride around the track, and no matter what you make of yourself, rich or poor, loved or miserable, life is too short.

Life is just too damn short. Death "is not a good thing."


NEITHER is the other D-word a good thing. Although virtually no one outside of Vic and whomever Loni told knew the truth about our marriage, my friends all realized how unhappy I was. Instead of being the guy everyone wanted to be, I was the opposite, and it showed. One day on the "Evening Shade" set, my cameraman Nicky McLain said, "Burt, I don't know what the problem is, but I've got a pretty good idea, and it's killing all of us. We love you."

Loni and I had good times together, but after two years of living a lie, I decided come hell or high water I had to be truthful to myself, and so I arranged to get a divorce. I was working at this time, directing and co-starring in a movie for TV with the wonderful young lady (and superstar of country music) Reba McEntire. My production company was co-producing with CBS "The Man From Left Field" for the coming fall season. Knowing the feeding frenzy that the divorce would stir up, I felt obligated to tell Reba so she could prepare to protect herself if any rumors affected her personal life after the divorce announcement. She said, "Thanks for telling me. These things are bad for everyone. You're a good man, Burt. I'm sorry. Just remember that time will heal a lot of things that are said. And I know how much you love that little boy of yours. I'll pray for you both."

She's quite a woman and one hell of an actress. When the picture ended, I broke the news to Loni. If my life was unpleasant before then, I was reintroduced to real misery afterward. For the next year and a half, the gossip rags reported on the proceedings virtually every week in excruciatingly painful and depressing detail. I couldn't stop at the grocery story without seeing something new emblazoned in headlines by the checkstand. I'd show up for work and the guard at the gate would just hold up the new *Enquirer* and ask, "Burt, you see this?"

"Yeah," I said shamefully, tired of it.

"So is she gonna take the five mil.?"

It got to the point where I asked, "Is this what I'm offering?"

Now I want to put that bickering and nastiness behind me. The wounds are still raw, the anger and pain are hanging just around the next thought in my head. To be sure, you don't pay someone $1.9 million (which I don't have) plus the third highest child support in history of the state of California and not feel some moment of depression. But I never want to be the guy in the purple suit (the outfit I wore on my "Good Morning America" appearance) again. At some point you have to step out of the mud and get a life.

Mine had been hijacked by the tabloids. I wanted it back for me and for Quinton. I don't want him to think I was so damned angry and insensitive to his feelings that I argued and pointed out every dirty detail of who did what to whom. I want to prove that I was the good guy. I want Quinton to always love his mother; I never ever have and never will tell Quinton anything but good about his mom. I truly believe that's the only way to do right by him. I'm no angel and haven't ever claimed to be in life, or in this book. But Quinton has made me a lot better man in so many ways. I'm sure I can be a hell of a lot better, and by God I intend to be.

# CHAPTER
## 58

AFTER MY "GOOD MORNING AMERICA" DEBACLE, Dinah told me to cool it. As she had so many times before, she reminded me that the cream always rises to the top while a lie will die its own death. No one made as much sense to me as Dinah.

"Honey, you have to remember the public loves you," she said. "But you're their bad boy. They have to spank you every now and then. Let 'em. Don't say anything. Which is gonna be hard. You're gonna want to say something. But you just call me instead. I'll always be here for you."

Although Dinah and I saw each other about once a month until the divorce mess, we kept in touch fairly regularly with phone calls, although even they slowed during the thick of things. In the middle of February, 1993, I heard she was critically ill.

Strangely, I had been wanting to tell her that Loni and I finally settled the divorce. When I called, she sounded weak.

"It's just a cold," she said.

She laughed off my inquiries about her health and instead told me how she was preparing for her annual golf tournament in Palm Springs. I later learned this was a lie, but that was Dinah, wanting to spare me the pain that she was suffering by being so ill with cancer. I tried making plans to see her.

"I'm so fat," she said. "I need to get in shape first."

"I don't care if you're fat," I said. "First of all, I don't believe you. Second, you know I don't care what you look like. Please, I just want to see you."

Dinah was silent. I heard her breathing. I suspected she might also be crying silently.

"You know I love you," she finally said.

"And I love you," I replied.

"No, dear. I really love you. I want you to know that. I really love you."

"I love you, too, Dinah."

From the moment we hung up, I had a bad feeling. Less than a week later, Pam woke me up from a deep sleep. After working all night on the show, I'd gone to bed and told her that I wanted to sleep as late as possible, and not come over until late afternoon. But as she shook me awake I knew something dreadful had happened from the sound of her voice and the look in her eye.

"It's Dad," I said. "Is it my dad?"

"No, honey, your dad's okay."

"What?"

I had no clue.

"It's Dinah."

I expected her to tell me that Dinah was very sick.

"She's gone," Pam whispered.

I started to sob and couldn't stop all day. Nobody's death, not even my mother's, affected me like Dinah's. At her memorial service, held at the Directors Guild and attended by the most celebrated crowd of people I'd ever been part of, I sat among mourners and watched a lengthy piece of footage assembled from her long and brilliant career. I cried till I ached.

I was privileged to have been a part of Dinah's life. But with her passing, I had also lost a piece of my own fifty-seven-year-old life, an irretrivable piece of the jigsaw that gave me shape and substance. After a shitty two and a half years, I wondered how much more I could take.

Not much, it turned out. One day on the set, I collapsed. I as well as everyone else thought it was a heart attack as I clutched my chest, gasped for air, and was rushed to the hospital with a bunch of wires glued to my chest. If I'd died, I was informed later, my estate wouldn't have had to pay Loni the money we'd agreed upon. But I had no such luck.

In the emergency room, the doctor examined me and then told me the good news. My heart was as strong as a buffalo.

"Mr. Reynolds, what you had is called an anxiety attack," he said. "It's brought on by stress. Do you have an unusually demanding work schedule now? Or by chance are you having marital problems at home?"

My mouth hit the examination table.

"What planet do you live on?" I asked.

"Why?"

"Because I want to go there."


It was hard to muster any optimism, but I tried because that's the kind of person I am, and wanted to become again. Also, I anticipated a multi-million-dollar syndication deal from "Evening Shade" after we finished the fourth season. MTM and me, Harry and Linda were fifty-fifty owners. The previous year we'd put the show up for sale for $1 million per episode. It was just a tad high. If we'd dropped the price to $800,000, we would've sold it immediately and all reaped millions.

But the way my luck was going, I should have known better than to count on a single penny. In June, 1993, MTM sold the syndication rights to "Evening Shade" to the Family Channel for the incredibly low amount of $150,000 per show. We got robbed. Furthermore, with no backend, CBS canceled the series, and all of us were left with nothing.

Nothing.

I was irate. It was unbelievable. But screw it. You've got to go on. As any good fighter knows, you have to create the illusion that your opponent's punches aren't doing any damage. A lot of people have told me that had they been in my shoes the past three years they would surely have been dead by now from drugs, booze, a heart attack, or attorneys' bills.

But I was taught not to give up. I've got movie offers on my desk, networks calling to see if I'm interested in doing another series, and every once in a while I go outside to see if anybody recognizes me.

My dad and I are finally now at peace with each other. And unembarrassed at hugs and kisses. We are making up for many years of being unable to show how much we really love each other. Something Quinton and he have already worked out.

I'm convinced the best years are still ahead of me. Christ, I've got my father, my son, and my health. I can still see all right, my legs haven't given out entirely, and my hair—well, my hair will probably outlive the human race. They will find a skull with perfect hair on it.

The only unfortunate thing with which I've come to terms is that I'll probably never win the Big One of my profession—an Academy Award. But damned if I don't already have the speech prepared, and since there's no reason to let it go to waste, I'll deliver it right now:

*I want to thank the Academy for finally realizing that I'm not planted at Forest Lawn . . .*

*I want to thank God, whose sense of humor is even stranger than mine. But enough is enough already.*

*I also want to thank my son, Quinton Reynolds, who has made me richer than any amount of money ever could have, and who has also taught me more about life in a few short years than I ever thought possible.*

*And finally I want to thank the first director who ever yelled "action," because that's what it's all about.*